from digital to analog

Colin Lankshear and Michele Knobel
General Editors

Vol. 69

The New Literacies and Digital Epistemologies series
is part of the Peter Lang Education list.
Every volume is peer reviewed and meets
the highest quality standards for content and production.

PETER LANG
New York • Bern • Frankfurt • Berlin
Brussels • Vienna • Oxford • Warsaw

AGUSTÍN BERTI

from digital to analog

Agrippa and Other Hybrids
in the Beginnings of Digital Culture

PETER LANG
New York • Bern • Frankfurt • Berlin
Brussels • Vienna • Oxford • Warsaw

Library of Congress Cataloging-in-Publication Data
Berti, Agustín.
From digital to analog: *Agrippa* and other hybrids in the beginnings
of digital culture / Agustín Berti.
pages cm. — (New literacies and digital epistemologies; vol. 69)
Includes bibliographical references and index.
1. Digital media—Philosophy. 2. Digital preservation.
3. Copying processes—Technological innovations.
4. Copyright and electronic data processing.
5. Gibson, William, 1948– Agrippa.
6. Literature and technology. 7. Electronic publishing.
8. Information technology—Social aspects. I. Title.
ZA4045.B47 302.23'1—dc23 2015022716
ISBN 978-1-4331-2505-8 (hardcover)
ISBN 978-1-4331-2504-1 (paperback)
ISBN 978-1-4539-1667-4 (e-book)
ISSN 1523-9543

Bibliographic information published by **Die Deutsche Nationalbibliothek.**
Die Deutsche Nationalbibliothek lists this publication in the "Deutsche
Nationalbibliografie"; detailed bibliographic data are available
on the Internet at http://dnb.d-nb.de/.

Cover art by Manuel Coll. Title: "Download."
Site specific installation, Museo Municipal Genaro Pérez, Córdoba, 2014:
40 x 50 cm painting, movement sensor and printer.

© 2015 Peter Lang Publishing, Inc., New York
29 Broadway, 18th floor, New York, NY 10006
www.peterlang.com

To Nati, Mora, Irene, and Juan.
To Eli and Jorge.

TABLE OF CONTENTS

PREFACE
Pirate Havens and Digital Coyotes

...is more aligned with bad infinity: the pops and
hisses in each video signal exactly how far removed the copy is from the original. The viewer
is thus always positioned within an asymptotal
distance to the ur-event; bootleg video inscribes
its distance from the original onto the material
substrate.
-"Bootleg video," *Dead Media Archive*

The digitization of culture and search engines have modified the
very foundations of a culture based on printed texts and media-
specific objects. It is not only about digitized things becoming
findable or easily reproducible; the new cultural milieu itself is
overtly digital. But what does "digital" actually mean? A somewhat
misleading concept to talk about cultural artifacts, it is often
confused with dematerialization. So, do digits matter? Or put
differently: Is the materiality of digital inscriptions relevant? This
book is about that and some other paradoxes.

Abstractions

An illegal download of The Clash's 1979 version of the song "I
Fought the Law" in an information lossy .mp3 file format or the
BDMV application files in a Criterion Collection Blu-ray disc
containing Orson Welles' 1974 *F for Fake* are two extreme cases of
discrete entities that common sense (as well as technical sense)
deem as "digital objects." That is, a song and a film in digital

format, which is the way things exist in a digital milieu. And yet they differ, since the first may entail legal persecution while the second most likely would not. One could think these entities as a strange case of concreted abstractions; after all digital culture has been built on the assumption of such paradoxes. I will discuss the nature of these entities and their modes of existence in order to remap contemporary culture, the undergoing changes and the unsuspected perseverations.

Take this book, for instance. Maybe you are holding it in your hand or reading it on a screen, or even in a printed or loose xeroxed page (some places some old technical habits die hard). Like most things digital, it is just another example of a new mode of existence of things. The following chapters trace the materiality of digital works as well as the affordances of being digital. To do so, it follows the back roads of digital culture and looks into a series of awkward cultural artifacts, both artworks and by-products, legally sanctioned or not. By sailing pirate waters, crossing the heavily policed boundaries of contemporary art and clipping the fences of mass culture intellectual property one may gain a deeper understanding of what these *things* are. Digital objects are taken for granted in our daily dealings with digital technologies. But one easily forgets that the measure of normality is often provided by the contrast with the anomaly, hence the importance to pay attention to those things that do not meet the standard. Any history of technology is, in the end, also a history of oblivions, erasures, outcasts, and massive deportations.

Concretions

In the eighties and early nineties, playing games on a PC involved a series of somewhat cumbersome procedures and artifacts, more so in developing countries. For example, in the city of Córdoba, Argentina, where this book was written, the potential gamer had to buy blank diskettes, and then had to walk or take a bus to get to a thirteen-square-foot bootleg game cave in a rundown commercial mall downtown. There the shop owner would produce a folder containing printed lists displaying five rows: a code number, a game name, its genre, how many 5¼-inch diskettes it used, and the minimum technical needs to run it. The potential gamer would then look through the lists or ask the seller for the newly arrived games and decide which games to, ahem, "buy." Since the best games generally had copy protection, while the game was being copied, the potential gamer would receive a xeroxed page containing the codes required to play. The page was not for sale, so it was necessary to stroll the hallway to a drugstore at the other end of the mall, photocopy the code page at the copying machine, and then return the, ahem, "original" to the game glass cave where, hopefully, the digital copying process was completed. Once the disks were received, the potential gamer would go back home and run them on the PC. Most of the time the games would work. Having fulfilled such eminently material tasks, the gamer could then have a proper digital experience.

Record and Data Trafficking

In the early nineties, before the expansion of the Internet, hacker subculture was a sum of interconnected local, grounded, scenes. After all, people still traded information in storage devices, which meant that, although theoretically transmissible, digital code was perceptually bound to things one could touch and, eventually, open or manipulate (some would say adulterate).

This was not new, of course. Any history of art is also a history of forgeries. Bootleg copies have haunted popular music at least since the apparition of cassette tapes. And the underground of rock culture thrived on such recordings, true hand to hand tokens. The fact that pirated (i.e., unlicensed) VCR copies of films were subject to criminal prosecution kept video rentals high enough to help cinemas survive the seeming obsolescence caused by home VCR players. But there is one aspect that is often overlooked in these discussions: magnetic copying implies a degradation that turns copies into tokens of a paradoxical uniqueness in the technical reproduction of music and video. (The degradation of analog copies was not considered as a relevant problem by Walter Benjamin in his seminal essay on "The Work of Art in the Age of Mechanical

Reproduction"[1].) Piracy and bootlegging, or the work of art in the age of illegalized technical reproduction, are not exclusive of digital media but do find there a fertile ground to flourish.

Over a decade before the advent of .mp3, game piracy had already spawned bizarre copy protection systems and brought about copyright enforcement to ordinary consumers' everyday life. For centuries plagiarism had been a matter of companies, artists, and authorities: a book company printing texts for which it had no copyrights being sued by the author and/or the book company withholding the rights to publish her/his work; a forger having his clandestine workshop raided by law enforcers. With the digital turn, potential consumers would also become potential offenders.

Many of those cracked or pirated games presented science-fiction scenarios and stories. Think of the absolute video game classic *Space Invaders*, for instance. But sci-fi itself was also looking towards digital screens. The 1982 film *Tron* is a fine example of this fascinated look at arcade games. Upon growing up some gamers would also become readers of a grimier, computer-heavy iteration of science fiction, cyberpunk. While the dazzled gaze at the colorful sprites of early arcade games and the (then) astounding FX of *Tron* laid the perceptual foundations for an idealist take on technology that focuses on its screen manifestations, the imaginary dark digital futures of cyberpunk still provide some deep insight for a materialist avant-garde.

Contemporary Necromancers

Books have always kept the thoughts of the dead alive. Later on, phonography and photography preserved their voices and their looks. Records of all kinds have always worked this powerful magic. But some things get lost in translation. To record is not only to produce an impression inscribed on a physical storage device but, as Latin etymology indicates, is to have something return to the heart: the Latin verb *recordor* comes from *re-* ("back, again") and *cor* ("heart," but also "mind"). Records deter death.

Science fiction writer William Gibson is considered the first to bind the idea of a digital space with the physicality of online computers, coining the term cyberspace (or at least turning into a *Zeitgeist* resuming word). In the prophetic year of 1984, *Neuromancer* made Gibson a frequent consultant to any interviewer wanting to inquire on the future. In *Postmodernism, Or, the Cultural Logic of Late Capitalism*, Frederic Jameson, defining his subject, also quotes him:

> the postmodernism looks for breaks, for events rather than new worlds, for the telltale instant after which it is no longer the same; for the 'When-it-all-changed,' as Gibson puts it, or better still, for shifts and irrevocable changes in the representation of things and the way they change.[2]

Insisting on back roads, if one looks at the first endnote, referred to in that first page of *Postmodernism*, one finds out that there Jameson asserts Gibson's work is "the supreme *literary* expression if not of postmodernism, then of late capitalism itself."[3] This is not the place to discuss the importance of Jameson's book for thinking neither about contemporary culture, nor the concept of postmodernism itself, although it has pervaded this research; but it is worth noting that this influential work was published in 1991. At the end of 1992, a peculiar artist's book and electronic poem appeared: *Agrippa (A Book of the Dead)*. It was a work by writer William Gibson, artist Dennis Ashbaugh, publisher Kevin Begos, Jr. and a number of collaborators (ranging from programmers to typesetters). On April 30, 1993, the European Organization for Nuclear Research (CERN) announced that the World Wide Web would be free for anyone who could connect to it, and, once again, it all changed. And typesetters went on to become designers, among many other things. One of the perceived perils of this change was that, rephrasing Marx, everything that's solid melts into the web. Rather than assuming the idea of dematerialization, digital existence may be better understood as a form of representation based on abstractions and multiple material realizations. And realizations always occur somewhere. This book is therefore about grounding digits. Regarding *Agrippa*, and rephrasing Jameson, some eight years after publishing *Neuromancer*, once again, Gibson could be considered the supreme *literary* expression if not of digitalism, then of digital capitalism itself.

Deep Roots

The theoretical basis for this research is as hybrid as its objects. From book history and aesthetics to philosophy of technology, new literacies studies, and digital studies, this book owes a lot to very diverse landscapes and road companions. If I were to draw a map, it would include the some of the following touchstones. The influence of several books by Matthew K. Kirschenbaum, Matthew Gold, N. Katherine Hayles, Alan Liu, David Bolter, Richard Grusin, and Espen Aarseth is evident and they have been the source of many intuitions that have guided my research. I have also drawn heavily from past and current debates in the role of technology in aesthetics, including those sustained by thinkers as influential as Walter Benjamin, Theodor W. Adorno, Max Horkheimer, and Vilém Flusser, as well as more recent articles and books by Lev Manovich, Christian Ferrer, Claudia Kozak, and Arlindo Machado. The relevance of studies on technology to (re)think the artifactual aspect of the objects discussed in the following chapters is based on the theoretical work of Gilbert Simondon, Bernard Stiegler, and Bruno Latour and, to a lesser extent, to other prominent names in the field such as Trevor Craver, Wiebe Pinch, Andrew Feenberg, and Lawrence Busch. The history of the book has been also extremely relevant, from Guglielmo Cavallo and Roger Chartier's seminal work to the more recent work of Ted Striphas. Several seminars taken during doctoral and postdoctoral research fellowships over the last decade also provided deep insight on the topics of the different chapters. Among these it is worth mentioning "Written Culture and Literature: Sixteenth to Nineteenth Centuries" dictated by Roger Chartier and organized by the Library of the National University of Córdoba; "Poetics of Transmedia and New Technologies. The Construction of a Latin American Critical Space" by Claudia Kozak; "Conceptualizations, Theorization, and Research in New Literacies" by Michele Knobel and Colin Lankshear; and "Creation, Appropriation and Dissemination of Knowledge in the Knowledge Society" by Carlos Correa, all organized by the postgraduate programs of the Faculty of Philosophy and Humanities of the National University of Córdoba; and, finally, the seminar "Science,

Technology and Society: The Case of Philosophy of Technology" by Diego Lawler, organized by UNC Teachers and Researchers' Union (ADIUC) and the Center for Advanced Studies.

This book would not be possible without the ongoing support of the members of *Dedalus*, a technology studies research group led by Javier Blanco, with whom I have thoroughly discussed the concept of "digital object." *Dedalus*' members Dario Sandrone, Anahí Ré, Leila Luna, and Andrea Torrano have greatly contributed with comments, suggestions, and corrections. Susana Romano Sued, Anahí Ré (again), and Tomás Vera Barros from the *Expoesía* experimental literature research group were also central to the origins of this research and many of the ideas presented in this book can be found in shared papers and presentations. Finally discussions held within Luis García's research group on the culture of the Weimar Republic, which I co-directed, were central to gaining a deeper understanding in the Benjaminean take on technology that underlays all the chapters of this book. The several graduate and undergraduate seminars in which I have participated with all these groups over the last eight years have served as an ongoing source of inspiration and new information. This book would have not been possible without the endless patience and help from the staff of Peter Lang Publishing, especially Chris Myers, Stephen Mazur, Sophie Appel, and Suzie Tibor. Finally, the research and detours that resulted in this book were made possible due to a post-doctoral research fellowship granted by CONICET, the Argentine National Council of Scientific and Technological Research.

Previous versions of some sections of this book have had their own oral and written iterations. The introductory chapter, "Milestones between Matter and Digits," is a revised version of an essay published in the special issue on technics of *Nombres. Revista de Filosofía* (vol. 27, 2014: 253-269). Chapter five, "The Book of the Dead and the Death of Books," is a lengthy expansion and revision of my first approach to the subject that was published in *Representaciones* (vol. 6, no. 2, 2011: 5– 28). Some passages of chapters two, three, and four have been taken and rewritten from presentations and lectures given in the II, III, IV, and V *Colloquiums of Philosophy of Technology* between 2011 and 2014 held in Villa General

Belgrano and Buenos Aires, the XXIV and XXV *Conferences of Epistemology and History of Science* in La Falda and Los Cocos, the IV and VI *Symposiums on Representation in Science and the Arts* in La Falda in 2008, and 2012, the *Ludión/Paragraphe Seminar* in 2011 in Buenos Aires, the *Interdisciplinary Colloquium Photoliterature, Visual Literature and New Textualities* held in Paris in 2012, the *I Conference on Science, Technologies and Cultures* held in Santiago de Chile in 2008, and the *II Expoesía: Conference on Poetry and Experimentation* that took place in Córdoba in 2007.

Some less scholarly or less systematized works have influenced this book. Namely, William Gibson's novels, tales and, particularly, articles on popular culture; Japanese *anime* director Mamoru Oshii's interpretation of the ontology of cyborgs, especially his *Ghost in the Shell* films; and the works of Argentinean writers Jorge Luis Borges and Julio Cortázar. Along with Benjamin, both have been recurrently mentioned as foreseers of digital culture and I will not be an exception. Gibson's introduction to Borges' most well-known English language anthology, *Labyrinths*[4] is, to my personal judgment, the best link of Borgesian bookish worlds with digital culture.[5]

Kirschenbaum, a leading scholar in the field, has cleverly suggested humanities students should learn to write code. Complementarily, at least in South America, one might add that humanities students should also learn to crack code (and in fact have). Anyone teaching in the developing world can acknowledge that this is already happening.

CHAPTER I
Introduction: Milestones between Matter and Digits

Extending the perception that all things material are being digitized, this book's primary claim is that all that is digital (also) materializes.[1] And derived from this claim are the facts that lack of bandwidth, overlapping temporalities, poorly enforced copyright control and expensive and inaccessible cultural products all become key issues when defining a materially minded approach to digital studies.[2] The other side of digital culture is the machines operating mathematical abstractions; machines that compute. Looking into what machines are and how they work and change is an unavoidable need when trying to understand contemporary digital culture.

Empires were built by standards. As were large scale modern nation-state based cultures. Transnational, global, or cosmopolitan cultures (pick the perspective of your choice), as well. Though not overtly evident, the technical fact of standardization underlies most major cultural changes and digital technologies are no exception. Digital culture is based on myriad of standards, from the inch size of now obsolete floppy disks to the voltage charges running Internet protocols. What is less obvious is that these standards emerge and settle through a series of complex negotiations and disputes where technical and social aspects intertwine.

Our contemporary hyperindustrial culture is experienced through standardized products of cultural industries still impregnated by Romantic dictums of originality and personality. (Surprisingly enough, in our industrialized culture, standards have very bad press.) In the late sixties, Italian semiotician Umberto Eco identified a dialectics between the apocalyptic and the integrated views of mass media communication and products. As of today, a synthesis has been reached (it may even be stated that it had already been reached then): even the most apocalyptic experience of culture is an integrated one. Almost no one relates to culture and cultural works without the use of media technologies. However, standardization remains a dark omen, the source of all dystopic nightmares from Huxley's soma drug used to chemically homogenize emotions to the violent and bureaucratic programs, led by Agent Smith, that administrate code alterations in the shared virtual reality where everybody "lives" in the 1999 film *The Matrix*. And yet, the digital milieu is perceived as a place of freedom. This book will address that fact based on two assumptions. First, there is no loss of humanity in technology (if there is any loss it should be located in economy and in politics). Therefore, an effective change in policies implies a deep understanding of technology. Secondly, in digital technologies there is no virtuality, no dematerialization, but only an acceleration of materiality enhanced by standards. Thus, I would like to discuss the hybrid condition of digital works that explicitly evidence their simultaneous existence as material concretions *and* mathematical abstractions. To do so, to understand the mode of existence of those entities we perceive as "works" we must gain an understanding of their modes of existence. And there are no digital works without standards. Furthermore, there are no reproducible analog works without some degree of standardization.

Standards have been laying foundations for modern technology for a long time before the emergence of digital technologies. A distinctive feature of standards is their ubiquity; they pervade practically all aspects of contemporary life and its technical administration. This is the reason why they are mainly studied as part of homogenization, bureaucratization, or rationalization strategies. Their epistemic value is not usually considered, much less their human-made origin. I would like to suggest that standards help explain the basis of contemporary technical change in which automation plays a decisive role to ensure an ever growing synchronicity or, in other words, interoperability. Digital culture today is a result of these technical phenomena and the changes they introduce in how we relate with the physical world. But there is no linear progression of technical development, and it is necessary to identify the tensions between cultural contingencies and technical necessities implied in the settlement of different standards and their effects within culture. One of the classic dichotomies arising since the very origins of digital studies has been analog production and reproduction technologies *versus* digital ones. While the difference may be illustrative, it oversees the shared industrial origin of both technologies. Analog and digital reproduction devices imply a standardized concept of discrete entities (embodied in discrete storage devices such as cassette tapes, VHS, compacts discs, and diskettes) that sets them apart from other less stabilized technical conventions (e.g., a canvas or the materials for a stone sculpture).

The discussion of standards and their features rarely appears outside technical handbooks and frameworks where operative definitions are usually provided. However, since standards do define how we perceive the world, some philosophers of technology have suggested that standards are epistemic tools inasmuch as they constitute the reference frameworks for the production and organization of knowledge.[3] There is, indeed, a surprising absence of studies on the epistemic value of standards, which I will discuss later. Regarding aesthetics, standards also play a key role in the production and perception of sensory stimuli in contemporary culture; in music, video games, literature, and film their relevance cannot be downplayed from this angle of analysis, either.

1993 could be identified as year zero for digital culture. As with any other statement of this nature, this starting date is, of course, a matter of debate but it is a discussion this book will dodge deliberately. Instead, I focus on the early nineties as a time of cultural turmoil where some of the most distinctive traits of digital culture emerged; most specifically, the idea of an ongoing and unavoidable dematerialization of cultural works (frequently received at the time with a mix of grief, nostalgia, excitement, and utopianism). Some twenty-odd years later, one can speculate that this dematerialization was due to the convergence and subsequent expansion of digitization and telecommunications. Both predate the web, of course, but their social impact has changed contemporary culture ever since. Needless to say, these changes have been radical (along with other major political changes worldwide, starting with the disappearance of the Soviet Union a few years earlier, and the slow emergence of a new world order). Nevertheless, interconnected home computers and, later on, mobile devices have brought about changes whose radical impact has been contained by an interpretation forced within the mindset of twentieth century cultural industries.

A piece of code is not a "thing" and yet we relate to it as so. What is more, a piece of code is not immaterial but its physical boundaries are ontologically different from those of industrially produced artifacts such as books, records, or videotapes. And that leads us back to the anomalies. There are few examples of works that explicitly assume the material nature of digital technologies. One such work (or at least a part of it) first surfaced in a bulletin board system in December 1992, just months before the birth of the modern Internet. This piece was *Agrippa* and it constitutes a milestone in the development of digital culture and, at the same time, a privileged example of the materiality of digital works. This peculiar artifact is one of many products of the time when digital culture was a relatively small realm that had not taken over culture in general. Nowadays, just two decades later, there is no cultural industry that is not intertwined with the digital world.

What is so relevant about an artist's book containing an electronic poem at the dawn of mass digital culture? As I explain in the following chapters, this particular work holds many keys to understanding new forms of existence brought about by digital technologies and the way they relate to the old ones. *Agrippa* is a forerunner to some of the most distinctive traits of contemporary digital culture while at the same time establishes bonds with the previous print and analog cultural mindset that dominated during the twentieth century. However, to understand this peculiar work, preexisting art and humanities concepts may lack sufficient specificity to work as useful comparisons. As prominent e-literature critic N. Katherine Hayles noted, anomalies call for a media-specific analysis. In order to do so, to define what is specific to a given media, some concepts of philosophy of technology can provide powerful descriptive tools. This discipline in particular, rather than semiotics or cultural studies, may prove a more fertile approach to defining what is "new" in new technologies and how we can study its products. With this toolset, I would like to undertake a critical approach to what was happening in terms of the origins of digital culture.

The main drive of digital culture today may not seem to be hardware or software but contents, uncontained entities freed from the material ties of paper or tape (e.g., eBooks or .mp3 files). To attain such freedom, contents are managed as digital objects, a new form of entity that is built on the assumption that objects that worked in an entirely different technical milieu can exist in a digital milieu.[4] The idea of digital content, deprived of its material container, along with its cultural implications, is a recurrent topic of this book. Building on ideas in a paper by Nick Monfort[5], Kirschenbaum has referred to a naïve (and extended) take on digital culture; that of "screen essentialism" that builds on the primacy of the screen output of computing over other possible outputs.[6] This is at the heart of what Kirschenbaum has called "medial ideology," a set of aesthetic practices linked to Western consumer culture that ultimately depict "information as an essence unto itself, or more properly, information as a synthetic (at times even haptic) commodity."[7] In this book I will present the idea that medial ideology is organized around a *content dynamics*, a perception of digital products that emphasizes abstraction and ignores material concretion. In some ways this development within Western culture carries the agenda of an integrated relation to mass media further. Following Eco, by integrated I refer to the acritical assumption that mass media and cultural industries are part of an unstoppable process of technological progress that must be embraced.

To analyze medial ideology it is necessary to understand the deep intertwinement of contents and containers, and the different affordances at stake in these material relations. Some peculiar intertwined artifacts, or *hybrid works*, as I will define them later on, are objects that illustrate negotiations between the abstract and the concrete that make up the digital world. Hybrids are usually sterile, or, in technical terms, they do not meet nor set a standard. They loom in a vague area between the prototype and the failed work. Likewise, for centuries, works of art were ontologically bound to uniqueness. The reproduction technologies that set the works free from their unrepeatable, physically located existence, in turn, generated mass oriented cultural industries that produced standardized containers carrying copies of a given content (for example, the seemingly ubiquitous prints of van Gogh's *The Starry Night* painting found in so many offices today). Apocalyptic views have regarded mass culture as a loss in terms of the specificity of art. And yet, photography, later cinema, and more recently video games and even television series have been admitted (even if grudgingly at times) into the domains of art. We have come to terms to the fact that the contents that make up most of our present aesthetic experience are industrial products, regardless of their analog or digital mode of existence. In fact, the tension between art and entertainment is really settled only in the field of contents, because containers are perceived as transparent, meaningless transports of something else. My first interest in hybrids is that they prevent us from considering them *only* as contents. The hybrid condition upsets technological media and illuminates areas that reproducibility renders invisible. Therefore, the first problem to tackle here is the relation between technology and reproduction (which is not the same as reproduction technologies).

Outside Ourselves

Discussions in philosophy of technics or technology begin with the very name of the discipline. Its different traditions (and the main languages in them) make its inscription susceptible to diverse interpretations. Gilbert Simondon suggested that "technology" is a "discourse on technics."[8] Building on his ideas I consider technology as an iteration of philosophy of technics that places emphasis on the materiality of objects. Assuming the premise that everything that is humanly possible is so by technics, any discourse will be, by necessity, technological.[9] The history of thought is, thus, the history of the storage devices that have made ideas transmissible, and interpretation is nothing but a method for manipulating those specific devices. When thought becomes effective outside the body, when it is enunciated, it can only be so through a technical mediation, through the embodiment of abstractions in material marks, be they acoustic, graphic, or voltaic. Or put otherwise, thoughts and expressions are realized in the form of sounds, letters, or bits, between the most frequent occurrences.

Thinking is necessarily a technology, since it reflects on the technics that mediate it. We keep forgetting that we are technical beings; we have always been so. Bernard Stiegler suggests that technology, the necessary condition of culture and not its result, is an *ur*-problem that is inseparable from and co-constituent of all human making. I build directly on that premise. Stiegler's main thesis is that there is no technics without humanity in the same way there is no humanity without technics. Technics is, in fact, the distinctive trait of humanity, the replacement for that which is lacking and the reason why humans are prosthetic beings. In due turn, technics can only exist as the possibility of "anticipation" that separates humans (who acknowledge mortality and try to deter death) from other organic beings (that are only perennial and not properly mortal; i.e., not at all aware of their mortality).

But there is another difference between humans as opposed to inert objects. There is also organized inorganic matter created by humans (that is, tools and inscriptions) that must be taken into account in any consideration of digital culture. This mode of existence, organized inert matter, is the one that enables the assumption that there are "exteriorizations;" that is, things out-side one's body that, in turn, point to the existence of a body "interior." None precedes the other. "Technics" is thus the lan-guage as much as it is the tools (or, as Stiegler would put it, the *outillage*), and neither can exist without humans, who are the elementary associated milieu of any technology. Stiegler locates the fundamental problem of technics in the co-constitution of humanity *and* technics originated in the absence of claws, of hair, of wings that cast humans into indetermination. Prosthetic sup-plementation to replace such lacking is, for that reason, the distinguishing characteristic of humanity. Resorting to prosthesis forces awareness of an exteriority to the body: the stone headed spear and the word are thrown outside into the world and, in doing so, humans catch a glimpse of an interiority that drives them. Moreover, projecting things outside oneself (the warning scream, the attack) demand anticipating the effect they will have. In doing so, prostheses *create* time.[10]

Discussing the impossibility of a myth of origins, of a fall, of a "natural" man, takes up most of the first volume of Stiegler's *Technics and Time*.[11] Let me summarize it at the expense of loss. If, according to Stiegler, there is no technics without humanity, but there is no humanity without technics either, then there could never have been humans living in a timeless interior as animals do. The main thesis here is that humanity commences when the supplementation of biological deficits begin. And it does not occur *ex nihilo*; it is the result of a long process of accumulation of exteriorization over exteriorization. The stones that can be shaped outside the body, the *silex*, mirror the malleability of the *cortex* inside the proto-human bodies. Reconsidering André Leroi-Gourhan's anthropology of technics, Stiegler analyzes three co-constitutions: (a) how the interior arises when primates start exteriorizing, (b) how, upon gaining awareness of mortality, an effort to deter death commences, and (c) how when this awareness "anticipates," it creates time. Temporality also implies that technics are transmissible and cumulative.

Successive existences exterior to the human body that can be recovered after the death of the particular individual who manufactured them are a co-constitutive part of humanity and technics. But why should this prehistoric fact be of any relevance to digital culture? Digitization is a particular form of exteriorization. And in order to fully grasp what distinguishes digital objects from other technical objects, it is fundamental to understand its roots as a human product. The problem is that the accumulation of exteriorization does not stay stable, it accelerates. The perceptions of technics as a promise and of technics as a threat are two complementary faces of that acceleration, of which digital culture is a new iteration. In fact, digital technologies make even more evident the acceleration of time, which is the acceleration on the change of technical objects.

The uncomfortable place of technics in the history of thought is based on a radical lack of understanding that makes it both opaque and transparent at the same time. Its transparency lays the grounds to assume a neutrality of technics that places all responsibility in human agency. This idea leads to an instrumental interpretation that cannot recognize the necessity of technical mediation in the action of thinking. Put differently, technics seem transparent because they are invisible or insignificant, which is the same as saying that they carry no meaning of their own. This is of utter importance for an informed critique on the digital dynamic of transplatform, allegedly non-media-specific, contents.

This bias does not exclude the opacity of technics that may be present even in discourses assuming the transparency of technology. The paradoxical complexity of the phenomenon, or to put it another way, the ignorance of the causes in spite of being able to partially deal with the consequences of technical operations, turns technology into a black box in which the incomprehensible becomes almost magical. And, like all magic, it is never absolutely controllable. Not many regular users know what actually occurs inside a working device, and when curiosity or malfunction have us opening the lid, it is very difficult to understand how the different parts relate and where each piece fits. If it was hard enough to understand the workings of a car engine when it failed, digitization has made the black box darker. I can make the best use of a text processor's functions to write and copyedit this book, and yet I do not have a clue as to how the program works. Aboriginal communities allegedly feared the automatic images produced by the photographic machine, but they did understand very well their own painting techniques. When the workings of our devices escape our understanding we risk finding ourselves just like an Inuit or a Selk'nam facing a camera for the first time; somehow we may end up being alien to our own (technical) culture. Thus technics induce an almost sacred terror, associated with what is perceived as an immanent direction that exceeds its creators, an unavoidable movement forward of technology that may result in the rebellion of the machines, as so many science fiction dystopias have depicted. These two interpretations are not contradictory and, in fact, usually coexist in the same discourse. Common sense has it that humans are responsible for how technical objects are used and, simultaneously, their existence is conditioned by technology whose control is beyond reach. This premise is false, however, since humans and technics are inseparable and the history of humankind is the history of technics. Understanding the ways in which humans become human requires also an understanding of how technics become time, and how time accelerates. The history of the acceleration of technics, a widely acknowledged fact, is also the history of the acceleration of humanity, a quite ignored fact.

Stiegler's "exteriorization" describes in more complex terms what others have defined under the concepts of tool, machine, device, instrument, and language. Exteriorization includes all forms that organized inorganic matter can take. From a silex-headed spear to be thrown at an enemy hominid with whom the access to a pond is being disputed, to the malware that empties our online banking account, we are facing different forms of exteriorization. (Of course, any list will be always insufficient since it would have to include to the totality of culture and its products.) Exteriorization includes organized inert matter (such as a wooden table, a bone spear or a bear skin garment, for example), but also to the domestication of seeds in the Neolithic or the manipulation of its genes since the second half of the twentieth century. And yet, there are strong differences between a Sumerian harvesting *akiti* (i.e., barley) and the corporate copywriting of soybean genomes; or between the products of the craft of an Italian *cinquecento* cabi-netmaker and the assembly of industrial furniture bought at a Swedish retail store. To think that it is only a matter of scale is a mistake. It is, rather, a matter of speed. A speed that allows an unprecedented growth of scales. Without yielding to the tempta-tion of finding the *télos* of technics, it is possible to think that, with forward and backward movements, scales tend to grow according to a time interval that tends to decrease, although that is tied to a series of restrictions imposed by material conditions and physical laws.

At this point it is necessary to discuss the problem of *diferance* inside the forms of exteriorization. Retaking Jacques Derrida's concept, Stiegler understands the *diferance* as the convergence of difference and deferment. The *diferance* is based on the degree of abstraction of exteriorization. Exteriorization implies, to begin with, a concretion and not an abstraction. But in order to speak of technics and not of genetics, to distinguish the bone in the hand of an ape from the club in the hand of a human, Stiegler identifies as exteriorization only those forms that persist and survive the death of its maker: these exteriorizations constitute "stereotypes."[12] The appearance of forms of exteriorization transcending individual makers sets humans apart from animals and indicates the co-beginning of technics and humanity. The first abstractions appear under the form of stereotypes, that is to say, the form of a *reproducible* exteriorization. This kind of abstraction implies the ability to anticipate, thereby introducing time into human existence. So, another aspect of the gap between animals and humans appears: the first are perennial, instinctively avoiding death, whereas the second are mortal since they are aware of their own mortality, can anticipate it, and act to defer it. Technics resides precisely in the hiatus between interior and exterior. And the unit of the reproducibility of exteriorization that make up technics, that is to say, that enables the conformation of a set of tools and actions that transcend the mere prosthetic discovery made by a single individual, is the *stereotype*.

Stereotypes

The "stereotype" is the vector for a kind of transmission that is not specific (or genetic) but ethnic (or cultural). It is that exteriorization that survives in its copies through an informed constructive action that anticipates its result. These organizations of inert matter allow the emergence of a tool grammar (*outillage*, in Stiegler's own terms), that runs parallel to language. These rules for the manufacture and use of tools comprise a set of transmissible and cumulative lore. Each technical intervention in the world involves abstractions aimed at an effective attempt to modify a given state of things. Such abstractions accumulate on preceding ones, allowing, for instance, the tracking of the footprints of the water mill gears in those of the cord clock.

Anticipating is an action that results as it was foreseen, aiming (in a broad sense) to defer death, although this deferment is not evident in every technical action, and the stereotype is the condition of possibility of such anticipation. In this sense, spying on the telephone calls and e-mails of an ally leader may not be very different from sharpening the head of a stone axe before storming the neighboring hominid group. Both actions imply anticipating and exteriorizing, both work as prosthesis, both *create* time, something only made possible by the mediation of technics. In one, the technical mediation is evident (the axe), in the other, it is less clear since we are facing what Simondon calls "technical ensemble," the organization of a series of technical objects and human agents under a single purpose.[13] Nevertheless, the main difference in the primitive and the contemporary action is speed. Technics are not permanent as instinct; inasmuch as technics *are* time, they fluctuate. As I suggested in the previous section, contemporary technics imply an acceleration of time, a meta-stable balance that changes state at an ever increasing frequency.

In one of the most famous scenes from Stanley Kubrick's version of *2001: A Space Odyssey*, Moon-watcher, an ape at the dawn of humanity, discovers that a bone can simultaneously extend his arm's reach and strengthen the force of his closed fists. The death of a tapir that falls under the ape's renewed range and power allows him and his group to project a new relation of force and attack the rival group, more numerous but unarmed, that had taken over the pond. After the foundational battle, Moon-watcher triumphantly throws his bone up in the air and film editing enables Kubrick to continue the turn of the bone into the orbiting movement of a space station: the hiatus has been saved, humanity arises because technics arise, and vice versa. From the mere awareness of facing death due to the drought that devastates the apes' barren lands and forces them to repel the invaders, to the calculation of the space trajectory carried out by an astrophysicist in order to cross the distances of deep space, there is a distance that can be measured by the effectiveness of the technical action, by the degree of anticipation. What separates the bone club from the space ship? A greater or smaller degree of foresight of the results? How does a greater foresight imply an acceleration of time? Perhaps the answers are in a particular form of stereotype: the *standards*.

Milieus

Let me pursue an intuition. If exteriorization helps explain the emergence of time, standards allow apprehending its acceleration. Standards demand a specific and normalized relation with the milieu that is not so determining in the stereotype stage of technics. The concept of "associated milieu" is central to understanding the definition of technical object presented by Gilbert Simondon. The only way to fully apprehend technical objects as discrete entities is through their relation with the world and the particular state that they attempt to modify. In order to accomplish its own function effectively, each technical object needs to be put in relation to the world within the specific milieu for which it is designed: a boat has no utility without its associated milieu, water, that allows it to float and, in that way, to move, just as the feathering of an arrow fulfills its function in a more effective way with the air as an associated milieu whereas it will find its effectiveness limited underwater. In that case, the harpoon, heavier, without feathers that would slow it and with a rope to retain it, will perform the specific required action in a more effective way, incorporating the milieu of water to its favor. These elementary examples point to a fundamental aspect of technical objects: their necessary adaptation to an associated milieu. The adaptation process implies an increasing complexity since the task of technics does not end in the creation of objects, but it extends also to the making of milieus, such as digital operating systems. The growing complexity allows differentiating inside technical objects among elements, individuals, and ensembles that include the lesser objects (e.g., a tool, a machine, and a factory). With the development of modern industry, the natural associated milieu (or "geographic," as Simondon would put it) begins to overlap with increasingly artificial milieus and, for most contemporary technical objects, the associated milieu is as technical as the object itself. There are fundamental differences between the technicity of a canoe and that of a train, which requires railroads to run on. But there are other differences in technical objects working in controlled environments such as machinery in an industrial plant or programs in a software environment. Following Simondon, a technical object is not solely defined by a given milieu and its adaptation to it, but also by the internal integration of its elements. Furthermore, the limitations that changing milieus may impose on an object will force it to gain in autonomy and "concretization." This last concept may be misleading and needs some clarification. The bottom line is that the less attached to an associated milieu, the more undetermined the object is; and the more efficient and interrelated its internal parts are, the more concrete a technical object becomes. For example, whereas a noria was a device that used the water power of a river, or a windmill used wind power, the steam engine did not depend on moving water or air, that is, in changing weather conditions. Steam engines did not need to adapt their materials to withstand operating with a specific kind of air or water current. Thus, steam engines began their own evolution according to themselves and not to adaptations motivated by the milieu. Another example is that of clocks. Ancient timepieces were limited by the contingency of their respective milieus: hourglasses dampened in humid milieus; clepsydras froze in cold milieus; pendulum clocks would not work in rocking boats. Clocks achieved indetermination with the mainspring watch, the first technical individual in this technical lineage, because it was regulated by itself and not by the milieu. Once the watch introduced indetermination, the process of concretization was solely driven by the improvement of its gears and pieces in relation to themselves and not to geographical contingency. That is the way technical objects "evolve" from a Simondonian perspective. Although the examples provided are a simplification of his theory, Simondon introduces a very powerful idea: technical objects tend to an internal perfection regarding how they work. This is due to their tendency towards a more efficient integration of their internal parts according to the laws of physics. So, in summary, the more concrete an object is, the more indeterminate it becomes and can be used in ways that were unforeseen in its original design. In the first half of the twentieth century compu-ting was primarily devised as a ciphered message transmission technology and a missile trajectory correction technology. Luckily for us, it evolved past those restricted (and antihuman) designs but the core of those developments can still be found in the more undetermined, open, concretized endless uses computing has today (e.g., sending e-mails, printing texts, playing music, and editing video).

Of course, the pieces that compose a technical object can take forms that comply with immanent material necessities; for in-stance, those necessities imposed by other technical elements that work as organs: the rotor of the train motor, for example. But, at a certain point in their development, technical objects become indivisible; at a given level of internal organization, the necessity of adaptations is overdetermined by the associated milieu. Since the history of technics identifies tendencies explained by the existence of a limited array of technical solutions for each specific problem, Stiegler detects a novel tendency of technics, industriali-zation, which exceeds the human scale.

The vector of industry is the standard, just as the stereotype was the early vector of technics (and of humanity). This statement is worth reviewing. The way in which objects exist in the world is more and more the history of the milieu in which they exist and not so much of the milieu for which they are designed. Digital culture provides endless examples of this: .mp3 files were just a compression system and not specifically aimed at taking the discman CD players out of the market. However, the milieu is becoming as integral a part of the design as the object itself. And closed software environments such as Microsoft's, Apple's, Ama-zon's or, to a lesser extent, Google's, are examples of this.

For human civilizations, the country and the city have been the associated technical milieus *par excellence*. The *country* is the standardized space for the production of food and other technical supplies, from cotton to biodiesel. (This distinction will leave aside purely extractive activities such as mining.) The *city*, on the other hand, is the model of associated milieu for a series of devices intertwined in successive levels that serve the preservation of what is specifically human: habitation units that protect from weather conditions, associated with the overlapping networks of electricity, gas, water, and telecommunications, in turn interconnected by streets, bridges and roads. By all means, a city is much more than that, but let us accept this *technical* reduction for argument's sake. For example, the operation of the hot water cycle of a washing machine depends on the first three networks as part of its associated milieu; the one of a television set, on the first and last. Once, if ever, the so-called "Internet of things" settles in, the milieu will become a digital and material hybrid.

The *wild* and the *desert* (as distinct from plowed fields or planned cities) are non-standardized spaces, as are the *air*, the *subsoil* and the *ocean*. These last cases are theoretically not possible to normalize, although fracking technologies for oil drilling, for example, may challenge this assumption. All of these, however, still constitute "geographical associated milieus." And the technical objects that are inserted in them operate based on a smaller scope of anticipation, considering the multiplicity of uncontrolled variables at stake. Airplanes continue overcoming air resistance; boats, marine currents; drilling machines, the hardness and the collapse of the earth. They are "given" milieus, although the development of the computer simulation tends to treat them as increasingly standardized milieus, due to the enhanced predictability of the behavior of variables. In either case, in the "domesticated world" and in the "world to be domesticated" there is a common feature that it is the base for the normalization and the simulation: the *standard*.

Standards

The stereotype is the minimum common denominator upon which the *outillage* (the tools as a grammar) is built. That is, the repeated features that make inventiveness exceed the individual creator and become a recognizable and usable technical object. Or, put differently, replicable prostheses that can replace the inabilities of several individuals of a community. Nevertheless, the stereotype has relatively ample margins of variation and its relation with the associated milieu is not too narrow.

From King Arthur's predestined sword, Excalibur, to B. B. King's famous guitar, Lucille, many objects have been individualized, assuming a particular correspondence between users and tools. This ultimately inserts the tool that defines the profession in the world of "beings," close to pets (who also receive the benefit of the name). And, given the control blacksmiths, tailors, and *luthiers* hold over their products, it is possible to understand the margin of adjustment to a specific user each stereotype has. At the time in which humans made their own tools, the user's body dictated the proportions of the prostheses. Today, the procedures of the modern industry have reduced the possibility of such unique tailored adjustment, of providing the objects their own name. No matter how hard we cling to them, beyond the deceptive "personalization" such as car tuning or the selection of screen wallpaper and a colored cell phone cover, tools are no longer unique specimens. Lucille is, after all, a series of successive Gibson ES-355 and not one famous guitar saved from a fire in a dance hall in Twist, Arkansas in 1949. Yielding to an apocalyptic view, there are no more swords waiting a single predestined hand. The reduction of the correspondence between owner and object is caused by the need for a greater capacity of anticipation, for the sake of a greater material (and economic) efficiency. The introduction of regularities in materiality and the production processes explains the acceleration of technical actions. Regarding this issue, Stiegler introduces an original inversion: it is not that modern industry invents standards but, instead, that standards invent modern industry.[14]

The derived question from all this is whether the concept of standard is inherent in technics or, at least, in a technical relation with the world. The first fact is that standards are discrete and necessary units but, in many cases, also arbitrary ones. Such arbitrariness would corroborate some theses of the studies in the social construction of technology that claim that the closure of interpretation of an object determines the stereotype. This implies that the standard for a given technology is eminently social.[15] An eloquent example of this position hides in one of the touchstones of modernization: trains. The standard railroad gauge, or Stephenson

gauge, is 4 feet 8 1/2 inches. One possible origin for this standard
is that of the axles of horse drawn carriages. The measurement of
the axles of the vehicles had been set, in turn, from the roads in
which these circulated; roads that in England were opened following the 2 *equus* measure that is, the back of two Roman horses,
following the old Roman imperial layout.[16] Similar paths may be
reconstructed for the reasons that led some countries to adopt 220
or 230 volts standards instead of 110 (thus allowing their citizens
to die of electrocution more easily). Or in the persistence of the
steering wheels on the right hand side of the car in the British
archipelago and some Commonwealth countries, yet another more
recent example of an imperial standard leftover. Or in the fact that
the .mp3 audio compression format, a steep sound curve reduction
for trained ears, is supported by the overwhelming majority of
devices that play digital sound instead of much more reliable .flac
format.

The establishment of certain features of stereotypes prepares
the ground for the emergence of standards that afford a more
precise anticipation, or, put otherwise, more effective prostheses.
Standards stabilize stereotypes and increase their transmissibility. By detaching technical objects from their particularizing
contingency, the materials and the parts of the technical object
tend to standardize, leaving aside the craftsman's personal decisions, and inserting them in the engineer's impersonal forecast.
Thus, it becomes possible to integrate technical objects in increasingly complex calculations. The process of mathematization of
reality that accompanied the development of modern science runs
parallel to the establishment of industrial standards. Both converge, for instance, in the use of the abstraction provided by
measure systems in practical applications. The history of the
relations between science and technology is, at least, winding, as it
has been clearly exposed by Latour.[17] Standards are, in fact,
central during the moments of more fluid relations between
science and technics, a dialogue plagued of misunderstandings but
certainly facilitated by calculation and consensus.

In his later work, and thinking specifically of the new scenario
unfolded by the expansion of digital technologies, Stiegler carries
this further and the standard becomes a necessary element of

what he calls "grammatization." This is the process of description, formalization, and discretization of "everything," even human behaviors such as voice and gestures. Grammatization is a blind technological and systemic process of categorization that precedes all intentionality.[18] But, if there is, in fact, an unintended technical process in course, what is the role played by standards? It seems to be a minor concept, and the debates usually discuss the parts played by objects, users, uses, associated milieus, or mechanisms. On the contrary, I believe that standards are the very base of contemporary (digital) culture.

When the stereotype becomes stabilized by the consensus or imposition of relatively arbitrary measures, when it standardizes, an unprecedented technical leap occurs. This leap introduces new problems: Does the evolution of technics necessarily imply standards? Is the standard a part of the teleology of technics? Standards play a decisive role in the development of a greater scope of anticipation, but this is not purely arbitrary inasmuch as it responds to physical limitations as well as to cultural decisions. But more importantly, standards introduce calculation in anticipation. With calculation, the automation of technical processes can be developed, and later, the automation of calculation itself. In his last book, Lev Manovich suggests that the introduction of automated calculation (after all, what computers basically do) alters our world in ways equivalent to mechanization in the preceding centuries.[19]

Automated calculation speeds up anticipation, and binary code is an evident example of the acceleration of time due to standards. Binary code implies a new stage of exteriorization that gains in abstraction and transmissibility, leaving behind the last ethnic characteristics of technics. As exteriorization, the pure mathematical abstraction of binary code means it can do without a particular, physically grounded associated milieu. When this occurs, technics lose their last ties to a territory, to a given physical milieu. On the opposite extreme, ethnic groups develop their technics based on the physical possibilities and the necessities that each associated milieu imposes: it is impossible to build igloos in the tropics, just as it is extremely difficult to sun bake bricks in the Arctic. The loss of ethnicity introduces a new form of anticipation, a form that gains planetary scale and where the transmissibility of exteriorizations becomes widespread. In order to arrive at that, allegedly, universal stage, however, a relatively arbitrary form of stereotypes, i.e., the standard, has to step in. In spite of its arbitrariness, it allows world scale modifications of the given states of the world. This does not mean that human will is all it takes. Anticipation is possible in concretion; in the effective accomplishment by means of a technical object that itself is intimately tied to the associated milieu, based on which it will concretize.

Abstractions

Another way to define technical objects is via their function. If we accept this premise we must accept that it is multiply realizable whenever it satisfies the function that defines it. Thus materials and forms may vary and a corkscrew might work pulling or levering with a sharp spiral (the most frequent occurrence), but a cork may also be removed by clipping it with two fine parallel metallic leaves, sucking, or by generating vacuum with a needle. However, before the increasing complexity of technical objects, the definition of "function" becomes more specific: a biplane and a jet are both airplanes but not helicopters. It is not only that they fly; they must do so in a particular way to be considered as classifiable within a particular kind. However, taxonomy of the mechanical kingdom is vain for approaching the problem of standards and the identification of the distinguishing characteristics of contemporary technics. Definition by function must incorporate the notion of associated milieu and also identify in which ways associated milieus are more and more technical rather than natural. The multiple realizability of the object is always limited by the associated milieu. For all the given types of the home corkscrew, there is a single possibility of operation with acceptable margins of efficiency that is determined by the forms and stereotyped matters of the cork and the glass wine bottle neck width. Thus, multiple realizability finds its reference in the associated milieu. The preservation of the qualities of wine during centuries could be satisfied with corks of diverse compositions and sizes that did not require, necessarily, a standard. Stereotypes sufficed.

Due to their industrial origin, airplanes and helicopters are much more standardized in their internal composition than wine bottles. Not meeting the standard for each piece involves the risk of not being able to replace the broken pieces, or that they fail during flight. Stereotypes do not suffice, at this degree of complexity, to satisfy the degree of anticipation implied in overcoming gravity and air resistance in a continued (and safe) manner. Or, what is more important, in a repairable way. Nevertheless, even in these cases, to be able to fulfill their function as objects they must be adapted to an associated milieu, which is given and not created (in the case of the airplane and the helicopter: the conditions of the terrestrial atmosphere). Therefore, the possibilities of multiple realizations are limited.

The concurrence of standardization and calculation that allows the development of computing has introduced some radically new features. The abstraction of the binary code affords an enhanced transmissibility and by multiplying its occurrences, the transit of information generates the illusion of dematerialization. In the end, it is still about exteriorization, but of a kind that exists and replicates automatically, at an unprecedented speed and in a scale that is unperceivable to the naked human eye. Even more, this occurs in multiply realizable storage devices (from the already anachronistic floppy disks and compact discs to hard drives, flash memories, and solid state drives). Digital abstractions operate following agreed protocols that guarantee its interoperability, that is to say, on standards that afford decoding the same files in different computers, and even in computers with different operative systems.

Some may argue it is premature to think that computers actually generate "digital objects" as Yuk Hui, a disciple of Stiegler, suggests.[20] I will reconsider his proposition. The constituent elements of the digital milieu are (partly) digital themselves. This has some consequences that can be seen as distinguishing properties of digital objects. If we define them by their function, digital objects admit multiple realizations, sharing this with "material" technical objects, even in a clearer way. But the very identity of digital objects can only be considered in a relational way, and that means the associated milieu is inseparable from them. A bit chain can be physically made in diverse ways, but its meaning as a digital object depends on the interpretation made by the programs of its digital framework. These programs are digital objects as well, and therefore they also admit multiple realizabilities, and they are also identified by their associated milieu or framework (that can include the framework that they conform, but they will not necessarily be identified with it). This chain of interpretations, of meta-milieus, meta-meta-milieus and so on can be extended, having no *a priori* conceptual limits for these extensions.

What is new here is the multiple realizability of the associated milieu. In the case of technical objects, the physical laws governing associated milieus restrict the possibilities of realizability; for instance, planes cannot fly underwater. In order to sort this problem, humans begin the long process that I have defined above as "normalization" in order to have a milieu that affords the required realizability, beyond the limits set by physical laws. Nevertheless, the realizability of the technical milieu is also limited. The conquest of nature, the efforts for the normalization of the world undertaken since the outset of the industrial era, collide with the complexity of the world, as studies on the impact of the human action in the ecosystem show.

Facing this state of things in which technics play a key role there are two major positions. The apocalyptic perspective stresses on the excess of the technical project, an excess that insinuates the loss of humanity.[21] The opposite is the integrated, optimistic escape forward that places hope in the development of a "correct," sustainable, technics that can conjure all excess. An example of this are the high expectations posed in the quest for indicators and patterns that will allow the establishing of standards (of carbon emissions, for example) that would make the technical way of existence of humans in the world a viable project. So that simulations work, it is necessary to count on technics overcoming the limits of the existing associated milieus. The digital milieu unfolds, therefore, a novel scenario. A scenario in which the milieus, and not only the objects, are also multiply realizable, without any other restrictions than those set by the existing possibilities of calculation and by the interoperability of the different material occurrences of the code. This alternative reinforces the illusion of a total abstraction that no longer depends on the object (or network of objects) that is carried out by computing machines. The complexity of the enterprise, that is to say, the simulation and patterning of all the variables of the world as an associated milieu for its effective normalization, is indicative of the size of the ambition and the hopes placed in this kind of project.[22] If we accept that standards are at the heart of industrialization, it is debatable that we are in a postindustrial era. It seems, on the contrary, that we are living in a hyperindustrial era. But, as the poignant idea of screen essentialism suggests, we are distracted by the lights emanating from our computers and forget to pay attention to the labor (and the screws and motherboards) that make them possible.

Territories

At the beginning of the eighties, in his first, typewritten, novel William Gibson imagined the emergency of an abstract and standardized associated milieu:

> Cyberspace. A consensual hallucination experienced daily by billions of legitimate operators, in every nation, by children being taught mathematical concepts... A graphic representation of data abstracted from banks of every computer in the human system. Unthinkable complexity. Lines of light ranged in the nonspace of the mind, clusters and constellations of data. Like city lights, receding...[23]

The global "consensual hallucination" suggests the suppression of the singular, local traits of stereotypes, an aspect of technics linked to a determined geographic milieu, marks of actual humans interacting with their territory. It is the passage from stereotyped technics, or ethnic technics, to standardized, or technics past ethnics. Gibson's portmanteau summarizes in a powerful way the novelty of a standardized multiply realizable milieu: in order to become "legitimate operators" in cyberspace humans must learn to deal with the mathematical concepts ruling that "place." Whether standards are the result of consensus or the reformulation of the rules of war by mathematical means exceeds the scope of this introduction. But in the following chapters I will present some of the disputes spawned by digitization and how it remapped contemporary culture and our experiencing of the world.

In summary, this introductory chapter presents some key philosophical concepts underlying the ontological nature of technical reproduction and of technical objects. The main concept is that of Stieglerian exteriorization as a co-constitutive trait of the awareness of an interior that distinguishes humans from other living creatures. One very relevant concept discussed here is the Simondonian concept of associated milieu that allows the definition and delimitation of technical objects. The next chapter discusses the idea of digital objects as an abstract form of technical objects, which is made possible by the development of standardized technics that allows an unprecedented abstraction and acceleration of human culture.

CHAPTER 2
Bit Rot

Digital Objects?

In this chapter I identify, characterize, and propose delimitation
for digital objects. In spite of the ubiquity of digital forms of
storage and information processing, we are far from reaching a
consensus about whether we are facing a new ontology or not.
Since the mode of existence of (and in) the digital milieu is usually
taken for granted, it is worth presenting some of the discussions in
the matter.

Some perspectives approaching the problem do not take into
consideration elementary technical aspects of the processes and
procedures that enable digital codification. There are different
kinds of codifications depending on their origin but in the digital
milieu they are equivalent. The most obvious is the ontological
difference of digitized things and things "born digital." However, it
is by the process of being digitized that pre-digital objects lay the
grounds for imagining the existence of digital objects. The ideas of
text, image, audio, and video files were devised thinking of things
that exist outside computers: films, books, discs, tapes, photographic copies, pictures, videotapes, pentagrams, theater plays,
handbooks.... Except for the last case, the ambiguous term "work"
is used to talk about any inscription delimited in these discrete
entities, which are deeply bounded to their storage devices. I will
mention several cases, each with its own specificities. This enumeration is as arbitrary as any, the limits between these forms being

blurry to say the least, but all the cases are interesting because each relates to the five basic forms of actualizing the code in our contemporary culture: text, static image, moving image, sound, and program. The first four imply an idea of finitude, bestowed by the limits of the object that make them an entity, a discrete thing, separated from the universe continuum. The separations, Stiegler's exteriorizations discussed in the previous chapter, can be mentally comprehended in the daily objects where exteriorization occurs (or, alas, used to do so).

Literary works can be described as a finite sequence and disposition of characters whose order persists (i.e., its "substantials") in spite of the diverse occurrence of "accidentals" in each edition, (that is, the material realization of a text). Following that same method, a static image is made up of the elements perceivable by the naked human eye contained in a limited surface. I will momentarily leave aside the difference between automatically-made static images such as photographs and handmade ones such as drawings and paintings. Sound recordings are usually bound by the beginning and end of the recording storage device and adopt too many technical forms to be listed here. Nevertheless, the material characteristics of the device (e.g., the length of the tape or the diameter of the disc) impose limitations that overlap those imposed by the established cultural forms (i.e., the perception units such as "song" or "symphony").[1]

Dramatic text or musical annotation, bounded by the pages (and the key), provide a more interesting example: they present sets of instructions to be executed. That brings them closer to the idea of program, but they are still limited.[2] What underlies works and discrete entities in the digital milieu is a form of mathematization of existence. The mode of existence of a special kind of objects that contain artistic, literary, and scientific works in contemporary culture is only possible by means of the standardization of these objects. Ultimately, this affords building an associated milieu in which they become computable entities. I will address this later.

When computers in their most diverse forms become ubiquitous, the phenomenon of digitization, that is to say, the codification of the different cultural forms so that these can be automatically

represented or reproduced, accelerates. Nevertheless, the phenomenon exceeds works and similar cultural objects, reaching
everything that is perceivable and that can be digitally
represented. The automated mathematization of the world brings
us back to the problem of the boundaries of objects in the continuum of the code. The definition of the limits of an object has been
a theoretical problem since industrialization; digitization forces us
to question about those boundaries in the code.

Although there is continuity between the industrial world and
the digital world, the ontology of objects introduces new problems
that are not automatically transferable from a given context (the
physical associated milieu) to another (the digital milieu). In spite
of this difference of context, attempts to define things and their
properties tend to make extensions from one milieu to the other.
Different approaches to the problem of culture in the context of the
so-called "new technologies" refer to certain entities as "digital
objects." In order to systematize, I will present three different
perspectives that can be distinguished based on their fields of
application: (a) pragmatic or institutional; (b) humanities; and (c)
computer science.

Digital Objects from a Pragmatic Perspective. Examples of
this are the instrumentalisation of digital collections (as it is the
use of DOI, or Digital Object Identifier) that replaces other identification standards such as ISSN or the ISBN, and is present in
business models that sell "works" in digital format (iTunes, Amazon, some of the services provided by Google). This pragmatic
reduction also operates in digital preservation institutions. For
instance, the "Glossary" of the *Linked Heritage Project* on the
Library of the University of Padova website provides the following
operative definition:

> A digital object is an entity in which one or more content files and their
> corresponding metadata are united, physically and/or logically, through the
> use of a digital wrapper. Digital objects (or digital materials) refer to any
> item that is available digitally.[3]

The key aspect of this approach is the definition of "digital objects" in quantitative terms. Defined properties can take standard, discrete values and, for that reason, afford automatic administration.

Digital Objects from a Humanities Perspective. A different concept of digital object appears in qualitative approaches such as *Digital Cultures* by Milad Douehi, some entries of *Tecnopoéticas Argentinas: Archivo Blando de Arte y Tecnología [Argentine Technopoetics: Soft Archive of Art and Technology]* compiled by Claudia Kozak, or *Debates in Digital Humanities* edited by Matthew K. Gold. What prevails here is a cultural interpretation of an implicit definition: the boundaries of digital object derive from a correspondence with the pre-digital ideas that have helped define what a work is. The boundary parameters correspond not to intrinsic aspects of the structure of the code but to established cultural guidelines, generally associated with objects that have allowed exteriorization and that are considered storage devices of the works at stake (i.e., books, songs, photo albums). In this point, it is worth noting the oxymoronic nature of digital objects, inasmuch as it implies the convergence of the concrete (the object) and the abstract (the digital code) around apparently discrete entities.

Digital Objects from a Computer Science Perspective. A third definition of digital object is that provided by the technical properties for the object's existence as such. One approach to this characterization focuses on the combinatorial properties over the gradual variations, the irrelevance of the specific properties of the individual entities (the bits) as opposed to the relevance of the relations between them. The specific form of the bit actualization is indifferent, it is not relevant for the operation and the interpretation of the digital systems, the only relevant value is its state: Zero or one? Jackendoff says:

> The power of the computer lies in the fact that the state of each binary switch (or "flip-flop") is independent of the states of the others. Thus, the action of larger components is not a sum or average of the actions of the parts; rather, it depends on the precise combinatorial properties of the parts. Furthermore, each part's changes of state depend on combinatorial properties of the other parts.[4]

If we follow this definition, digital objects are abstract, admitting diverse physical actualizations, and, another very important feature, they are semantic. This means they are not only defined by their structure as a sequence of bits, but also by the associated milieu (usually also digital) in which they exist.

Meta-milieus

It could be said that digital technologies do not bring about anything new. Information has always existed and has always been fundamental for the development of human societies. Nevertheless, it seems that in this case size does matter, and the unprecedented amount of information and the speed at which it is handled are producing a new phenomenon. That can happen because there are programs able to effectively process this amount of information. Programs, in a specific sense, are also digital information and they can constitute digital objects as well. According to Yuk Hui, digital objects are something with which we interact on a daily basis.[5] That is why he suggests it is necessary to think of them either as extensions of the classic idea of natural objects, or as a particular kind of Simondonian technical objects. And to do this, understanding the nature of the associated milieu in which they exist is indispensable.

In the first half of the twentieth century, computing was developed with the advances in the automation of mathematical operations. One of the fundamental concepts in understanding the scope of this new technical field is Alan Turing's notion of "universal machine." Rapidly summarizing a well-known story, Turing proposed a mathematical machine that could imitate all existing (mathematical) machines. In the twenty-first century, the expansion of computing derived technologies in almost all aspects of human life radically changes the rules of the game. The procedures and specific tools in each sphere of human labor have been progressively imitated by software. In *Software Takes Command*, Manovich suggests that today we face the effective existence of a properly universal machine due to its capability to imitate preexisting milieus:

> Alan Turing theoretically defined a computer as a machine that can si-
> mulate a very large class of other machines, and it is this simulation
> ability that is largely responsible for the proliferation of computers in
> modern society. But [...] neither he nor other theorists and inventors of
> digital computers explicitly considered that this simulation could also
> include media. It was only Kay and his generation that extended the idea
> of simulation to media—thus turning Universal Turing Machine into a
> Universal Media Machine, so to speak. [6]

Here he introduces a very powerful idea for a philosophy of
computers. This particular technical object is a true "metamedia"
that can simulate all preexisting media (and even itself or other
metamedia, as is the case of emulation software) but also give
existence to new media. It is worth noting, although "media" in the
communicational sense is not exactly equivalent to the concept of
"milieu" proposed by Simondon, Stiegler, or Hui, for the particular
case of the digital technologies that Manovich analyses works in
an equivalent way, since "simulated media" are the "associated
milieus" without which the digital objects cannot exist.

Digital Objects or Computing Objects?

The coupling between the object and the associated milieu is
constituent for digital objects. From a certain degree of abstraction
we can see a given digital object as a bit sequence, or even more
concretely, as its physical realization in terms of voltage, of a
distribution of magnetic orientations in a surface or as holes in
paper. But it does not seem possible to grasp the identity of a
digital object in terms of its physical realization. For example,
when we copy the digital image of a disc to a notebook hard-drive,
the respective physical realizations lose all similarity and yet,
from a human perspective, we are identifying them as equals;
using the word "copy" speaks for itself.

To consider a digital object as a sequence of bits is also somewhat problematic, since that same sequence can be interpreted in
very different ways depending on the digital context in which it is
inserted. It may be a program in source code, in machine code, a
photo, a musical recording, etc. Now, given a specific context, not

any sequence of bits is an object there, and context itself determines the conditions of possibility for digital objects that would exist in that particular digital milieu. A code error turns a song into mere noise or a program that interprets the code and reproduces songs into a program that repeatedly displays an error message.

The development of computer science and its increasing ubiquity in every discipline has given rise to a family of concepts whose scope oscillates and varies in different theoretical approaches. It is not about finding the ultimate and precise definitions for them – something as chimerical as premature. It is about establishing the different relations among them and analyzing their persistence in the different contexts from use as well as the, sometimes subtle, differences. This will provide us with concepts strong enough to carry out a critique of content idealism.

Usually, "digital" is considered synonymous with "computational." Since both concepts are used in a multiplicity of ways, indeed some conflations do coincide. A paradigmatic example of this is pan-computing, that expands the idea of computing to almost anything, reason for which the digital would be a subclass of computing. Nevertheless, the adjective *digital* can be applied to a wider variety of objects than *computing*. Furthermore, computing would not even be applicable in an intransitive sense. Computing can actually be seen as a matter of degrees: a pocket calculator will compute more than an abacus but less than the Babbage's Analytical Engine. Summarizing, there would be objects or systems that compute more than others. Pursuing this idea, the property of computing would be an intrinsically relational one.

But before discussing computing, let us return for a while to the idea of digital. Digital objects abound. We can review them, modify them, duplicate them, transmit them.... As Hui suggests, from a perspective where digital objects are considered as an equivalent of Simondonian technical objects, there are different degrees of concretization in different digital object formats, and this degree of concretization is not necessarily increased with new technologies. Hui considers the passage from GML to HTML as a web document format to exemplify the loss of concretization, since HTML is a simpler and lighter language. The appearance of, for example, XML as digital object representation language would account for this process of concretization,

> if by concrete here we mean that the concepts of the objects are more well defined and the relations between parts of the objects and between objects are more explicit—that is, no longer limited by hyperlinks but by parsing and comparing well-structured data.[7]

Hui characterizes the variety of existing digital objects in the associated milieu provided by the World Wide Web. This milieu has grown in an exponential way, opening up to new possibilities (that is, more and different digital objects) and challenges (such as maintaining interoperability and data coherence). These objects would be subject to concretization processes, in spite of the ambiguity they embody. There is no essential distinction between a text and a program, between code and data. This indifference is constituent of computing as a discipline and it is demonstrated in Turing's universal machine theorem. One needs to be careful here when considering the mode of existence of digital objects, since distinctions only are provided by context, and contexts can change. In fact, they do it all the time. A program compiled to run in a given Linux version in principle cannot be executed directly in MacOs; at a certain point it stops being a program to become flat text, or worse, an indecipherable bit sequence. It ceases to be a program and becomes a problem: how to make meaning of that object or how to make an abstraction "become" an object. A digital object that is incompatible within an associated milieu is not even a technical element in the sense of Simondon (a tool working as a part of a larger machine), since its very existence as digital object depends on the associated milieu that interprets it.

Hui tries to establish some differences between digital objects according to their possibility of manipulation (or their affordances). But it is necessary not to lose sight of the fact that the possibility of manipulation is not an intrinsic property of digital objects, but an established relational property set in a digital milieu that is, a reference frame (a compiler or interpreter, an operating system, a video or sound codec). A symptomatic example of this is the use of encrypted files, so necessary to avoid technological surveillance. If we have the access key, the object can be any object and have the most elaborated affordances; if we do not, and the cryptographic protocol is sufficiently sound, there is only noise.

Would not all digital objects be computing objects then? That is to say, some objects are programs, under certain conditions of the associated milieu. Others, in principle, could be data that afford manipulation by a specific program (again, under certain conditions, not *a priori*). Although the probability of finding rational code or interpretable data or an index that indicates some of these in, say, the molecular structure of a compacted soda can found in a trash bin is extremely low, search engines and decoders of all kind, aided by the standardization of formats, afford an intensive and always novel use of, as Google puts it, "all the information in the world." But, of course, endless milieus fall into disuse: What is today, for instance, a file created on text editors such as *Word Perfect* or *Chi Writer*? They have become incomprehensible digital relics rather than objects.

Multiple Multiple Realizabilities

The constituent elements of the digital milieu are usually digital objects themselves (although hardware is always necessary, the digital anchorage can be deferred as much as required as I explained earlier). That is the distinguishing property of digital objects. It is clear that, defined by their function, digital objects admit multiple realizations, sharing this characteristic with technical objects, even in a clearer way (i.e., very different programs can accomplish the same specific task). The very identity of digital objects can only be considered in a relational way, and that means the associated milieu is inseparable from them. As said earlier, a bit chain can be physically realized in the most diverse ways, but its meaning as a digital object depends on the interpretation made by the programs of its digital context that are digital objects as well. The matryoshka doll-like chain of interpretation contexts that are an object at a level and an interpreter in the preceeding has no conceptual limitations. Not just the technical object but also the associated milieu are multiply realizable.

Fabricating an extreme example, it is as if one could create the atmospheric conditions for a plane (and not a submarine) to *fly* underwater and still *be* a plane. That is actually what occurs in digital milieus. An example of multiple realizability of the associated digital milieu is the case of old arcade games in their coin-op cabinet, opposed to the same games running on programs such as *MAME32* (a Multiple Arcade Machine Emulator software) that rebuilds a machine specific digital milieu in a completely different context.

The possibility of copying digital objects gives rise to interesting questions about the unique identity of these objects. The multiple realizability of technical objects allows for speaking of "copies," or of "standardization," or "models" of a certain object. Nevertheless, the serial production of technical objects from a model does not give rise to identity, at least an identity of tokens. A car of a given model and color is not the same car, legally speaking, as the next in the production line. But we are accustomed to say, on the contrary, that the file I am editing and that I have just copied to my external drive (and, just in case, also backed-up in my cloud drive) is the "same" file that is in the flash memory at this moment. In any case, I do not identify my file with its physical realization, opposed to what I do with the car or the corkscrew.

Identity and Limits of Digital Objects

What are the limits of entities perceived as a part of a given technical lineage that exists in another associated milieu, such as the digital milieu? The typical case here concerns whether there is a specific technical relation between the book and the eBook. (A question derived from this case concerns whether a change of milieu allows the continuation of a "technical lineage" properly speaking). Summarizing the discussion on the previous pages, the first characteristic of digital objects is that they can be considered "discrete entities." This implies an idea of finitude granted by the limits of the object, which is an entity separated from the continuum of the universe.

The decisive aspect of the pragmatic-institutional approach to digital objects is the definition in quantitative terms of properties that can take standardized values affording automated management. From a humanities perspective there is a prevalence of a cultural interpretation that establishes correspondences with pre-digital notions in order to define what a "work" is. As already noted, the parameters to set the boundaries are not intrinsic to the structure of the code but a hybrid with established, non-digital, cultural perceptions associated with specific storage devices in which the works are inscribed. Finally, according to a computational conception, digital objects are somehow abstract and admit diverse physical realizations. Reconsidering Simondon's philosophy, I added the semantic aspect to this characterization. Digital objects are defined not only by their structure as a bit sequence, but also by the associated milieu in which they exist.

As I previously discussed in the first chapter, contemporary technics is based on a milieu that is as designed as the technical object itself. And, in the cases where it cannot be designed, it is standardized, patterned or modeled in order to provide the high degree of anticipation required. Computing plays a decisive role, by means of a normalization of the world (as the one caused by GPS devices, for example) or by means of the modelization (in the anticipation of the behavior of the soil in oil fracking or weather forecast, for example). Within the digital realm, the technical milieu also implies problems that deserve philosophical attention especially regarding the question, posed by Hui, about the delimitation "within" the code.

The coupling between the object and its associated milieu is constituent in the case of digital objects. But, as noted earlier, considering digital objects only as bit sequences is problematic, since any given sequence can be interpreted in very different ways depending on the digital context in which it is inserted. Not any bit sequence is an object in a specific context, and this determines the conditions of possibility for digital objects that can exist in that milieu. And, because of that, a codification error can turn digital objects into noise.

An associated issue here is the distinction between a program and a file as technical objects. Although this discussion might seem superfluous, it is not. A text processor is comparable to any physical technical object whereas the .rft files that it produces are equivalent to the products of a typewriter. But some text files can have programs inside them, as in the case of document macros or templates. These are affordances that texts produced with a typing machine do not possess. As spreadsheet templates show, it is difficult to think that they are "only" products of a program. If the divisions were that clear, there would be continuity between the *industrial machine* that makes objects, like the printing press produces books, and a *program* output, the word processor that program creates text files (that may or may be not sent to the printing queue). Such a naïve approach assumes continuity between material and digital milieus. The impression of continuity rests on the allographic perception of objects. Even conceding to a limited concept of digital object of this type, that is to say, that only programs would be true digital objects, two new problems arise when comparing it to the industrial context: that of identical copies and, derived from this, that of the identity of objects.

The possibility of copying objects digitally raises interesting questions on the identity of these copies. We usually think in terms of "copies," "standardization," and of "models" of certain objects. But as I have claimed above, the serial production of technical objects of a model does not produce an identity of tokens. Two cars can be of the same model, but this does not make them the same entity, something that, in addition to the inscription in state registries, car tuning, and the driver's skill (or lack thereof), makes them start differing one from the other once they hit the road. On the other hand, people usually refer to different instances of a file as the very same file. Eventually, due to the successive modifications on each of these instances people may consider them not as different things but as "versions" of the same thing (say, of an essay for a Modern English Literature course) and, in order to avoid its multiplication, people may just try to stop its variations by making it a .pdf file. In any case, we do not identify files with their physical realization, as opposed to what we do with cars or corkscrews or bullets. Forensics goes a long way when trying to ascertain the identity of things.

An interesting and informed approach comes from the field of digital conservation. Owens, continuing Kirschenbaum's approach on digital forensics, stresses the existence of an aspect of objects (not only digital) in which interpretation plays a key role. It should be noted that the "interpretation" is a phenomenon as technical as psychological. Or exterior and interior, retaking a Stieglerian perspective:

> I find it interesting that these two different senses of sameness, the allographic and the autographic are fundamentally mutually exclusive properties. [...] While conservationists do their best, from day to day there are changes in things like the water content in pages or other minor fluxuations in the chemical composition of any artifact. I suppose if the device wasn't particularly sensitive it wouldn't detect the difference, but even if it did say they were the same thing we would know that it was a lie, it just wasn't sensitive enough to pick up the subtle changes in the artifact. This is a key distinction between analog and digital objects. Digital objects are always encoded things, in this sense they (like the text of *Frankenstein* or the text transcribed by scribes) are allographic. Their essence is actually more allographic than those analog corollaries, as the encoding is much richer and leaves much less interesting information residing in the artifact itself.[8]

In some histories of literature the differences in the text of works are defined as accidentals, opposed to the permanence of the substantials. That is to say, errata do not affect the constituent properties of a text, which is removed from its particular printed existence. At this point it is important to distinguish levels, since a *work* (be it literary, artistic, or scientific, etc.) is not a technical object. The technical object is the book or the electronic reading device and the files it holds. Trying to avoid discussions on the nature of the work of art or the semiotic approaches that study works as "devices" or "artifacts," I would like to focus on another aspect that may introduce a different view on debates in art and technics.

A fundamental aspect of technical objects is the possibility of their replicability. Repetition is, in fact, the main drive of technics; what separates the individual discovery or "naturefact" (i.e., using a fallen tree to cross a river, holding a bone as a club) from the artifact, a thing made by human craft. Only when exteriorization becomes stereotypical, when an idiosyncratic use transcends individual use, one can properly speak of technics. Simondonian "technical objects" are beyond stereotypes, because they are only possible as standardized industrial products that integrate different technical elements. But when facing works, especially artistic and literary ones, we still have to deal with the (somewhat Romantic) idea of "uniqueness." It could be said that such works are always prototypes. And yet there is an inescapable difference within the vast universe that fits in the concept of work: that of *replicability*.

Even abjuring the exegetic excesses of Walter Benjamin's most famous essay, it is possible to think about the difference between "auratic works" and technically reproducible works. Auratic works are unique pieces with a distinct identity that carry the traces of their history (their physical changes and their changes of ownership). The "aura," the accumulation of time, inscribed in both the physical marks of wear, tear, and restoration on the materials and all the receptions of a particular historical existence that provides "authenticity" to an "original" work is lost even in the most accurate mechanical reproductions. Benjamin defined aura as the unrepeatable convergence of time and space on the objects, which in turn embedded them in "the fabric of tradition."[9] In Benjamin's theoretical work, "tradition" means a pre-industrial context of production. Put differently, auratic works are autographic works, while technically reproducible works are allographic. But even within this approach, it is always about products and not technical objects.

Let us consider printed texts. The purpose of this detour from bits and chips into characters and pages is only to identify some similarities between text and code. The falsification or authenticity of unique auratic works can be defined from an autographic perception (of the marks that distinguish it). Texts, however, have an allographic property. Traditionally, the interpretation of a given literary work does not depend on its realizations (i.e., editions) and its variations are accidents that do not alter its substance.[10] If accidents modify a work in a way that prevents recognizing it as such, textual integrity will have been lost. Put differently, it will not be Mary Shelley's *Frankenstein* but another work, probably the outcome of bad plagiarism.

As writing is the basic element of texts (in a narrow, non-semiotic sense), codification is the basic element of digital objects.

And its existence is, *a priori* allographic, as computing operations such as checksums or cyclical redundancy verifications that control the identity of abstractions demonstrate. In *Wikipedia*, as of January 21, 2015, the entry for "cyclic redundancy check" explained it

> [...] is an error-detecting code commonly used in digital networks and storage devices to detect accidental changes to raw data. Blocks of data entering these systems get a short *check value* attached, based on the remainder of a polynomial division of their contents. On retrieval the calculation is repeated, and corrective action can be taken against presumed data corruption if the check values do not match.
>
> CRCs are so called because the *check* (data verification) value is a *redundancy* (it expands the message without adding information) and the algorithm is based on cyclic codes. CRCs are popular because they are simple to implement in binary hardware, easy to analyze mathematically, and particularly good at detecting common errors caused by noise in transmission channels.[11]

Extending the concept of text to that of code may be hasty and demands some consideration. The most important consideration concerns code agency. The 2015 software that regulates traffic lights of a city is not the digital equivalent of a 1965 folder with the layout, plans, and schedules of an operating traffic lights system. Digital code does not only describe actions, it can execute them. From the perspective of digital objects, relationally delimited in the code, a "program" is the same as any other "file" that the said program can "open." But is not only a question of levels; some examples make distinctions complicated. Some digital objects are just displayed while others carry out a series of operations. Think of the difference of an image file or a video file compared to a videogame.

In the electromechanical industrial context, defining technical individuals and their degree of concretization based on the integration of the technical elements inside them does not demand the additional effort to identify the limits of such objects since they are self-evident. Perhaps delimiting the associated milieu requires a greater descriptive effort; but, nonetheless, physical limits do exist. On the contrary, in the digital context, that definition is necessarily relational. And unlike the case of technical objects, an

aspect to consider here is the "integrity" of the code in the successive replications, the fixity check. With closed software this does
not seem to be so problematic and is, in this sense, equivalent to
technical objects, but the permanent upgrade dynamics have no
equal in other technologies, not even for closed software packages.

Today's cell phone applications are constantly updated, and not
necessarily with the user's permission. Thus, the same object
remains different from its previous existence. This is why, in
principle, the definition of a digital object should include the
version number. Nevertheless, this claim loses sight of the indetermination of open source and free software, and of non-
restrictive programming. Hui, in fact, suggests that the Simondonian concept of concretization can be applied to describing change
within the new digital milieu. This assertion argues that proprietary software is in fact a kind of software that prevents concretization in a way similar to what Simondon calls "deceptive
aestheticization" to refer to those design decisions that prevent the
concretization of technical objects, namely in the car industry for
economic rather than technical purposes.

Another aspect I would like to insist on is the paradoxical dual
condition of digital objects: at the same time abstract code and
material inscription. In the field of digital conservation, this
double condition reveals the profound coexistence of allographic
and autographic characteristics in digital objects that becomes
evident in forensic approaches:

> What is wild about digital objects is that there are extensive forensic, or
> artifactual, traces of the media they were stored on encoded on inside the
> formal digital object like a disk image. That is, the formal object of a disk
> image records some of the forensic, the artifactual, the thingyness of the
> original disk media that object was stored on. The forensic disk image is
> allographic but retains autographic traces of the artifact.[12]

However, these traces of materiality do not become an obstacle for
the occurrence of another distinguishing feature of digital objects,
the multiple realizability of their associated milieus, that are, in
turn, digital objects in the context of other associated milieus.

The scenario that I have just introduced cannot offer definitive
answers, but only suggest a few common terms to identify some

recurrent problems. An intuition guiding my research is that some possible answers may hide in a deeper understanding of the relations between code and standards, for which it is necessary to understand the part standards play in technics and, inside the digital milieu, their importance in the processes of identification and replication. But how do things that do not meet the standard exist in these milieus? This, of course, exceeds the scope of this book but I nevertheless aim at taking a first step in that particular direction.

Arts Computing

Digital poetry has been a most fertile field for experimentation in digital culture. Nevertheless, critical studies on the topic face several difficulties due to the innovation and the decontextualisation (akin to avant-garde *ostranenie* procedures) generated by technical mediation. There are two intimately related problems that should not be avoided. First, the concept of work that in literature was somewhat bounded to its associated mode of circulation (i.e., books) and the associated practices they afford. Although books are not the necessary condition for a string of words to be read as piece of literature, its centrality in the conformation of Western literate culture is unquestionable. And, in the Modern age, literary works became intrinsically bound to a more specific kind: printed books.

There are three salient characteristics of modern literary works in their bookish existence: permanence, abstraction, and reproducibility. The first characteristic has been sustained by printing in paper and storing in books; the second originates in the conventional graphical representation of the acoustic matter (namely, the alphabet) enabling the practice of writing and reading; the third accelerates the effect of the previous two with the affordances introduced by the printing press. Printed books do not account for all the modes of existence of books as specific objects but they are the *de facto* overwhelming majority of their manifestations. And they are a product born of standardization. Literacy in the West is deeply related to the development of modern technology. Both the order of books and the order of industry emerge from standards. Typography, once the press reaches an industrial scale, is the standard for writing upon which a lasting, abstract, and reproducible order is built.

What is the relation of print, industrial, and digital cultures? Like industrial parts, both printing and digital technologies are based on discrete, standardized units. But there is a major difference. The units of the press are concretions: the metal glyphs of a typeface or font. Those of the word processor are abstract: the glyphs of a TrueType[13] font. Rather than the different locations of two different cultures it is a difference of speed, the acceleration of the production and transmission rate enabled by the digital standard. Literature in the digital milieu is always a construction over two layers of standards: those of the alphabetical writing (standardized by the national educational systems, the state, and cultural institutions) and those of the digital protocols (established by companies, national institutes of standards of certain countries, and international web ruling boards such as the ICANN, the Internet Corporation for Assigned Names and Numbers).

Although the stabilization of literary forms in the era of books was challenged by Dadaism, Surrealism, and other avant-garde movements, they did not radically change book culture. The perception of a "crisis" or "death of books"[14] is caused by a change in standards: digital text apparently becomes the hegemonic mode of existence. And new poetics challenge it. As it is well known, innovative artistic practices are themselves a "tradition" that from time to time questions the naturalized technical features of writing (both print and digital). Within experimental poetics it is worth looking into some aspects of "digital poetry" and their relation to standards. In order to do so, I will review some critical definitions. The not too narrow concept of digital poetry can be included within other wider concepts such as "e-literature," "techno-texts," or "technopoetry." Each emphasizes a specific feature.

e-literature is a concept that includes digital poetry as well as hypertextual narrative and other genres of the digital milieu. However, it should be noted that the "e" suffix for "electronic" places the emphases on the means of production (and, to a lesser extent, reception) of works:

Electronic literature, generally considered to exclude print literature that has been digitized, is by contrast "digital born," a first-generation digital object created on a computer and (usually) meant to be read on a computer. The Electronic Literature Organization, whose mission is to "promote the writing, publishing, and reading of literature in electronic media," convened a committee headed by Noah Wardrip-Fruin, himself a creator and critic of electronic literature, to come up with a definition appropriate to this new field. The committee's choice was framed to include both work performed in digital media and work created on a computer but published in print (as, for example, was Brian Kim Stefans's computer-generated poem "Stops and Rebels"). The committee's formulation: "work with an important literary aspect that takes advantage of the capabilities and contexts provided by the stand-alone or networked computer."[15]

In parallel to e-literature, Hayles refers to technotexts, "when a literary work interrogates the inscription technology that produces it, it mobilizes reflexive loops between its imaginative world and the material apparatus embodying that creation as a physical presence."[16] This concept retakes the idea of inscription as a constituent technical element of any language and demands to consider the specificity of each material manifestation (or mode of existence). Hayles calls this process "media-specific analysis."

Finally, Kozak indicates that

[w]hen an assumed confluence between poetry and technology becomes manifest, we are in the realm of technopoetry. The term yearns for inclusiveness, since it does not aim at a specific state of the technology but points out a close and aesthetically productive relationship between poetry and technical media given by their specific materiality, as well as the dialogue that poetry establishes with the technological context in which it arises. This relation is the object of experimentation, and therefore technopoetry could be called technological experimental poetry. [...] [E]xperimental technopoetry is poetry with a strong intermedial and/or transmedial vocation that leads it to fusion different degrees of image, word, sound, body and movement and that [...] finds a territory to explore in the contemporary technological availability, which allows easy manipulation of such "materials." [...] Although there is a frequent tendency to relate technopoetry with those working with the cutting edge technical means of each period [...] technopoetry can also occur in anachronism.[17]

The concept of technopoetry draws attention to the historical condition of technics. In the same book, Kozak emphasizes the necessary intertwinement between technological poetics and technological politics,[18] noting that different relations with technics will also imply different political positions.

The above-mentioned conceptualizations implicitly or explicitly introduce the need to pay attention to the material properties when conducting critical research in contemporary arts and literature. Both authors likewise indicate two particular characteristics of poetry in the digital milieu: the importance of the visual aspect of the poetic form and its kinetic properties. As I said before, digital poetry retakes some typical avant-garde procedures, such as interactivity, tactile perception (derived from kineticism and interaction), convergence of resources originating in other arts (text combined with image, audio, and video), automation of text generation, programming, and use of contents external to the work itself (newspapers, databases, etc.).

An issue not very much addressed by critics is the most salient characteristic of the text in the digital milieu, its "addressability." The concept comes from computer science and defines the result of the objective quantitative classification by means of discrete, standard units, which afford protocolized and, later automated, treatment.[19] Today digital technologies "refer" in such terms to any coded object in any sphere or field of contemporary culture. Text, image, sound, or video in the digital milieu are codifications that programs can address in defined, discrete segments of the code and operate accordingly. Any operation on a digital string is carried out by addressing it.

In order to study digital poetry it becomes indispensable to consider addressability because it illuminates how each technological poetic *operates* be it *against* or *within* an hegemonic technology. Addressability is also fundamental to identify the diffuse authorship of these works as well as their underlying idea of technics. Furthermore, addressability provides a deeper understanding of the change operated in the passage from analog to digital (and vice versa in some cases).

These works' most shared feature is being built from the standards established by different softwares (such as Flash or Time Based Text). These usually exist online and that necessarily implies the use of standards that afford the different pages to work properly. In other words, that the browsers can interpret them and run them in the computer screens with all their different functionalities. Within the general context of digital experimental poetics, most are located in a specific group, that of standardized experimentation. This provides a visibility and transmissibility that is not present in works that pursue aesthetic experience by means of destandardization or by rendering standards inoperable.

In this second group we can locate works as *Agrippa* by Gibson, Ashbaugh, and Begos Jr., Mauro Césari's asemic writing[20] or the novel by Pablo Katchadjian *Mucho trabajo* [*A Lot of Work*]. *Agrippa* proposed a self-consuming work composed by an unreadable book object, illustrated with erasing etchings and containing a disc with a self-destructing digital poem that allowed only one reading. Césari constructs visual poems using anachronistic technologies in unexpected ways generating results that resemble works of digital art. *Mucho trabajo* is a novel printed in Times New Roman 2.1 font size. Its printing necessarily implies the use of digital technologies, first to write it, then to reduce the font size, and finally to print it. The result is an almost unreadable book, unless one undertakes the laborious task of reading it with a magnifying glass. The three cases are examples of technological misuses that demand deciphering and that, at the same time, destandardize. That is to say, these are works that by their own technical procedures conspire against the preservation and transmission possibilities afforded by analog and digital technologies.

On the contrary, typical works of net-art are interpreted by the browsers. And before the Internet as we know it today, early e-literature also operated "within" standards, and sometimes even contributed to establish them, as is the case of early hypertext fiction *Afternoon: A Story* by Michael Joyce created using *Storyspace*, a hypertext editing software developed by Joyce and Jay David Bolter to create and run this and other pieces of the same e-literature genre. This does not imply in any way that poetics operating with standards imply a conservative position opposed to the allegedly daring subversion posed by destandarizing poetics, which in turn could be hastily dubbed as neo-luddites. What is interesting in both kinds of poetics, those operating *with* standards and those operating *against* them, is whether they challenge or not the established technical discourses and ideologies by either showing their possibilities, finding the limits, turning the attention to otherwise naturalized procedures, or inventing new categories that avoid hegemonic standard-based technical tendencies.

Indiscretions

The concept of *unaddressability* refers to the loss of digital text affordances. There are at least three extended ways to digitize text: to type it, to scan it, or to apply OCR software. The first is simpler and it depends on human input; the third it is more complex, and is based on automated input and software interpretation: the use of a scanner to produce an image that is then subject to optical character recognition (OCR) software that codifies the scanned image of a text in a discrete character string. In both cases, the attention is centered in reproducing the content of the text, its semantic content, at the expense of its form and/or materiality. The second way to digitize a text is to scan it in a format predetermined by the device (such as .jpg, .tif, .gif). In this case, the text separates from the linguistic code and stops being addressable *as text*: it will no longer fully afford elementary digital text functionalities such as "find" or "copy & paste." Nor it will be an information rich indexable object, since its words will not contain machine code interpretable as a linguistic content, not characters but pixels. Unaddressability is a procedure by which a text that was originally indexable (that is to say, that it preserved its discreteness, affording automatic reading), losses that quality to become only a digital image. On the other hand, this loss will enhance other material aspects of the text: its visual traits and its physicality, depending, of course, on the resolution of the used scanning technology. Unaddressability recovers an aspect of texts that had been somewhat disregarded during nineteenth and twentieth century print culture: its visual value, to be seen and not necessarily to be decoded. By becoming digital images, books partially recover their condition as historically situated objects.

A *poetics of unaddressability* may include examples of very different origins. The following list aims to identify cases from different arts. All contain elements contributing to blur standardized categories that would justify inserting them in established artistic technical procedures and genres. Such blurring can be seen in the ways in which the standards operating in each artistic procedure are put into question. In the case of the relation between literature and visual arts, there are numerous experimental works, both analog and digital, that challenge the closed and finished condition of works, and the clear authorship in the case of printed books; the legally sanctioned transmissibility in the digital milieu; and the modes of permanence, legibility, and access in both technologies. Some examples of poetics of unaddressability are the material/digital hybrid *Agrippa*;[21] in the case of properly digital literature, the poem *petite brosse à dépoussiérer fiction* by Philippe Bootz;[22] in the case of print literature, the above mentioned novel *Mucho trabajo*.[23] Another interesting example of hybrid analog/digital unaddressability is artist's book *Humument* by Tom Phillips, a work in progress since 1973 that has its own iPad app version.[24] Even the unorthodox scholarly work *Writing Machines* by N. Katherine Hayles in collaboration with designer Anne Burdick might be considered as an example of unaddressability. The book presents a methodology to analyze experimental and digital literary works subverting the standards for academic publishing, and it would not be farfetched to consider it as an attempt to unaddress literary theory.

Principles of Analysis

An inquiry into the relation between works and their storage devices demands accurate definitions of the entities that oscillate between the poles of the idealist (allographic) abstraction and the pure auratic (autographic) expression of a trivial and fetishistic materialism. For that reason, I will retrieve from histories of art, literature, books, technics, and technical reproduction the origins of some artifacts that can illuminate the transits between idea and realization, between representation and codification, between storage device and reproduction.

In his "Opening Lesson" to the seminar "Writing and Culture in Modern Europe," Chartier enunciates some principles of analyses that come in handy when approaching writing and culture in the context of the digitization.[25] Chartier identifies three key problems: "The proclaimed or discussed authority of what is written, the mobility of its meaning, the collective production of the text."[26] In relation to these problems, there are three methodological principles to approach such corpus. The first is locating the construction of sense between the transgressed restrictions and endorsed liberties of texts. The second focuses on the double dimension of representation: (a) a "transitive dimension" for which any representation "represents" something else, that is, it is a transparent vehicle of sense; (b) a "reflexive dimension," its declamatory opacity by which any representation also "presents itself" representing something else. The third principle is inscribing objects in synchronic and diachronic axes. This allows researchers to locate written productions in their own time, and to link them to other contemporary productions from different registers of experience. Second, it allows relating written productions with the history of their particular genres. These principles will guide the analysis of all the digital objects presented in this book and especially the case of *Agrippa*, discussed extensively in the chapter "The Book of the Dead and the Death of Books." I have followed them in order to reconstruct the boundaries that this peculiar project sought to transgress, its opacity and its presentation, as well as its inscription in very diverse historical series (ephemeral art, experimental poetry, electronic literature, artist and writers collaborations, artists' books). Hopefully this will provide new insights into the particular moment and the importance of work and storage device intertwinement at the beginnings of massive digitization in Western culture. The three principles, therefore, articulate the reconstruction of the *Agrippa* project and its relevance for a critique of medial ideology.

Storage Devices

The social and economic conditions that made the printed book a consolidated industrial object cannot be separated from the extended perception of texts as deprived of materiality. Likewise, works produced with digital technologies are frequently considered as devoid of any materiality. Alphabetical codification affords the possibility of abstractions that keep the characteristics perceived as substantial in several accidental presentations. In the case of digital code, the abstraction of content from containers produces a technology-specific dynamic of contents that effaces the material aspects inherent in any representation due to the inaccessible opacity and automation of inscription and representation technologies (for example, of hard drives or flash memories). Kirschenbaum's digital forensics[27] and Hayles' media-specific analysis (MSA) are useful perspectives to approach contemporary works and other practices without losing sight of the principles indicated by Chartier. According to Hayles,

> MSA attends both to the specificity of the form [...] and to citations and imitations of one medium in another. MSA moves from the language of text to a more precise vocabulary of screen and page, digital program and analogue interface, code and ink, mutable image and durable mark, computer and book.
> [...] The power of MSA comes from holding one term constant across media (in this case, technotexts) and varying the media to explore how medium-specific possibilities and constraints shape texts. Understanding literature as the interplay between form, content, and medium, MSA insists that the texts must always be embodied to exist in the world. The materiality of those EMBODIMENTS interacts dynamically with linguistic, rhetorical, and literary practices to create the effects we call literature.[28]

The reference to the materiality of works so that these *make* sense is necessary in order to produce an informed critique of content dynamics. A claim typical of medial ideology is the existence of pure contents that can circulate in diverse forms that we perceive using "transparent" reproduction devices. It is just a contemporary iteration of what Eco described as the integrated position towards mass culture, since it acknowledges the apparent democratization digitization enables but omits the reinforcement of intellectual property concerns, copyrights, and the expansion of cultural industries. It also ignores the constitution of new attention and perception regimes each technology bestows. Against a naïve assumption of a neutrality in technology under the illusion of its transparency, the concept of content dynamics shows a form of aestheticization of perception akin to the one identified by Walter Benjamin in analog reproducibility technologies in the first half of the last century. But, as he foresaw, technics also do hold the possibility of a cultural revolution. In other words, technics is not a neutral means to an end, nor necessarily an apocalyptic impulse, but a scenario of disputes, and for that reason, a political space. The idea of pure contents governed by copyrights and intellectual property is guided by the profit driven cultural industries in late capitalism. That is not the sole drive of culture, nor has ever been, nor has to be.

Digitization widens perception and modifies the statute of works, redefining the concepts of art in ways similar to what had happened with the apparition of analog reproduction technologies such as the printing press and the photographic camera. But aesthetics can only provide partial answers to adjust to shifting paradigms. Digitization produces a new technological sublime based on the acceleration and the abstraction imposed by content dynamics. That sublime is the base of a new stage of aestheticization, which is tied to an idealist content-centered cultural capitalism rather than to the totalitarian cultural propaganda of Benjamin's time. Nevertheless, there are works, along with other social practices that politicize technics and introduce non-teleological approaches that avoid the nostalgia so frequent in apocalyptic views. The technological sublime is the digitally mediated contemporary perception of reality. In this form of perception, materiality yields to the constant novelty and the "pure" forms causing an aesthetized perception of the world, in which technical phenomena, impossible to represent in their complexity, are reduced to mere stimuli. Ultimately, these stimuli are determined by contingent technologies, of which users have no deep understanding, but just practical interface interaction built by habit. Ideas, more elevated than materials, separate from the worldly storage and reproduction devices in which stimuli originate. Once their importance is discarded, subjects can, at least momentarily, set aside the material contingency of objects.

The *Agrippa* project and copy protection systems in early computer games are examples that embody the tensions between work and storage devices, between unsanctioned digital circulation and commodification. And Gibson's persona in particular, a science fiction author, both cult writer and popular best seller, is particularly relevant due to the part he played in the making of the technological imaginary associated with the digital world that built the particular perception of technology that Kirschenbaum describes as medial ideology. The context of the emergence of *Agrippa* is also interesting. The project was produced by people participating in the contemporary art circles of New York, where some nodes of the hacker subculture were located at the time. And in the crossing-paths of different artistic and technical traditions the project caught the attention of diverse audiences including collectors of art and hackers, to begin with, but also literary critics and, as Striphas suggests, the editorial industry.[29] Whether intended or not, it was a subversive or, at least, visionary twist on the established models for the circulation of works that anticipated the contentization of culture. The unsanctioned circulation of video games is another emergent aspect of that phenomenon.

Summarizing the arguments of this chapter then, the concept of digital object is neither purely technical nor purely cultural and that implies important methodological considerations for digital culture studies. Therefore, the use of media-specific tools should incorporate an informed philosophical substrate, and also rely extensively on the existing consolidated methodologies in the humanities. Some cases in digital art and literature, as well as in video games, in the last two decades of the last century provide complementary starting points to approach paradigmatic changes in the age of digital reproducibility and in the perceived crisis of books and other media-specific storage devices as the privileged vehicles for literature, and the emergence of a content dynamics organizing the mode of existence of cultural works in the digital milieu. But first, we must understand how digital technologies recontextualize pre-digital culture.

CHAPTER 3
Crossing Borders

...Allá fui por mi *grincar*
Me fui dejando todo *pending, baby...*
-Indio Solari, "To beef or not to beef"

Digital/Digitized

The transition from analog to digital is not as linear or uniform a process as it would be expected. Several factors of diverse orders converge in the passage from one recording, representation, and inscription system to another: the specific development of the techniques and technologies, the historically determined cultural contexts and, most importantly, the conflicts between producers, industries, state institutions, and the public. This chapter presents a systematization of the modes in which works are digitized, as well as some differences between distinct modes of digital existence. Piracy and other unforeseen practices help understand the aestheticization caused by the concurrence of abstraction and the ignorance of the technical phenomenon. In previous chapters, I have described that phenomenon as a part of the content dynamics in order to refer to the circulation of digital and digitized works when presented as pure abstractions, independent of their storage devices or reproduction platforms. These modes of symbolic production and consumption are summarized in the cliché of "convergence" by which distinct forms of representation and different media are adapted to be experienced through a single device, the computer. The idea of convergence is a good example of the perceived transparency of technics sustained by the medial ideology. The tensions between aestheticization and politicization are also present in the search of a stability of works under the ideas of preservation and controlled conclusiveness, as opposed to the emergent phenomena of mutation such as the one presented by remixing, leaks, and other forms of what can be defined as *inconclusiveness.*

Centuries before digital codification, there had been several crisis in the ways of preserving and reading of texts: the appearance of the *codex,* the introduction of paper in Europe or the invention of modern press. However, each event is not really a new beginning since new technologies do not always fully replace the previous ones and they often coexist and influence each other. With the emphasis on the circulation of texts, some specialists suggest a break equal to the emergence of the printing press: "This fanciful scenario is meant to suggest that the place of writing is again in turmoil, roiled now not by the invention of printed books but the emergence of electronic literature."[1] But from an artifactual point of view, as Chartier points out, the invention of the printing press did not change the fundamental structure of books, which are still composed, as they were before Gutenberg's press, by a number of paper pages bound together, preferably with a hard cover.[2] Chartier also has also suggested elsewhere that with regards to how we read, the digital technologies cultural revolution is more akin to the emergence of the codex than to the invention of the printing press.[3]

The possibility of identical copies is a common denominator between both technologies that does not receive as much critical attention and involves the specific affordances of technical reproducibility. The problem of the so-called crisis, therefore, comprises several dimensions: the material production of highly stereotyped and standardized storage devices, the stability of texts, and the circulation of the entities derived from both (contents and containers). The conceptual ambiguity around the storage devices obscures the relationship between the book as an object and the text as a delimited work. The abstraction of texts from their material realizations has been a source of disputes since the dawn of Western culture, with the well-known example of Plato's criticism of writing in the *Phaedrus* and the effect it has on learning and thinking.[4] From a Stieglerian perspective, I will assume the necessary exteriorization of knowledge and thus the inescapable dependency on storage devices for human culture to exist. The history of *how* we write, count, depict, read, and see is also the history of *what* we can think. How do we think when exteriorization becomes digital? To try to address this matter this chapter introduces a provisional classification for different types of literary works in particular, but also other artistic works in general, in relation to the digital milieu. This will provide a starting point to discuss how digital technologies shape contemporary culture while being shaped by it.

Any digital or digitized work implies a common trait: a digital representation. This implies some new affordances, fundamentally the convergence of several arts in one device that enables a form of perception and manipulation, commonly known as multimedia. In his introduction to the book *The New Media Reader,* Manovich established a division between new media objects and objects from other media that exist there: "new media are the cultural objects which use digital computer technology for distribution and exhibition,"[5] such as websites, computer games, virtual reality, digital special effects or the Internet itself. Cultural objects that do not use computing for final distribution would not be new media. That would be the case of television, radio, magazines or books in the nineties. That definition has become rather dated, as Manovich acknowledges in his last book, since the digital milieu has become a universal media machine that can emulate all preexisting media,[6] the obvious examples being radio and TV streaming, eBooks, and newspaper and magazine editions for tablets and phones. However, that early distinction still sheds some light on the emerging features of digital technologies.

New media is a combination of traditional conventions of representation, access, and manipulation of information (textual, aural, and visual narratives) and new (numerical) conventions. The combination is defined by the author as an aesthetic of the early information culture[7] and is the result of the convergence of two particular social forces: the existing cultural-specific, storage-device oriented mindset, and the conventions of human-computer interfaces. In an influential 2001 book, Manovich had identified some properties present in new media objects, namely: (a) digital or numeric representation, (b) modular composition, (c) variability, (d) authomatization, and (e) transcoding.[8]

"Numerical representation" is the property of new media objects to be formally described. As mathematical representations, they afford algorithmic manipulation; thus, new media products become programmable. "Modularity" is the possibility to aggregate and disaggregate the discrete elements that make up an object. This implies that, at a certain level, an object can be composed of multiple aggregated objects while some things can be removed without causing the object to disappear or to be incomplete. For example, a digital image can be composed of a series of layers, or a webpage can include hyperlinks, images, text, and audio that can be added or removed without the page ceasing to exist as a discrete object. "Authomatization" (what I refer to in this book as "automation") refers to the quality by which computers replace (and accelerate) procedures that were previously carried out by humans. There are two levels of automation, according to the scope and complexity of the procedures in which human agency is replaced by software. For digital texts, some obvious examples of low level automation are word counting, index generation, font changes or endnote and footnote functions. Automation in digital images is present in elementary functions such as filters, color and contrast correction, cut and paste, the calculation of perspective for a three-dimensional image, etc. Examples of high level automation are the applications of artificial intelligence in games to animate characters not controlled by players, or the input and output generated with sensor directed devices of an art installation to respond to the audience movements. The fourth property, "variability," will receive special attention in this chapter for its impact on the conclusiveness of works and on the relative stability of literary and artistic institutions; as well as cultural industries that build around, and against, this property. It depends on the previous three properties (numerical representation, modularity, and automation) and is one of the most notable features of new media objects:

> Old media involved a human creator who manually assembled textual, visual and/or audio elements into a particular composition or a sequence. This sequence was stored in some material, its order determined once and for all. Numerous copies could be run off from the master, and, in perfect correspondence with the logic of an industrial society, they were

all identical. New media, in contrast, is characterized by variability. [...] Instead of identical copies a new media object typically gives rise to many different versions. And rather being created completely by a human author, these versions are often in part automatically assembled by a computer.[9]

The latest feature, or "trend," as Manovich chooses to call it, is transcoding, a more ambiguous idea because it does not point to formal aspects of new media objects. Transcoding describes a transit inside culture, the transition between a cultural layer and a computational one and the way in which reciprocal influences are generated, though heavily determined by the processes of digitization. It is, summarily, a process of "cultural re-conceptualization" derived from the ontology, epistemology, and pragmatics of computing.[10]

The concept of new media object proposed by Manovich includes a wide array of entities including works but also cultural heritages as a whole, individual cultural products, and other entities not necessarily related to artistic fields, such as databases or the Internet itself. Based on his general approach, this chapter discusses the specific features of the new and old media literary works focusing in their storage devices. This classification, based on the characteristics of the digital milieu, sometimes includes works of art coming from disciplines other than literature.

In a narrow, literary, sense, there are three large groups of works: (a) *printed works* keeping the common sense perception of modern literature, mostly associated with print culture, from *Don Quixote* to *Neuromancer*;[11] (b) *digitized works*, i.e. those originated in literary works in print culture (or analog recordings) coded to be accessible through digital reproduction platforms such as those offered by the *Ayacucho Digital Library*, *Project Gutenberg* or *Google Books* or by museums and media online archives, but also the sophisticated digital emulations of the book's artifactual existence, as the book reading software for tablets that graphically represent page movement;[12] (c) *digital works*, digital born works created in, and accessible through, reproduction platforms that execute digital code.[13]

This general classification aims to identify particular issues regarding the analog to digital transition. Within the limits of these three groups, there are many problematic, hybrid works that share the materiality of printed texts with the possibilities offered by digital technologies, as is the case of *Agrippa*. The existence of derivations from other works predates digital technologies; plagiarism, imitation, and parody go a long way but they have been empowered by digitization. This includes (a) memes, (usually parodic) variations from digital or digitized works; (b) many forms of reutilizations of digital and digitized works (some unintentionally parodic), similar to what occurred in analog form; and (c) leaks, that is, the digital circulation of works, frequently in an unfinished state, obtained without permission during the production stages prior to the release authorized by copyright holders.

Benjamin pointed out that technical reproducibility changes the ontology of works of art and transforms them into commodities by increasing the exhibition value over the cult value. When, thanks to photography, a work of art can be reproduced it loses its auratic quality, the traits of uniqueness and timely existence of a work associated with a distinct container. Photography and phonography decontextualize the work of art (and any other source of located sensory stimuli) and make it accessible beyond the narrow limits of its particular existence. From the Stieglerian perspective I presented in the introduction, the new reproduction rate of exteriorizations is that of standardization. And that accelerates not only production but also perception. On the other hand, the 1656 painting *Las Meninas* by Diego Velázquez exhibited at the Museo del Prado in Madrid, or the performance of the *Mass in B minor* "Sanctus" conducted by Johann Sebastian Bach at the 1724 Christmas service in Leipzig can be considered as previous forms of exteriorization: inasmuch as unique, inaccessible cult value objects and events they belong to the more diverse and slow age of stereotypes. In his seminal essay Benjamin perceived the novelty implicated by a work leaving its location to meet audiences wherever they might be. But the change in the spatial condition of works included a change in their temporary condition as well. He had duly noted that photographs and phonographic recordings also extract works from timely existence, although he did not pause to reflect on the problem of acceleration, which industrial reproduction technologies also introduced. Digital reproduction produces a similar phenomenon, due to the ongoing process of digitizing all existing cultural production and an enhanced acceleration of reproduction.[14] Nonetheless, there are important differences to be observed.

Derivative works are one of the hallmarks of this new paradigm of circulation, although this kind of work had not been originally foreseen. Derivative works uproot digital and digitized works from the land of copyright in an operation akin to that by which mechanical reproductions uprooted the works of art from the context of tradition. But, more importantly, they also uproot the works from media specific storage and reproduction devices. That is, they change the associated milieu of exteriorizations.

Returning to texts in the digital milieu, almost every text today is "born digital." Even those still associated with print culture are produced by digital media.[15] However, this should not lead into the frequent error of understanding digitization as a unidirectional and irreversible process.[16] Digitization is not an absolute and definitive change but is part of a cultural oscillation. In fact, the illusion of immateriality, rooted in an idealistic approach to technique itself casts a veil on the transition from analog to digital (and vice versa):

> The relevant points are that writing and reading to and from the disk are ultimately a form of digital to analog or analog to digital signal processing–not unlike the function of a modem–and that the data contained on the disk is a second-order representation of the current digital values the data assumes for computation.[17]

The transition from digital to analog is much more physical than it is usually thought to be, and it is not an irreversible process. What does radically change is the perception of digitized works, objects, information, and phenomena, in a manner comparable to the way in which photography changed the perception of painting. Nowadays, something that cannot be digitized represents an obstacle in the assumed teleology of progress because it cannot be computed, and therefore cannot be accounted for in what is becoming the only sanctioned, standardized, and objective possibility of record.

The transition occurs in the storage devices, but there are also other marginal practices that are consubstantial to the problem and are usually associated with the illegalized circulation of digital and digitized works both in analog and digital technologies: the typing of texts to upload them, the circulation of audiovisual content via camcorders present in the so-called "camrips" of Hollywood blockbusters uploaded just after they are screened in theaters, or older widespread practices such as book photocopying, printing scanned books, the unauthorized making of bootleg tapes, and home tape recording.

At this point it is worth reconsidering an aspect of the analog-digital dichotomy that is especially relevant for the digital reproduction of works of art. Not all analogical records imply continuity; there are discontinuities in the frames of a film, for instance. However, in cinema, the discrete levels of representation were not quantified by the apparatus and therefore were not subject to computational manipulation, which is the crucial step that is reached with the digitization, and with digital production.

The difference between digital and analog reproductions is that of allographic representation against the autographic representation: an allographic work fulfills its ontology in reproduction, an autographic one betrays it.[18] The gap between a copy of *Las Meninas* and the original painting is insurmountable; the one between two editions of the novel *La invención de Morel* [*The Invention of Morel*] is, theoretically, irrelevant, at least for print culture perception standards. Errata or the use of a particular typeface will not alter the status of the work (or that of the copy). Allographic reproduction does not require a perfect (or autographic) fidelity to be perceived, it only requires that it be kept within the range of variation that allows it to be perceived as a distinct entity and not mistaken for another. This occurs in the perception of the absolute differences on which the alphabetic writing is based. An "a" is always an "a" and it cannot be a "b." When confused, abstraction is lost in particularity. This fact underlies all forms of text idealism that considers works as abstractions. Chartier has described this as the oxymoron that leads to characterize text as an "intangible thing" that establishes a separation between essential identity of a work and the indefinite plurality of its realizations, that ultimately are the justification for the property of literary work. This is based on the assumption that a work may be recognized as always identical to itself without taking into consideration its mode of publication and transmission.[19]

The identicallity of digital copies rests upon the cyclic redundancy check that provides the screen realization of the information contained in a digital code stored in the hard drive or other storage devices. This check allows returning a result that is always identical, regardless of the physical inscription in the storage device (at least ideally). Making a somewhat forced comparison, one could tell a computer to update information on the hard drive in a manner similar to that of the reader that understands the following text despite its obvious mistakes:

Tihs senetnce has tyops in almsot erevy word.

We can understand the meaning of the sentence (and identify the words) precisely due to our abstraction ability with regards to a particular realization of writing and the errors presented based on the discrete character of writing. By making sense within the grammatical and semantic context we perform an abstraction of the inscription that allows us to read: "This sentence has typos in almost every word." Digitization implies a greater automation of allography, within a process of increasing abstraction.[20] This can be tracked in the path that goes from the inscription of voltage differentials on the surface of the drive to its interpretation by the computer first as machine code, which often is the compiled code, which results from the source code. This chain of abstractions attains also realization as an output that may be a screen display, a sound emission, or a printing on paper, just to mention some possible examples.

In other terms, and from a very acute perception of the social phenomena introduced by mechanical reproduction, Benjamin pointed out that copying and counterfeiting were ontologically different. There are no copies of a photograph, since there is no "original" in the mechanically reproducible.[21] However, there was a dimension of the phenomenon that he did not fully envision. In pre-digital reproduction technologies, there is always an unavoidable degradation in the copies made from the original analog inscription. Such degradation bestows in the first inscription a quasi auratic material existence that, symptomatically, receives the name of *master*: the dominant record that rules over its offspring, the one that must be preserved from degradation. Digital copying implies a novelty, the possibility of copies without degradation with regards to the first inscription due to the allographic property of digital recordings (at least theoretically speaking).[22] Operations with texts, musical notations, and mathematics that demanded much effort in the past are now automated and this also extends to the realms of sound and image. However, the allographic dream of ever identical copies is still to come, since storage space and transmission speed impose limits to technically feasible copying. As of today, the overwhelming majority of digital content circulates on lightweight information lossy formats, such as .jpeg for image, .mp3 for audio, or .avi for video. Needless to say that compression implies degradation when compared to the source.[23]

Pre-digital Works in the Age of Digitization

A pre-digital work is any literary work that originated in print culture as well as previous works whose survival has been associated with books, although originated in handwritten and/or oral cultures. To be readable any text must accommodate to a somewhat stereotyped symbol system. However, alphabets and binary code are not simply two different types of code or two levels of code. While writing requires readers for its realization, binary code requires the mediation of a machine that interprets it. Considering devices as "readers" is a simplistic metaphor that does not account for the radical difference between both agencies, that is, human reading and machine decoding. On the other hand, computer code implies a form of automatic agency that alphabetic writing lacks.[24] The texts as digital objects, whether they originated in the digiti-

zation of printed or handwritten texts, or they are digitally produced, always imply a string of code that is not equivalent to the
broader concept of text associated with digital and digitized works.
As I noted earlier, in digital environments, the text is something
that devices realize following instructions from the code. It is
necessary to clarify what may be a no-brainer because of the
extended use of vague metaphorical allusions; by which any type of
coding (namely, the serialization of DNA, a poem, and a hand-
drawn map) are "texts." If everything is text, then nothing is.
Therefore, to address the classification of works in the digital
milieu I will adopt a narrower definition: *text* is a set of sentences
written in a code that humans can interpret without the aid of
decoding technologies, i.e., groups of words written using a given
alphabet. Under this definition, texts produced under very different material conditions coexist: digital, print, and handwritten, in
turn stored in hard drives, pages, parchments, stones, etc.

Each bears specific marks of origin that imply specific material
conditionings (such as the writing tool–quill, pencil, pen, etc.–, the
cost of galleys, the possibility to delete, or the existence of multiple
versions, just to list a few) that have a direct impact on the final
result. But all these types of text have a single common feature:
alphabetic writing affords the abstraction of their material existence. Unlike other periodizations of technology from an aesthetic
perspective, Czech philosopher Vilém Flusser suggests that the
shifts are caused by successive processes of abstraction and imagination.[25] For Benjamin, for instance, the technical reproduction of
texts and images are parallel processes that enthrall the loss of the
possibility of making experience and the decay of the auratic
quality of objects. That occurs due to the preeminence of the
exhibition value over the cult value of the work of art and the
preeminence of the transmission of information over the transmission of experience derived from the authority of the narrator. The
result is the uprooting of works from the traditions on which they
were inserted. Flusser, on the other hand, suggests that reproduction technologies account for different instances: imagination,
textualization, and remagization. Each stage is defined by a
growing degree of abstraction leading to technology as a black box
whose internal workings are inaccessible to humans. In order to

regain freedom, the black box of technology needs to be open, allowing an intervention on the device's program rather than having humans merely actualizing the possibilities set by the program. The idea is similar to that of medial ideology presented by Kirschenbaum. As discussed early, medial ideology is the result of abstraction afforded by computers accompanied by the concealment of the physical nature of storage on the hard drive turning it into a "black box."[26] In another periodization, focusing on the specific writing technologies, Chartier suggests that the ruptures owe more to the emergence of new storage devices than to innovation in the forms of reproducibility. His periodization presents an early stage defined by the parchment, followed by that of the codex and then by the different types of digital files that represent the text on the screen. However, none of the affordances of digital text depend in any way on Gutenberg's press, but on a mode of text publication invented in the early centuries of Christianity, breaking apart from the ancient writing scrolls: the *codex*, that particular device made of bound leaves we now call a "book." On one hand, the digital revolution is closer to the codex revolution than to the one spurred by Gutenberg's invention, because it changes how the text is distributed on its storage device.[27] Nevertheless, the digital text technologies can be compared to the printing press in the acceleration they introduce.

From a technical perspective, abstraction is what allows the universal technical reproducibility of texts in particular storage technologies. Each change of storage device involves a number of specificities in its modes of production, reproduction, and manipulation that establish the boundaries between one and the other. The practice of medieval copyists was open to comment, to deliberate intervention on the text itself, and to involuntary error; printing, to standardized particular versions, defined by the actions of printers and editors. But it also encompassed other particularities: errors in the layout process appear as traits of serialized texts and with them comes the role of copy editors and, subsequently, of publishing as a (costly) stage of authorial verification. Digital publishing extends editing and design decisions to authors (and cheapens the cost of galleys and copyediting), while causing a proliferation of versions. This does not exhaust the particularities of the various stages in the history of texts, but it must be noted that various technologies (and temporalities) coexist under the book object. The expansion of digital technologies to the publishing world and to society in general (i.e., to authors) blurs the boundaries of previously clear distinct stages because most of the processes associated with the composition and realization of texts converge on the computer.[28]

The classification that follows is intended only for descriptive purposes in order to contextualize the emergence of new forms within what could still be defined as literature. In the debates on the cultural impact of technology, published paper books are seen as an endangered species based on the naïve idea that they are still the same books that existed in the pre-digital era. But, as already noted, now digitization is present in every stage of the book production process, from its conception and writing to its editing and reproduction. Thus, in the digital milieu paper books are but one of the many possible outputs of a digital text.

Digitized Works: The Passage of Books

For the arguments presented in this book, digitized works are digital representations of works that originate in print culture (or previous ones). But the devil is in the details, and digitized works may implicate very different forms of digital objects. A book that is digitized as text is not equal to one digitized as image; they do not have the same affordances. And within the subcategory of digitization as image, there are also big differences when the image has undergone OCR and when it has not. The scan of a printed page and the display of digital text file with some restrictions on copy and paste affordances, frequent in proprietary .pdf or .ePub files, are not equivalent.

That being said, I will present a systematization of the modes of digitization with the necessary warning that it can never be exhaustive since it is a dynamic and currently ongoing cultural practice. Hopefully, the systematization will provide a general overview of the problem and the specificities of the three main practices involved in the digitization of texts: (a) typing, (b) scanning and (c) optical character recognition.[29]

Digitization by Typing: The Modest Reauratization of the Copyist. The most elementary mode of digitization is typing whole texts on a computer. Similar but not equivalent to the medieval copyists, this practice also reintroduces one of the typical features of manuscript copying: *errata*. In the first case, the error was what determined the uniqueness of the handwritten copies; in the digital milieu errors multiply, originating a new phenomenon: the multiplication of versions, in a very broad sense of *version*. The first digital scribes, however, did have the halo of a crafted skill similar to the role of the typographers in the early print houses.[30] There is a unity of action in digital typing, the unique, unrepeated moment of the relationship between reading and typing in the hands of the voluntary bibliophiles who invested extensive hours to "liberate" texts into digital existence. This is evident in an answer of founder of *Project Gutenberg* Michael Hart to the question of how the digitization process is carried out:

> -q: *What about you? Do you still manually type books or do you use a page scanner?*
>
> I'm mostly just holding on to the reins. I'm mostly an administrator. I don't get a chance to do the real thing. I've done both, and I can tell you from personal experience that it's a lot more fun to type a book. Once I typed in a book that was 1,000 pages and it took nine months. Then I scanned the sequel, which was about 750 pages, and it took maybe three weeks. It's a huge amount more efficient, and a huge amount less fun.[31]

In the opposition between pleasure and efficiency hides the dilemma of personal experience, the uniqueness of typing versus the standardized results of scanning. Any technical process is gradual and implicates temporal coexistence and oscillations with previous technologies, rather than a radical break. Typed copies are in some ways akin to early photographic copies as a craft trade until the mid-nineteenth century, carried out by solitary proficient technicians. However, typing text digitizes it and that introduces a form of infinite reproducibility that separates it from its storage device of origin (most frequently, a book). Thus, texts are converted into code and, after that, may be subject to all manipulations, indexa-tions, and interventions afforded by digital technology.

Forerunners of Digitization: Free Contents for All. Created by Hart in 1971 at the University of Illinois in order to promote the creation and distribution of free electronic books, *Project Gutenberg* provides a model of text circulation that defies the logic of the book as a commodity and strives for the creation of a univer-sal library. On the project's website there are manifestoes, essays, and interviews presenting the ethical and political positions of the project regarding digital reproduction. The history of the project also reflects the history of the modes of existence of texts in the digital milieu: from digitization by typing to the use of scanners and character recognition software. Another very relevant aspect is that texts are controlled by volunteer proofreaders.[32] *Project Gutenberg*, like similar cultural initiatives, assumes the idea of literacy as a way to democratize societies while opposing the commodification of knowledge and cultural heritages. This was explicitly affirmed by Hart in several posts and is one of the first examples of the idea of free access to culture in the digital mi-lieu.[33] The overwhelming presence of English language culture over others, and especially of English literature, is evident (and probably unavoidable, given the dominance of English language and English-speaking academia in the early stages of digitization). However, that has been complemented by a commitment to the translation of works and the inclusion of other languages, with a special interest in those with very few speakers (and readers). The choice of the name and the selection of the first texts to digitize (namely, *The Declaration of Independence of the United States, The Bible*) might seem to define an editorial policy. But these choices also show a political stance, an adjustment to the existing technic-al affordances and a historical inscription. The name chosen for the project assumes a direct identification with Gutenberg's invention and the social changes that it spawned; thus publishing the same work that made the printing press a cultural game changer was not a religious biased choice. The first text also introduces the idea of democracy (albeit in its peculiar U.S. inter-pretation) that oriented the project. But sticking to those interpretations without considering technical aspects may be misleading, because there were storage and copyright issues at stake at the time.

The rate of title accumulation and the selection criteria over a forty-year span also shed some light on the relationship between digitization and the development of storage capacities and the devices associated with the process. Although today it is a commonplace assertion that culture dematerializes with the spread of digital versions (with the respective praises or woes this causes in the integrated and apocalyptic ranks), digitization still occurs in physical storage devices, as Hart himself was well aware back then:

> The Project Gutenberg Etexts should cost so little that no one will really care how much they cost. They should be a general size that fits on the standard medium of the time.
>
> i.e. when we started, the files had to be very small as a normal 300 page book took one meg of space which no one in 1971 could be expected to have (in general). So doing the U.S. Declaration of Independence (only 5K) seemed the best place to start. This was followed by the Bill of Rights —then the whole US Constitution, as space was getting large (at least by the standards of 1973). Then came the Bible, as individual books of the Bible were not that large, then Shakespeare (a play at a time), and then into general work in the areas of light and heavy literature and references.
>
> By the time Project Gutenberg got famous, the standard was 360K disks, so we did books such as Alice in Wonderland or Peter Pan because they could fit on one disk. Now 1.44 is the standard disk and ZIP is the standard compression; the practical filesize is about three million characters, more than long enough for the average book.[34]

This aspect of digitization is a clear reminder of the historicity of technology and the material constraints that determine all cultural forms, in this case the digitized texts. The problem shifts from the possibility of identical reproduction acknowledged by Benjamin to the possibility of infinite identical reproduction by becoming code. This does not mean accepting that an actual dematerialization takes place. In fact, the exacerbated aspect is the loss of uniqueness, as well as the deferment of the problem of wear, but not the lack of materiality. Moreover, one of the problems for digitization in its origins was choosing which code should be adapted as a standard, which mode of becoming code favored universality better without risking a restrictive particularization. Such a choice involves a specific concept of text. Digitizing in "Plain Vanilla ASCII" entails the assumption that, at least considering the existing technical constraints, texts are mainly worthy for their words and not for other paratextual aspects such as typography, textual layout on the page, editing in general, etc. The fact that the universal is an "American Standard Code" clearly evidences the relationship among power, technology, and production of knowledge and cultural heritage that has been a constant of digitization, at least in Western countries. The problem of standards is not only that of a false universalism; it conceals the political direction inherent to the correct operation of the devices. As I discussed earlier, standards build empires. Regardless of the explicit political objectives and their dispute against restrictive models of circulation of knowledge and cultural assets, any digitization project must negotiate with the socio-historical conditions of production: the development of the digital culture is also the translation to a specific system of symbols. That being said, and despite the assumption of neutrality of the technics that some may see underlying *Project Gutenberg*, Hart assumed ethical positions in relation to the digitization process and against the advance of copyright, criticizing its expansion and questioning the sincerity of statements claiming to aid the development of the Third World by those not actively involved in the defense of the free circulation of eBooks.[35]

It should be noted that one of the most famous cases of the limitation of private rights in order to assure the social appropriation of technology was precisely that of an invention that affords reproducibility: the case of the acquisition of Daguerre's patent of the photographic camera by the government of France in 1839. This policy differs radically from the restrictive positions favored by countries holding sway over the technological global trends nowadays. (Of course, there were other geopolitical interests at stake, such as restraining the British intention to gain control over the nascent photographic technology.) As stated in one of the most famous statements of scientist and politician François Arago, advocate for the government Bill of Pension for Daguerre, *"[c]ette découverte, la France l'a adoptée; dès le premier moment, elle s'est montrée fière de pouvour en doter libéralement le monde entier.*[36] It must be noted that during the nineteenth century representations became commodities. Digitization has only exacerbated the disputes over the ownership of representations as well as of the ways of generating representations, that is, the control over recording and reproduction technologies. Since the end of the twentieth century, the ownership of the decoding technologies that afford realizing representations has become one of the most prized spoils of these technological turf wars.

The case of *Project Gutenberg* compared to other collections is particularly interesting since it belongs to the so-called "heroic times" of the development of digital technologies, during which utopian projects, which today would be considered economically unviable, thrived. Such collections, usually linked to public libraries and educational institutions, challenge both the service model (for example, the one driving the first book digitization project proposed by *Google Books* in exchange for receiving customized advertising)[37] and the virtual bookstore commodity model such as Amazon's, Apple's, or Barnes & Noble's.[38] Surprisingly, this is the basis of what Chartier has identified as the paradox underlying the idea of literary property formulated in the eighteenth century. Only when written works were separated from their particular materiality, literary compositions could be considered property. And that is the origin of the oxymoron that characterizes texts as "intangible things."[39]

During the late eighties and early nineties some author- or collection-oriented digitization projects with planned file access policies and a careful scholarly curation appeared. These projects tend to focus on canonical works. However, as time passed, and their webpage design grew obsolete, the device-specific nature of the sites became evident. They were meant for computer screens and, in some cases, for printers, which today are just two of the many possible alternatives. Some examples of the so-called Web 1.0 illustrate this problem, as is the case with the Massachusetts Institute of Technology's *The Complete Works of William Shakespeare.*[40] The site claims to be the first web edition of the complete works, online since 1993, following the second series of the widespread classroom standard Arden Shakespeare edition.[41] The starting year of the website is meaningful: 1993, a few months after the appearance of *Agrippa* and in the same year in which the World Wide Web was made public.

This first type of web collection is an example of the perceived crisis of print culture, where the traditional text storage devices seem to lose relevance against the ubiquity and transmissibility of online texts. Collections of this kind are an eloquent sample of the previously discussed textual idealism that assumes the storage device as an accessory, a mere means to an end. The obsolescence of these webpages in terms of their basic textual structure, their austere design, and the predominance of text over image, sound, and other resources is indicative of the underlying textual idealism. New collections organized by academic institutions explore other possibilities of digital technology and include new affordances such as file downloading, tactile access, accessibility for the visually impaired (through audio or Braille terminal outputs), and display settings adjustment depending on the access device, just to name the most frequent. An evident contrast with the previous example is *The Shakespeare Quartos Archive* digitization project.[42] This scholarly digitization model also shows the development of digitization and digital representation technologies. This project evidences the intention of preserving the original materiality of texts. In order to accomplish it, the website offers digitizations by scanning; i.e., images of the original quartos, complemented by digital text versions. This double, text and image, digitization affords all the possibilities introduced by addressability while preserving the visual reference to the materiality of the texts. Obviously, this form of digitization is rare due to both cost and required expertise, and it is usually more feasible in the cases of canonical works. The digitization of the works of the English language's most iconic literary figure is financed by some of the most prestigious universities and cultural institutions of the United States and the United Kingdom. It is not, in fact, a case of enthusiastic volunteer digitization, as the one commanded by Hart, but its specificity is also the opposite to the Google model of universal digitization that I will discuss ahead. Finally, another key aspect this last kind of collection introduces is the effect of the other two technologies that come after digitization by typing.

Digitization by Scanning: The Age of the Text Picture. The history of scanner technology (and subsequently of optical character recognition) provides some insight into the relationship among telecommunications, sound, and image. Their convergence is central to the current modes of book digitization. Some forerunners of the digital scanner can be found in devices related to the telegraph as Giovanni Caselli's ill-fated electric pantelegraph that transmitted images and handwritten word, patented in 1861 and also bought for the public domain by France. Another case is Édouard Belin's 1913 belinograph that was adopted by news agencies and resisted obsolescence for almost a century until it was fully replaced by digital networks. The first digital image using a scanner was produced by a team led by Russell Kirsch for the United States National Bureau of Standards. The source image was a photograph of his son; the resulting digital image of Walden Kirsch is suggestively ghastly, almost an involuntary reminder of the first daguerreotypes.[43]

Over the years scanning technology would evolve enough to afford producing images of texts that were readable on screen. But the result is still an image, not text, and there is a loss in abstraction. This creates a paradox: while it produces a more truthful representation of the storage materiality (and eventually in color, an improvement over photocopies and microfilms), it clogs the circulation and manipulations of it as a pure text. Instead of an abstraction, the text is concreted, infinitely reproducible but as a particular, specific image. Due to file size issues digitizing works as images limits their circulation while providing a decreased readability, compared to that of typed texts, due to screen flickering. And, most importantly, as an image, the text does not have the same affordances as digital texts, such as fluidity, searching, or indexing, due to its limited addressability.[44]

In relation to the personal experience of typing a work pointed out by Hart, establishing a personal relationship between the copyist and the text, one might think of the scanner as a different stage of digitization in the age of technical reproduction, which transforms digital copyists into assembly line workers while minimizing errata. The stage of scanning has been a bridge between the digitization by typing and digitization by optical character recognition that I will discuss in the next section. However, before doing so, I would like to point out an important aspect of digitization by scanning. Images draw renewed attention to the materiality of previous text storage devices. Books regain relevance as objects with a history of their own. Digitization by scanning allows a series of operations on the image of texts, as zooming, comparing versions by superimposition of images, etc. Another fundamental aspect is that digitization by scanning diminishes the aura of collections. With digital collections, scholars do not have to observe the limitations and careful procedures imposed by ancient document conservation protocols, nor travel to where the collection is stored. Researchers and readership alike leave these steps aside and have no contact with the materiality of volumes and scrolls that now accommodate in the screen in ways impossible to those working on tables in a library or archive. The oscillation between cult value and exhibition value described by Benjamin to address reproduction technologies is, in this example, its application to the book as an object and not as a text. Of course, this does not mean that materiality loses relevance, as classical studies include many procedures that still need the physical presence of the storage devices to conduct for instance, chemical tests. But it has certainly caused a shift in methodological approaches in the field.

One of the subjects in which digitization by scanning generated more expectations are the works where the separation between text and book is impossible without loss as is the case of illuminated manuscripts. One of the first digitization projects that took advantage of the scanner is the online repository dedicated to William Blake started in 1996.[45] Almost twenty years later the *Blake Archive* has become digital archive material itself. As many products of the early web, the structure of the site may seem confusing and cumbersome in terms of current usability standards. However, at the time, it was an incomparable choice for the study of works that otherwise would have been inaccessible to most researchers. Obviously, considering the difficulty of the material access to these works, the effort and times involved in the use of the *Blake Archive* were considerably lower than travelling and obtaining funding for allowances. But the accessibility and acceleration enhanced by contemporary digital technologies turn perfectly reasonable times for scholarly practices into signs of obsolescence and death by boredom to the general public.[46] Online archives and repositories have since incorporated new technologies, such as digitization by optical character recognition, allowing the combination of text as image and text as code that introduce a new series of affordances. So-called artist books are the opposite of a pure text in their unavoidable reference to materiality that these sites care to preserve by making use of increasingly complex techniques. The tensions between idealism and materialism to approach the digitization become visible in editorial decisions such as cutting the result of scanning to keep only the contents of the page, and removing the image of the rest of the pages, or, in more recent projects, maintaining a broader scanned image thus facilitating the perception of the location of the page inserted in the book as a whole.[47]

The growing attention to the image of the texts highlights the tensions between cult value and exhibition value. Although in this case, being digitized, both text and image are ubiquitous and infinitely reproducible, the image is not, yet, as addressable as the text. The affordances of one and the other are different and, above all, involve distinct degrees of abstraction.[48] Optical character recognition tries to solve the problem of the addressability of the text contained in the image and is a step forward on the residual cultural primacy that subsists in the images showing ancient pages.

Digitization by OCR: The Ghost in the Machine. Optical character recognition is a technology that interprets the words of an image and renders them into digital text. Its genealogy includes prototype devices for book reading machines for the visually impaired as Edmund Fournier d'Albe's 1913 optophone, the demands of different intelligence and military agencies, and since the fifties the urge of large companies for information management through the incorporation of computers. The contribution of the OCR was instrumental in the acceleration in the digitization of texts by enhancing automation not only for the passage from analog to digital but also for the conversion of images into texts. This introduced the possibility of applying automated error correction that was exponentially faster than human correction, since scanning made the text addressable once its characters were recognized, that is, recoded as text. The emergence of a market for digital editions led to an automated mass digitization and a fierce dispute over the contents including practices similar to the proliferation of pirated popular books in the eighteenth and nineteenth centuries. Automated digitization, especially when applied to works in the public domain, has been accurately described as "zombie editing,"[49] a form of digitization for print on demand services that unearths uncopyrighted material. The undead are not only unearthed, but also linked to the idea of plague; thus, zombies serve as a powerful metaphor of the digitization by OCR and the blind automated multiplication of unreliable digital texts.

Machine automated digitization reveals the continuity of print culture into digital culture practices but also sheds light on the specificities of each context. Piracy (or privateering, pick the perspective of your choice) is a key element of the digital progress as it was in the expansion of European capitalism from the sixteenth century onwards. Digitization has pirates of its own, but some, such Amazon or Google, have managed to obtain letters of marque in the agitated sea of copyrights and the troubled waters of electronic commerce. Much of the success of *Google Books* originates in the confluence of the digitization by OCR and the automated correction based on grammars and lexicons, as well as to the permanent improvement by means of pattern generation. Because of Google's behemoth-like scope and aims, this project has changed the mode in which the digitization of information is organized in almost all aspects of culture. Due to the economic success and the ambition of the objectives set by the company and the way in which it constantly feeds on each particular use that is made of their services, Google has become a true universal standard generator for absolutely everything by means of turning everything into information that affords encoding, indexing, and patterning. The only limit so far has been drawn by the logics of commodity that its own business model undermines. Copyright laws defended by the publishing industry, paradoxically colluding with some national libraries, constituted the main legal impediment for a project that already has the necessary technology for the creation of a ubiquitous and infinitely accessible universal library in a very short period of time.[50] In fact, (almost) all books in the world are already digitized, though they cannot be accessed by everyone. Digitization of books most usually often refers to the books of the past since contemporary books are born digital, although they may not be available online for reasons unrelated to their conditions of production but to intellectual property concerns.

With the apparition of *Google Books*, the ability to catalyze human resources, technology, and archives to a planetary scale, digitization stopped being a technological problem only to become an economic, legal, and cultural one. The dilemma is if texts are a product or a service. In the first case it is assumed that there is something intangible, unique, and original whose reproduction is limited by intellectual property. In the second case, the text forms part of a collection whose access is supported from revenues generated by tailored advertising to which their storage devices and digital representations contribute whenever we use them, by abstracting our online searches and behaviors into patterns; or from the charging a membership fee.

Copyists in the Assembly Line. An example of the convergence between digital use and involuntary contributions to digitization was the reCAPTCHA system devised to improve OCR results while avoiding the automation of SPAM or other abusive forms of nonhuman access on the Internet, those peculiar entities that usually receive the name of "bots."[51] This was achieved through a reformulation of the validation request input known as CAPTCHA, a catchy acronym for Completely Automated Public Turing test to tell Computers and Humans Apart. reCAPTCHA provided webpages with a security check that guaranteed an actual human access by requesting the user to recognize two words or phrases in an image. The display showed at least one word that Google's OCR had not been able to properly identify and another to validate access. When the word was recognized by human agency the reCAPTCHA results were included in the Google digitization project. With this system, the last human mediation, the error correction in the digitization process, was automated. Using scanned content with the reCAPTCHA, Google provided a security check, while also having users manually enter or verify scanned text for free. As bots evolved reCAPTCHA changed but it still provides feedback for Google.[52]

This is clearly illustrated by comparing the texts resulting from automatic OCR with those from OCR combined with a reCAPTCHA. If we accept the idea of a distinctive experience in human typing and correction, reCAPTCHA ended up diluting it by handing out the words that OCR failed to recognize among millions of users throughout the world. Totally decontextualized word recognition is not equivalent to reading, a moment of personal attention, a particular personal experience. It is a paradox: words are decontextualized to be recognized in order to verify the presence of a human and by doing so contribute to a digitization devoid of the human agency in the typing of texts. As any automation process, the goal is to minimize human agency (and human contingency). As it has been duly noted by Marx and his countless interpreters, the change introduced by industrial assembly line compared to hand craftsmanship is also a change in the relationship with the objects. When craftsmen lose the idea of the totality of their production and deal only with isolated parts, their product is subtracted from the tradition that gave context to their practice, which allowed them, in sum, to be able make assimilable experience.[53] Modern urban life and factory work can only produce inassimilable, decontextualized stimuli. Similarly, and even if Benjamin regarded silent book reading as another form of the degradation of subject experience (parallel to the decay of the aura of objects), reCAPTCHA took the process further, going from the time span demanded by attentive reading that gives sense to the series of words according to their context, to the reading and quick input of a single, decontextualized word, turning readers into unaware operators of the text digitization assembly lines.

Consider the craftsmanship involved in early book printing. All the different positions involved (writer, editor, printer, composers, etc.) in publishing houses are intimately related to the material aspect of literary and other kinds of textual works. As Fyfe points out, the figure of proofreaders does not arise until the seventeenth century, and settled as an in-house position by mid-eighteenth century. What is more, the proofreader role in the production of books was located in an ambiguous situation between the established posts (with fixed salary) and precarious ones or in the process of learning the trade:

> Then, as now, the corrector occupied an ambiguous middle ground between editorial and production, between managerial and technical realms. [...] Though expected to be well educated and to exert editorial influence on the copy, they were not in the echelon salary of a house's publishing or commercial management. Though paid piecemeal, working with the compositors and printers assembling them, they were not allied to the working press. The corrector overlapped with each domain and properly belonged to neither.[54]

The awkward place of errors (along with necessarily associated figure of the person meant to avoid them) in the allographic expectations of print culture is an aspect as important as unknown of the material dimension of literary works. Errors are obstacles for the illusion of a faithful and infinite reproducibility over which the commodification of art and literature in the age of technical reproduction is built. As Chartier points out, accidentals are an essential part of the material history of the works.[55] In the context of digitization, editorial correction is one of the many roles undergoing a serious crisis after centuries of unstable existence. Benjamin has suggested that during the last stage in the history of storytelling before the hegemony of printed novels, the master craftsman was a confluence of the two archaic types of storyteller, the seaman who brought news of distant lands and the peasant who preserved the local memory. In craftsmanship a convergence of time and space took place in the encounter between the settled master and the travelling journeymen that,

> worked together in the same rooms; and every master had been a travelling journeyman before he settled down in his home town or somewhere else. If peasants and seamen were past masters of storytelling, the artisan class was its university. In it was combined the lore of faraway places, such as a much-traveled man brings home, with the lore of the past as it best reveals itself to natives of a place.[56]

Fyfe indicates a similar meeting point between master and apprentice in the printing trade: figure of the *reading boy* or *copy holder* that read aloud the editorial tests. This informed technical action was indeed a "professional performance with its own auditory conventions; a reader pronounced grammatical marks and used sing-song inflections for variations in type."[57] Printed books prior to the modernization of the publishing houses are artifacts created precisely in the crossroads of guild craftsmanship and industrial production. The proofreading position gradually disappeared between the ends of the nineteenth century and the beginnings of the twentieth century, replaced by a growing demand for authors and composers to avoid errors in the galleys. This led to an increasing dominance of the sense of sight in printing technology, also thanks to the expansion of writing using typewriters, which developed on par with the consolidation of a book industry.[58] During the same period, massive silent reading was born with widespread proliferation of romantic novels in the idle urban middle classes.[59] It is not bold to see parallelisms between twilight of oral storytelling described by Benjamin, and the disappearance of loud reading in the print trade and the shift from aural to visual correction pointed out by Fyfe. Both phenomena happened when publishers became a part of advanced capitalism and the then nascent cultural industries.[60]

Indulge me a brief digression. The concept of errata is also related to the glitch, the kind of errors that do not affect the performance or stability of a program, and therefore cannot be considered a defect in the software (or bug), but rather an unplanned trait. Such errors also appear in a series of social and artistic practices that seek to exploit such failures. The unpredictability of error, its multiplication, and its persistence conceal the possibilities of tracing the history of the works, through the cracks that show when the screen essentialist illusion of perfection staggers.

Returning to the cultural impact of automated editorial correction using scanning and OCR, let me suggest that the use of reCAPTCHA is a form of "work in a state of distraction" that expanded the "reception in a state of distraction" that Benjamin detected in early film audiences.[61] reCAPTCHA worked with a countdown that created, by its immediacy and vertigo, a single, decontextualized, momentary, time of reading and writing.[62] The use of software such as reCAPTCHA is an example of "human computation," the process by which the input of users feeds automation to minimize the role of human correctors in digitization:

> We believe the results presented here are part of a proof of concept of a more general idea: "Wasted" human processing power can be harnessed to solve problems that computers cannot yet solve. Some have referred to this idea as "human computation."[63]

Ironically, at least until 2013, every time we tried to access various webpages we were, willingly or not, *reading boys* in Google's digitization project. (But there was no one listening us reciting.) As this peculiar example shows, cyborgs, the human and machine integration, do not necessarily resemble grotesque images of robotic prostheses, meat and metal intertwined as in low budget sci-fi blockbusters.

Standing on the Shoulders of Lilliputians. *Google Books* is supported by the core of Google's business model. That is, the offer of free services in exchange for advertising, combined with the possibility of patterning user activity to produce automated service improvement. This clever use of otherwise wasted resources has resulted in the making of a social and cultural institution of a magnitude unparalleled in history. Its capabilities in various fields exceed by far those of comparable state institutions dealing with the same issues, such as libraries, secretaries of commerce and communications, intelligence departments, statistics departments, and research laboratories. The project has laid the foundations for the existence of an actual universal library, or at least for now, a Western world library. And the basis of this has been the minimal daily contributions of millions of users, "crowdsourcing" in the technical jargon: the more or less known fact that everyone pays Google a tribute of input in exchange for their free access services.[64]

Google Books does not provide a clear figure for how many books it has digitized although some estimates claim it would have passed from some hundreds of thousands in 2005 to nearly twelve million in 2010. Barbara Cassin provided in 2007 some figures that allowed envisioning the size of *Google Books* compared to other digitization endeavors: the *Project Gutenberg*, launched by Michael Hart in 1971, eighteen thousand books; the *Million Book Project* at Carnegie Mellon University, six hundred thousand; and *Gallica* at the French National Library, seventy thousand volumes in image mode and one thousand two hundred and twenty in text mode.[65] These figures of course change on a daily basis. As I write this chapter, the *Project Gutenberg* page declares forty eight thousand and twenty nine free eBooks, *Gallica* offers three million two hundred sixty two thousand five hundred and fifteen "documents" of which five hundred fifty four thousand one hundred and twenty four were books. Outside independent projects and national libraries in the corporate world, the only competitors at the scale of Google, are quite far from boasting similar numbers: Apple claims that its online *iBooks* store offers two and half million electronic books "and counting," a search for "Kindle eBooks" on Amazon's site sheds three million one hundred eighty five thousand three hundred and fifty six results, Microsoft abandoned its *Live Search Books* project when it had reached about seven hundred and fifty thousand copies, Facebook has no book digitization project of its own. The only project keeping the pace is Microsoft's Live Search former partner, *The Internet Archive*, which declares six million "fully accessible public domain eBooks."[66]

As time passes, the gap just grows wider. In a blog post a Google employee stated that they had established, temporarily, the total number of existing books: "After we exclude serials, we can finally count all the books in the world. There are 129,864,880 of them. At least until Sunday."[67] According to this estimate, as of the writing of this chapter, Google has digitized over fifteen percent of the books in the world.

Leaving aside the political and social implications of the unprecedented power of digital technologies corporate behemoths such as Google, Amazon, Apple, Facebook, and Microsoft (along with the fears that an oligopoly of such magnitude spurs), the affordances of the *Google Books* digitization project have radically changed the ways in which we relate to texts. Although this impact has been buffered by laws governing intellectual property, the process of digitization and the improvement of reading devices providing a perception closer to the experience of paper reading will only foster this phenomenon.

The brief history of book digitization presented in this chapter introduced considerations regarding digitization on other arts and in culture in general, especially the importance of discreteness for standardization and the changing affordances of different book digitizing technologies. It also introduced some differences between digital born and digitized works. Finally it presents some of the social and political implications of large and long scope digitization endeavors such as that of *Google Books* in comparison to other similar projects, and the particular role of users as well as that of the State and other institutions. In the next chapter I turn my attention to what is happening with culture, in a broad sense, inside the digital milieu.

CHAPTER 4
Illegalized Aliens in the Land of the Copyrighted

Digital Works

Based on the scenario described in the previous chapters, this chapter discusses an instrumental definition of "digital work" that incorporates the problem of storage. Taking on from Hayles' definition of electronic literature, by digital works I specifically refer to born digital works and not digital objects that are the product of the digitization of works originated in print or previous cultures. Any of these works represents an instance in which a code is executed, although they are not solely defined by this feature. A formal analysis, following the distinction between formal and forensic proposed by Kirschenbaum,[1] assumes that digital works exist in the code. The code is interpreted by a device and it is realized according the possibilities and configurations afforded by the physical and logical output of the latter. A digital work is, in a narrow sense, pure code but its perception is deter- mined by the output therefore requiring the mediation of repro- duction platforms, that is, screen, printer, speakers, Braille monitor, etc. Comparing the code with the score, realization possibilities depend on technical capabilities similar to the case of musical execution, involving not only the skill of the musician but other factors such as the material conditions of the instrument, acoustic and environmental conditions that affect the dissemination of sound, etc. While the comparison may be somewhat forced, it helps with considering all aspects involved, in the same way the materiality of books and their relationship with the texts provides a new and more solid insight on literary works as historical objects. But even as code, digital works possess materiality: they are inscriptions on standardized storage devices and comply with technical requirements so that they can be realized. This materiality makes them similar in stability, but not equal, to literary works stored in books, while implying a complex set of hardware and software constraints that make their actualization somewhat comparable to the execution of a score.

Philippe Bootz' model of digital poetry analysis proposes that the instance of the code corresponds to a second domain, that of "technical intervenients," the physical constituents of the work. Bootz' model adds some complexity to thinking digital works by incorporating the idea of storage and technical realization. To this end he considers digital works as entities:

> endowed with three dimensions: an essence, physical constituents (extensive parts: material and symbolic elements) and relationships that link them with the essence. This essence is a power to act in the world. This power can be used only by contacts between a set of actors and the work, i.e., communication between these actors via extensive parts of the work.[2]

Bootz' model incorporates the materiality inherent to the moment of the output or the realization of the code on the screen, speaker, printer, or any other device that displays it. In his conceptualization, the realization is defined as the "observable transitory." Although the works are code, they are interlocked to the materiality that enables their perception and therein lies what the French scholar calls "technical liability," that is, the technical aspects, both in hardware and software, that may modify the observable transitory, due both to change in systems and computers in time (the diachronic lability) and their differences in a given period (their synchronic lability).

From a historical and contextual approach, a digital work is not only a piece of code in the same way that a work of literature is not only a text. However, the reference to the code is an essential aspect to define at least one specific trait of digital works. Although the code is also part of contemporary printed works uncritically (and fallaciously) inscribed as part of print culture (since they originate in digital archives), digital works imply the execution of code and an instance of realization, or back to Bootz, an observable transitory.

Code is therefore not a defining characteristic but a necessary one that is completed with another excluding feature: the need of an execution that results in an observable transitory. (This definition might be extended to a "perceivable transitory" to include digital works whose realization does not require the sense of sight.) It should be noted that there are digital works that do not imply a problematic definition, especially those presenting limited degrees of formal and technical experimentation. Two examples of this are hypertext novels such as *Afternoon* by Michael Joyce and visual poems that use Flash, such as *Wordtoys* by Belén Gache. Some collaborative products specific to the digital milieu are the *Wikipedia Books*[3] and the blog *fanfictions*.[4] All of the above are textual forms in which the digital genesis is decisive. The boundaries of the more established genres of digital literature and art such as hypertext fiction, interactive fiction, installation art, or Flash poems are established from non-problematic cases such as these in which a correct execution of the code is the basic element for the perception of the work.[5] Other genres interlock digital code and specific new technologies and devices, such as SMS short fictions, geolocated narratives with GPS coordinates, virtual reality works, interactive theatrical pieces with remote actors, algorithmic random works, generative art, codework, and works that articulate digital and printed instances. In these cases the dematerialization discourse does not hold up so easily but all of these cases imply particular perceptible transitories defined by the realization possibilities that are intertwined to the material technical affordances of the devices at stake.

Drifters in the Digital Realm

...I'm an alien I'm a legal alien
-Sting, "Englishman in New York"

...I am just a shadow of a shadow of a shadow
Always trying to catch up with myself
-Nine Inch Nails, "Copy of A"

They had forgotten the shield-hung hull
Seen nearer and more plain,
Dipping into the troughs like a gull,
And gull-like rising again
-Rudyard Kipling, "The Pirates in England"

Outside digital art, there are odd digital objects that do not usually receive critical attention: *derivative works*. These works originate in technical recording and reproducibility practices enhanced by the digital milieu. The importance of derivative works is that they are actually where the digital *doxa* are defined. Without these productions, one cannot fully dimension the phenomena of the digitization of works of art and other cultural forms and how the digital culture map is drawn. It is impossible to attempt a critique of works challenging the established limits of the digital realm without considering those that establish them and those that try to transgress them with no artistic or experimental intentions. Furthermore, the dichotomy between digital and digitized dilutes in derivative works. From a market perspective, which ultimately determines the rules of digital existence and circulation today, derivative works can be classified into two large groups: sanctioned and unsanctioned, legalized and illegalized realizations. Since the problem of the copyrights is one of the key debates in relation to digital reproduction, I will follow the prevailing commercial criteria for descriptive purposes before presenting a critical interpretation of the cultural implications of this model. Copyright issues also include areas in dispute within the digital milieu, usually deemed as piracy, a problem that relates to disputes over the digitization of printed books discussed in the preceding chapter. For example, some of the scanning models associated with piracy by the market dictums are by-products that illuminate the aestheticization of abstraction on which medial ideology is based.

Anachronisms, Remediation, and Programmed Obsolescence. The conceptual basis for legal derivative works is an idealistic reduction of art to pure content and of literary works to mere text. Such a transit enabling the abstraction of one medium into another is not new. The *Odyssey* is not only the history of Ulysses' long return to Ithaca, it is also the eventful journey of the text from the voice of the rhapsodists through a series of storage devices (parchment, paper, codex) until finally reaching the homely digital shores of *Project Gutenberg*.[6]

Brazilian theorist Arlindo Machado points out the existence of a problem in audiovisual media that can be extended to textual media. Without artistic experimentation, Machado suggests, every new medium is filled in with the contents of previous media, producing a formal anachronism. Original works are adapted to forced conditions of reproducibility. As he notes,

> [w]ithout the intervention of a radical imagination, machines succumb to the hands of production operators that do nothing but fill them up with "content" from previous media, repeating in new languages solutions already crystallized in older languages. VCR machines reproduce the history of film, holograms mimic Greek sculptures, *computer art* programs simulate styles consecrated by painting.[7]

The idea of "content anachronism" is a crack in the idealist content-centered conception of art that drives contemporary digital culture. Anachronism recurrently persists in new media; the ongoing survival of something belonging to a different technical era contradicts the naïve faith in the teleology of technical progress, the assumption that each new medium is an improvement on the previous one. At the same time, through difference, anachronism highlights the often unperceived materiality of storage devices and their specific affordances: the distances separating 35 mm film from magnetic tape images, marble from pixel textures, and vinyl from 64 Kbits/s .mp3 encoding sound outputs... Several authors discuss the artistic languages according to their material specificities and aesthetic effects, such as Manovich's definitions of new and old media or Hayles' media-specific analysis. However, these do not frequently address the gaps generated by the successive adaptations, or the translations from one device to another, or from one software to another.

Bolter and Grusin's remediation does address the circulation of content from one reproduction technology to another. One virtue of the concept is that it discusses the intertwinement of content, reproduction devices and storage devices by describing the polar oscillations between "immediacy" and "hypermediacy," and between "transparency" and "opacity." Immediacy implies a trustworthy representation, the perception that a new media renders its content better than previous media by making the mediation invisible, imperceptible (for instance, in the image resolution of DVD players compared to VHS, which in turn are surpassed by Blu-Ray). Hypermediacy, on the contrary, reveals the mediation of the technical representation device that by showing itself through the proliferation of marks in the content representation becomes opaque. Some marks are evident, such as interface icons while others are less obvious, such as film subtitles, photo captions, and metadata. Hypermediacy highlights the historicity of media, challenging the implicit teleology of technological determinism and identifying physically located cultural and technical disputes: "New digital media are not external agents that come to disrupt an unsuspecting culture. They emerge from within cultural contexts, and they refashion other media, which are embedded in the same or similar contexts."[8] The appropriation and reappropriation dynamics described in *Remediation* also implies an oscillation; old media can also remedy new media. This back and forth movement of remediated content looks towards media itself, and shows the illusion of content transparency.

Another process in the dynamics of remediation (and anachronism) is obsolescence, a degradation in technical agency. Eventually, the elements that make up a given technology may be discontinued and the technical milieu in which it is inserted dismantled, losing its agency, as occurred with magnetic tape, photochemical photography and 35 mm film. A commonsense extended notion is that technical objects become obsolete when they are surpassed by others that are more efficient, thus inserting objects in a linear history based on an ideology of progress. Yet the processes may be reversible and some discarded technologies may resurface.⁹ But the obsolescence of a work that depends on a particular reproduction technology implies also decay in its reproducibility. And so it follows that the exhibition value will recede and, inadvertently, it will gain cult value since it will only become reproducible in devices progressively harder to get, most likely located in museums of technology, in archives, or in forgotten boxes in the attic.

In this discursive dispute between the teleology of progress as the unavoidable rule of technology and the overlapping and coexistence of technologies that in fact occurs, unsanctioned remediation creates a novel scenario in which illegal derivative works dispute the logics of content as a commodity. Medial ideology is based on the concealment of difference under the illusion of an increased transparency, an alleged improvement in the content realization compared to older media. Content dynamics is a form of aestheticization sustained in an idealist concept of work that is the current basis for contemporary cultural industries. This calls for a critique of the myth of ever pristine works in the succeeding remediations in order to reconsider the history, the materiality and the conflicts inherent to any cultural object. Looking into the opacity and noise of each form of reproduction is the first step to undertake a serious critical approach.

One of the typical forms of digital derivative work is, in this context, the result of the intention of adapting a pre-existing content so that it can be reproduced as output on another device or, as Bolter and Grusin would put it, to remedy it. The double dynamics of remediation reveal the oscillations between transparency and opacity, and between immediacy and hypermediacy. For instance, legal digitization considers eliminating noise one of its major accomplishments. There is a quest for representation transparency enabled by technical progress. Illegalized digitization also deals with noise as a problem but explicitly assumes the possibility of generating it, in the battles over the appropriation of copies. By doing so, by digitizing in subpar conditions they introduce unexpected improvements motivated by the particular circulation dynamics in which they are immersed. A collateral remediation, if you will. The following subsections discuss the specificities of both forms of derivation and the way in which illegalized ones subvert the content aestheticization established by their legal counterparts.

Short Note on Franchises. My concept of derivation should not be confused with another derivative phenomenon typical of the cultural industry, that of cultural franchises. A franchise is the paradigmatic product of contemporary cultural industries and can be described as a thematic and aesthetic universe, relatively coherent, covering multiple genres and artistic disciplines, which is rigorously controlled through the administration of intellectual property and copyrights, and is ultimately oriented towards the maximization of profits. It must be noted that franchises are not content, which is a more abstract concept that includes some of the many different types of products that may be included in a given franchise. A cultural industry franchise *par excellence* are Walt Disney animated characters but there are also digital born franchises such as the one generated around the online role playing game *World of Warcraft*, comprising comics, novels, and a film (still in preproduction), or the one that has been mounted around *The Lord of the Rings* and *The Hobbit* film sagas by Peter Jackson including video games, a theme park, and a republishing of the works of Tolkien adapting its editorial design to that of the film aesthetics. Today any potentially profitable work tends to generate a franchise around itself, from B movie monsters such as Freddy Krueger or Jason to teen heroes as Harry Potter, from Don Corleone to Mr. Spock, from dreadlock wearing pirate Jack Sparrow to Rastafarian singer Bob Marley. Franchising aims to retain revenues generated from any remediation, derivation, and adaptation provided they respect the copyrights and intellectual property as well as the aesthetic guidelines set by the owners of the franchise.

An interesting example is the case of the music album *Rogue's Gallery: Pirate Ballads, Sea Songs, and Chanteys*, produced by Johnny Depp and Gore Verbitsky (actor and director of the film adaptation of Disney's park ride *Pirates of the Caribbean*, respectively). The album compiles old pirate songs versioned by contemporary rock musicians. The abundance of blood, semen, and obscenities made it unsuitable for the family oriented franchise and it was launched separately. Manovich suggests this type of derivation usually originates in a "source," usually a literary work or film, although there are cases of franchises generated from video games, music stars, and, as this case shows, even park rides.[10] The next section does not address this type of derivation; instead, it focuses on digital variations coming from works perceived as stand-alone units.

Legal Derivative Works. Digital commonsense defines an electronic edition of Homer's *Odyssey* as an eBook. The work is a derivative work resulting from the digitization of a pre-existing work, regardless of the process by which it has become code. But the definition of an eBook is an exemplary case of how something seemingly simple implies a multiplicity of technical, aesthetic, political, and economic aspects. If the concept of book itself is still a subject of debate due to the relation between the text and its materialization in a specific storage device, the definition of "electronic book" is even more problematic. From a technical point of view, it could be relatively simple: a digital code whose output is readable. The real problem is to determine what makes a given digital text to be culturally perceived as an eBook. Italian librarian Laura Testoni provides a cultural definition of eBooks: "An eBook is a digital object, with textual and/or other content, which is the result of the integration of the familiar concept of a book with features that can be provided by an electronic environment."[11] Although the definition suffices for a general understanding, it has the problem of referring more to a form of storage, the book as an object, than to a textual work contained in a specific storage device. In fact, the closeness of the object book in itself also is a subject of debate, as Striphas suggests: "Books *conventionally* have edges, but they don't *necessarily* possess them. For all practical purposes people today tend to treat books—with the exception of anthologies—as if they were discrete, closed entities."[12] But, as he points out, it has not always been this way and in early printing single bound volumes could contain several works. Thus the relation between the work and the book as storage did not always coincide. He also calls the attention upon the taken for granted fact that today readers receive "finished works," in the sense that they do not demand any material action to be complete. But for economic reasons in the past, books were shipped by the printers with the pages unbound. The conclusiveness of printed text is also a technical matter. As Striphas points out, perhaps "they were books all along. If so, then the word 'book' denotes not so much a hard-edged product than a supple, diffuse, and ongoing process."[13] The process described by Striphas is surprisingly closer to an idea of fluidity more frequently associated with eBooks rather than paper books.

An undeniable feature in the definition of eBooks is that they require an energy source to be readable. Outside of that, all other approaches towards a definition depend on different combinations of cultural and technical factors. An inclusive approach can be considering as such any electronic edition of a text. From this point of view, digitally produced works and digitized ones are both eBooks. Each file format determines a number of affordances, as the capacity of the text to fit the reading device screens, usually known as "text fluidity." The current standard, the open .ePub format, allows other affordances such as changing font size, copy and paste, or performing searches within the text. The opposite of this dynamic output is the "fixed text" frequent in the realization of texts as images, where the layout and typography are definitive, so common in .pdf format using its more restrictive settings, which may afford as little as just zooming on the text. Between these two extremes there are reading device specific formats like the ones supported by Amazon's Kindle, as well as forms less constrained but with lesser affordances as the most basic text, UTF-8 encoding format.

The problem of eBook standards is something that does not exist for physical books, whose readability, if the book is in good condition, is only constrained by the skills of readers (human readers, of course). Digital technologies, on the other hand, are associated with protocols (which work on the basis of discreteness demanded by the decoding operations). The nearly effective universality of the physical book associated with the reading skills assured by biological and cultural abilities are in a way more versatile than the alleged but restricted universality of eBooks

that are determined by the predominance of one technology or
another depending on the development of market strategies and
the survival of certain standards in order to avoid obsolescence.
The battle for the standards is also fought between a business
model based on providing services against one selling goods. This
description is, of course, a simplification; some companies pursue
both models selling either separate items or granting access in
exchange of membership fees. But the underlying fact is that both
dynamics are based on the same idea of *content*. The dynamics of
the artworks as commodities has already been well studied by the
critics of the cultural industry such as Theodor Adorno and Mark
Horkheimer whereas the basis of Google's business model as a
cultural industry has not yet been fully discussed and the analyses
are restricted mainly, and separately, to economic, social, and
technical issues.

What pervades culture today is the extension of the already
fuzzy attributes of works acknowledged within a print culture
mindset that are extended to the context of digital technology,
where there is an ongoing dispute between free circulation and
copyright based marketing. The tensions nesting in the different
technical cultures surface when the models of digital circulation
clash, as in the case of eBooks. In this regard, Federico Heinz from
Via Libre Foundation ironically suggests that:

> Calling these digital files "eBooks" is like calling transatlantic passenger
> jets "winged tricycles": it describes them in a way, but grossly underes-
> timates them. This underestimation is useful to publishing houses:
> thinking in terms of "eBook" sets limits on our imagination about what
> can we expect from them.[14]

For a cultural critique of technology it is necessary to stress
that eBooks exemplify one of the most outstanding aspects of the
crisis of traditional storage devices. Cultural industries, after a
period of tensions, place hope in solving the dilemma through the
establishment of a circulation model based on pure contents. The
most salient aspect is the fracture between the text that becomes
code and the book as an object. The storage devices are diluted in
the code inscriptions on the hard drive or in the volatile memory of
devices. The digitization of texts affords new modes of reproduc-

tion that recover almost discarded book related practices as is the case of the audiobooks generated through automatic reading or Braille output softwares. In this case the text is set free not only from its traditional storage device but also from visual perception. Abstraction affords a series of remediations that ultimately lead to works becoming just content.

The Rights of Many and the Copyrights of a Few. With the application of DRM (Digital Rights Management), code measured in eBook units becomes a controllable infinitely reproducible commodity. This is made possible by the confluence of the abstraction enabled by alphabetic writing along with that of digital reproducibility and manipulation. In the kingdom of copyright, text is more than ever content, a pure idea whose access is only limited by price.

A long tradition of plagiarism and apocryphal works with deep roots in print culture quickly set foot in digital culture. Since the advent of mass use of the Internet, cultural industries and governments have been trying to control the dissemination of works that does not comply with the limitations imposed by copyright holders. Since digital copies require nothing but transmission and storage space while extracting nothing from the original, the problem that gave rise to the idea of copyright resurfaces: the possession of an abstraction, text. The dispute moves on now to the ownership of another form of abstraction, code. However, unlike text, digital code is capable of agency, in this case the ability to realize representations.

Accelerated copying speed, storage miniaturization, and ease of manipulation afforded by digital technologies provide the context of emergence of a series of practices that, though prior to digital technologies, have found in digital circulation a fertile milieu. However, not all derivations are equivalent and each type poses different challenges to the work-centered organization of Western culture and the hegemonic cultural industries.

Viral Reproduction. A paradigmatic case of derivation and viral dissemination are *digital memes*, usually parodic variations of digital or digitized works. Knobel and Lankshear provide a broad definition encompassing the many artistic disciplines from which this digital practice feeds and its applications in the context of digital culture. The concept of meme was popularized by geneticist Richard Dawkings and digital memes share some features with the neuroscience understandings of the mind. The original concept of meme described contagious patterns of cultural information that passed from mind to mind generating world ideas and significant forms of behavior in social groups. Some typical examples of memes are popular melodies, witty phrases, architectural styles, ways of doing things, icons, and jingles. It is, in short, about short forms. According to Knobel and Lankshear, digital memes have three key characteristics that identify them as "successful," that is, that they become viral: fidelity, fecundity, and longevity.

The first characteristic describes those meme qualities that can be copied without losing meaningful information; this has nothing to do with being true, just memorable. The second characteristic identifies whether the meme can spread quickly and thus capture enough media attention. A specific trait of this characteristic is the meme's susceptibility, and the timing and location that make it fecund due to its relation to ongoing events, trends, or expectations. The third characteristic means that the longer the meme lives, the more it can be copied. This is an aspect fundamental to the chain of replication and mutations involved in a meme's existence cycle.[15]

The artistic relevance of memes is minor but they are an undeniable part of the new sensorium marked by the acceleration of circulation, reproducibility, and variability. What took much work and hard-to-come-by skills in the past, once coded, becomes easier to quote, intervene, comment, or parody. The combination of plagiarism, parody, and viral circulation also show an important trait of digital reproducibility. Memes thrive in a sensorium receptive to the ridicule and the *kitsch* spawned by cultural industries. Technical reproducibility is no longer the only factor at stake, technical mutability is also central to the modes of existence of digital objects:

> In many ways, these "mutations" often seemed to help the meme's fecundity in terms of hooking people into contributing their own version of the

meme. A concept like "replicability" therefore needs to include remixing as an important practice associated with many successful online memes, where remixing includes modifying, bricolaging, splicing, reordering, superimposing, original and other images, sounds, films, music, talk, and so on.[16]

While digital memes are generally anecdotal derivatives, they highlight a fundamental aspect of digital circulation: the intervention on the copies. The gap between the source and the juxtaposition with other representations destabilizes the reduction of works to closed or controlled contents managed by cultural industries. On the other hand, the viral nature of its circulation does not only blur the authorial figure in the disseminating crowd, it also reinforces the always provisional character of works and the reproducibility that makes it more comparable to a biological phenomenon than to a technological and social one. The difficulty to bind digital entities is a recurring issue of digitization that is also evident in other derivative works that confront with legal digital derived works: the derivatives popularly known as leaks.

From High Culture to the Low Fidelity. Leaks may be considered as involuntary derivative works. Any digital entity, such as a work, a document, or a program, obtained without permission during the production or circulation stages prior to its release or its official publication is a leak. This concept extends well beyond art and literature, with the case of journalistic organization *WikiLeaks* being the most well-known example. Internet pages publishing leaked corporate or government information is another typical example of digital circulation. Contrary to memes, leaks do not imply a modification during their digital circulation. Instead, they strive to preserve as much resemblance and accessory information regarding the source as possible. In the case of leaks related to literature, arts, and entertainment, there are however two major differences with regards to the authorized versions: (a) leaks often cause either viral dissemination of an *unfinished work*; or (b) of a finished work in *subpar reproduction conditions*. Leaks originating from cultural industries introduce aesthetic dilemmas concerning the perception of works in the digital milieu since they decisively influence way we relate to culture.[17]

Ubiquitous and free circulation has been the cause for the rede-
finition of a model based on the sale of copies, akin to that forced
by the appearance of industrial scale text, image and sound
reproduction technologies since mid-nineteenth century. The
unforeseen impact of free access afforded by digital copies is
changing the cultural industry business models. From one based
on the sale of objects storing a specific content (i.e., books, posters,
and other storage devices such as disks, eight track magazines,
cassettes, CDs, videotapes, DVDs, floppy disks, etc.) cultural
industries are moving towards a different, hybrid, model that can
also profit from different ways to access digital and digitized
contents. The process is still ongoing and has not yet reached an
instance of relative stability similar to the one achieved by the
cultural industry majors during the second half of the twentieth
century. The need to change a business model based on the sale of
physical copies began with the crisis of the musical industry due to
the digital circulation of songs in the popular .mp3 audio compression format and has since extended to film, publishing, and television industries.[18] The process has been accompanied by a
convergence of information and communication technologies (ICTs)
due to the digitization of previously specific and separated technologies. It is seldom remembered that recording and communication technologies did not develop together, although they have
frequently crossed paths, and that each developed its own specificities due to their affordances and the social practices they cata-
lyzed without necessarily having been planned or even foreseen.

An oft sidelined topic of Benjamin's essay on the work of art is
the status of mimesis in relation to reproduction technologies. The
representation of an absence, which is the basis of any record or
telecommunication, remains the central element of what today
comprises all the different exteriorization technologies grouped
under the term ICT. To the already complex relationship between
content and container, technical reproducibility adds the problem
of its circulation. The idea of a pure content, stored in a neutral
container that evenly distributes it through a neutral medium, is
an idealist simplification. This assumption discards materiality
and historical inscription that interlocks content, container, and
their associated milieus. What is more, contents and containers

are co-constitutive and content remediations also usually imply the simulation of the previous storage devices to retain its mimetic power.

However, when Benjamin postulated that technical copies uproot works from pre-industrial tradition, he was not considering that it also implied rooting them into another (technical) tradition, since the new reproduction technologies also had a history of their own. Although serial production represents a decline in the aura of the unique storage devices, standardized devices do belong to another tradition, that of the industrial objects. In a way similar to what happened to the *incunabula*, the books printed before 1501, nowadays some objects gain a distinctive and particular cult value due to the singularity and individualization time and obsolescence bestow upon things that were once just part of a standardized series. There is a paradoxical aura in discontinued industrial objects as first editions, super-8 film, vinyl records, or Atari games (and that even extends to the technological devices used to play them).

In the history of data storage, the miniaturization afforded by digital inscription is another step forward in the abstraction process introduced by analog reproduction technologies. Its material existence becomes even more inaccessible, inscribed in the black box of digital storage devices. This illusory dematerialization, however, makes the materiality of prior storage devices visible and their taken-for-granted specificities become evident.

Remediations are the touchstones of a technical tradition that free circulation of digital copies undermines. In the context of ever growing network coverage and the multiplication of devices that afford reproducing digital and digitized works, a particular kind of remediation, digital leaks, poses a serious threat for the cultural industries. The urgency that accompanies the acceleration of the contemporary sensorium along with the ease to copy and distribute have generated a series of practices that clash with intellectual property regulations upon which different cultural industries have thrived during the last hundred and fifty years. Among the practices regarded as "piracy" by copyright holding business conglomerates, a leak is the digital circulation of a work "before" it is made available for legal consumption by the industry (under the form of publication, release or screening). Due to the predominantly digital origin of contemporary cultural products, be these texts, audio, or fixed or moving images, the overwhelming majority of the creation or registration and of the correction, editing, and post-production stages generate multiple versions previous to the so-called definitive, concluded work.[19]

There are different kinds of leaks. The most obvious are direct leaks; that is the circulation of contents before they become available to the public at the stage of production or post-production. A subsidiary practice is the apparition of low-fi leaks, such as the so-called camrips, clandestine personal camera recordings of movies previews or screenings, which populate peer-to-peer networks and feed the illegal DVD copies industry. This example eloquently illustrates an oscillation from cult to exhibition values, which chooses immediacy over image quality. Having attained the very high quality standards set by the 35 mm film, today well on the way to being replaced by allegedly equivalent digital projectors, the reproductions obtained with a handheld camera can hardly be considered "copies" in the strictest sense of the term. For this reason I prefer to include them among derivative works, paying attention to their constituent material differences, even though, at a formal (and at a legal) level, they can be considered the "same" film (and their unauthorized derivations can be persecuted accordingly).

This type of derivation is a particular case of the remediated content anachronism previously discussed, although driven by the public rather than by the cultural industries. The practice is also related to another widespread form of digital leak, the circulation of private recordings of artistic events (concerts, samples, performances, etc.) that can be traced back to the circulation of live concerts' bootleg records, usually produced by sound engineers without the awareness of musicians, which were common in popular music between the seventies and the nineties. The common trait of these leaks is the loss of fidelity over immediacy. If early bootleg tapes could still claim the auratic value of being the nonindustrial registry of a unique occasion, in the context of the digital circulation the leaks are but one more sign of the depreciation of sound fidelity for the sake of urgency. Leaks are a paradoxical validation of content dynamics. There is an idealist perception that chooses to ignore the noise generated by the leak process or that minimizes its importance, ultimately deeming materiality as a contingent or directly irrelevant aspect. German critic and theorist Hito Steyerl has presented a brilliant defense of leaks in what she calls "poor images" and the subversion of cultural capitalism. In the final paragraphs of her essay she states:

> The poor image embodies the afterlife of many former masterpieces of cinema and video art. It has been expelled from the sheltered paradise that cinema seems to have once been. After being kicked out of the protected and often protectionist arena of national culture, discarded from commercial circulation, these works have become travelers in a digital no-man's-land, constantly shifting their resolution and format, speed and media, sometimes even losing names and credits along the way.[20]

In previous unpublished presentations of my research I termed the massive public acceptance of low fidelity compressed image, audio, and video formats as the ".mp3 paradigm." The case of music was the first cultural industry to be hit by the digital revolution, and where information lossy compression formats thrived. Although despised by audiophiles, the small size of .mp3 files was in the right place at the right time when the first file sharing technologies settled in and young people started stuffing their hard drives with music.[21]

For decades, the practice of photocopying has been a widespread form for readers to relate with books (and that practice is still alive and kicking in many developing and underdeveloped countries).[22] The case of illegalized eBook circulation is slightly different. There are some common traits with other unsanctioned derivations, as in the case of the already discussed zombie editions (for example problems with proper authorial and publisher information and other paratext). But the most distinctive trait, which relates them to leaks, is their lack of digital affordances. Most frequently leaked books exist under restrictive functionality fixed text formats, such as pdf files or text as image originated in scanning without proper OCR re-textualization. On the other hand online bookstore versions are expected to afford fluid text, under .ePub and other device specific text formats.

Summarizing, the contemporary sensorium favors a depreciated mimesis for the sake of an exacerbated mobility. Given the ubiquity and free nature of illegal content, the polar oscillation towards exhibition value reaches its highest point whereas cult value dilutes in a form even more pronounced than the decay of aura Benjamin detected in the early analog copying. Although unnecessary from a technical point of view, the more efficient digital abstraction of the text yields to the text as digital image, the high definition lines of images pixelate, and the digital sound frequency curves flatten.

Piracy in the Age of Technical Reproduction. The impact of the leaks (and of illegal copies in general) has led to the identification of copies with what is known as digital watermarking. These can be evident, i.e. visible or audible, or hidden in the code to be detected analyzing the file instead of playing it. Of course, a digital copy may include various types of watermarks. This information is not to be confused with the file metadata, the additional information within the code that enables digital manipulation and its affordances. Digital watermarking, on the other hand, does not imply a human perceptible improvement of the works.

In response to the viral logic of leaks, imperceptible water marking allows tracing the origin of the leak, granted each copy generated in a given stage of preproduction, production, and postproduction has been properly watermarked. While this procedure is complex and costly, it is a part of the defensive line set by major music, film, and publishing production companies (along with persecution of illegal downloads and of in-company leaks). An early phenomenon was watermarking at the expense of the usual reproduction standards through permanent or sporadic presence of sound or visual noise in the reproduction of the file used in previews, although this did not seem to affect the immediacy driving leakers and their public.

This is not the place to judge the lawfulness or utility of such measures. What I want to highlight is that leaks indicate that allographic perception seems to be the norm, at least for a significant percentage of the public, instead of the autographic perception afforded by the specific reproduction technologies, as is, for instance watching a film in a theater instead of a cell phone screen. Perceiving well is not as important as perceiving now. The oscillation from fidelity to immediacy transcends the boundaries of commodities, forcing a reformulation of contents in order to keep them marketable. The widespread zeal in the production stages of any high profile literary, cinematic and musical work is a symptom of this phenomenon, which also finds its obverse in the open works and works in progress. Conclusiveness is more and more a feature of a distinct cultural tradition: the age of finished works related to media specific storage devices.

"If the e-reader is the digital equivalent of the brown-paper wrapper, the romance reader is a little like the Asian carp: insatiable and unstoppable. Together, it turns out, they are a perfect couple," wrote journalist Julie Bosman in 2010.[23] It should not come as a surprise that romantic novels, a guilty pleasure, were one of the early boosts for eBook sales. There is a direct relationship between the cultural industries and each storage device affordances. First, in the case of printed books they allowed silent private individual consumption, and now, secret reading, even in public: eBooks do not reveal their covers to other people in the bus, the queue, or the waiting room. Digital reading devices extend the private sensorium inaugurated by the Sony Walkman in the eighties to the realm of literature.[24]

The history of culture provides an endless list of unfinished works. My own academic background provides me a short list, by no means exhaustive: *Dead Souls*, whose second part was fed to the flames by Nikolai Gogol nine days before his death apparently due to a religiously fed feeling of guilt; the ironic and paradoxically incomplete novel *Bouvard et Pécuchet* by Flaubert where he mocks the ongoing attempts to catalogue all the scientific and historical knowledge of the day; dementia was the cause for the interruption of Mervin Peake's fourth part of the *Gormenghast* series and only the first three pages of the *Titus Awakes* made it to print.... Outside literature, I could add to this series Walter Benjamin's life endeavors whose result is the myriad of notes and quotations compiled as *The Arcades Project* and Alejandro Jodorowsky's hallucinated film adaptation of Frank Herbert's *Dune*, which allegedly would feature surrealist painter Salvador Dalí, Orson

Wells, the set and character design under H. R. Giger, and music composed by Pink Floyd and Karlheinz Stockhausen, among many other eminent collaborators. A common trait of this enumeration is the idea totality, and an ambitious plan to represent it all: all of Russia, of knowledge, of the Castle, of the city of Paris and the nineteenth century, of the universe, and so on. Truncated for different reasons, these works contrast with those works whose plan was actually executed; for instance, Dante's *Divine Comedy*, Cervantes' *Quixote*, Goethe's *Faust*, Joyce's *Ulysses*, Flaubert's *Madame Bovary*, Adorno and Horkheimer's *Dialectic of the Enlightenment*, David Lynch's *Dune*.

But these mentioned works, both finished and unfinished, have found, after the death of their authors, their final form associated with objects (books, scripts, films) that, ultimately, establish their limits. The last page or the last photogram still set the boundaries of these narrow universes that are usually between eighty and five hundred pages, or between one hundred twenty thousand and two hundred and sixty thousand film frames, materially speaking. Today, the relationship between conclusion and storage device has changed with the emergence of digital coding. Digital commodification under the form of ubiquitous content available for download (or streaming) and reproduction *versus* the possibility of the unsanctioned circulation shifts the previous debate between high and low culture towards a dispute between high and low definition. The value of the work blurs in the tension between novelty value and fidelity value. There is a new oscillation in the sensorium from watching, reading, or listening *well*, to watching, reading, or listening *now*, or, better still, *before*, as leaks suggest.

This unfolds new possibilities for the inconclusiveness of works that transcends the author's megalomania, madness, or death, or the producer's fatigue, deadlines, or bankruptcy, whichever happens first. Leaks are not actually a falsification of the original. They are its acceleration. When a work, conceived as pure content, leaks, it is subtracted from the cultural industry consecration rituals that bestow the serial object with a fabricated aura or transform it into fetish. The screenings of films, the release of books, and of records are events that mark official beginnings: the mystique of the premiere, the autographed copy, the first edition.

And, in this peculiar relationship between copies and their storage devices, the fetish is wrongly called "original copy." But, as noted by Benjamin, the opposition between original and false makes no sense in a mechanical reproduction paradigm; there is only an *original* in the case of auratic objects.[25]

The precise term is not original but *legalized*. Put differently, the object has a number that inscribes it in the series as opposed to illegal copying, which, without identification, evades the payment of the royalties to the author, to the copyright holders, and to the State that looks after their rights. Legalized books or discs, as authorized copies, have a relationship with the author, no matter how indirect, that *authorizes* us to acquire them. Pirate books or discs do not. The acceleration imposed by leaks is a different mode of existence for works. It is not truly a falsification since it is an incomplete work in the more traditional sense of the term, and the author has not yet completed it (or, at least, the producers or publishers still have not defined its final details).

The specificities of cinema, music, and literature are many and complex. I only wish to suggest some common traits by looking into the commodification implied in their reduction to content. When a literary, cinematographic, or musical work leaks, some details reveal its unfinished nature to the public educated on the subject: the final mix of the audio is deficient or not consistent with the quality standards of industrial recordings, image quality or film editing are not optimal, or the text appears as a work in progress.

Let us compare some cases from global contemporary culture: the leak of Argentinean rock star Charly García's album *Kill Gil* [*Kill the Moron*], that of the Brazilian movie *Tropa de Elite* [*Elite Squad*], and the publishing zeal to prevent any details of the last four installments of the British *Harry Potter* saga from leaking. The three examples are profoundly associated with cultural industries, and the artistic qualities of the works themselves are not particularly relevant to the problem of leaks. These are all works that originate in consolidated cultural forms prior to the emergence of digital technologies, namely, a rock album, an action film, and a teen fantasy novel series.

The case of Charly García's album presents many aspects worth analyzing. A prototypical rocker, his self-destructive rebellion, his growing paranoia, his declining stardom at the time of recording the album, contributed to the idea that the album's name was just a prank. But it was actually a serious album that its leak left unfinished for a couple of years. No label wanted to edit it because a demo version leaked and circulated as .mp3 files on the Internet. In an interview for *Rolling Stone*, journalist Mariana Enríquez described the notorious differences between the leaked *Kill Gil*, that is, the only available *Kill Gil*, which was just a bad album by García, and the one García himself made her listen to at his house, the finished original, perhaps brilliant, but inaccessible at the time, unless one was lucky enough to be invited to sit down and have its creator play the copy.[26]

Tropa de Elite is the other side of the coin. The Brazilian film portrays urban violence in Rio de Janeiro. The film was leaked to pirate retailers (abundant in Brazilian street markets) months before it premiered in theaters. This motivated a criminal investigation that accused two people in charge of the film subtitles and one of the actors. Contrary to *Kill Gil*, the informal success of the filtered version, in addition to the media coverage of the police case and the claims of the director that the film was different from what it had been leaked, helped *Tropa de Elite* became one of the biggest box office hits of Brazilian cinema. By that time, the film had already won the Golden Bear award of at the Berlin Film Festival. What happens when two films share the same name but not the same final cut, and when both circulate, homonymous, as pure content, authorized and pirate, in different storages? As said before, leaks undermine the idea of work conclusiveness. Three answers can be suggested here: (a) the film that filtered had not been concluded; (b) the leak forced the producers to change the final cut to recover the investment; or (c) it is the result of a very complex marketing strategy that incorporates the cultural dynamics of the circulation of works in the context of the digitization to its own benefit.[27]

The last case, J. K. Rowling's *Harry Potter* novels, is indicative of the changes occurring inside cultural industries. This case exemplifies the zeal and the managed secrecy that are part of any high profile publishing, record company release, or large budget film premiere. The millions of copies and sterling pounds involved in the last four volumes on the adventure of the young wizard required a rigorous organization attempting (with relative success) to keep the secret about the crucial aspects of the plot while providing immediate access to books in the English-speaking world. That is, managing logistics to maximize the number of sales of a specific book object based on its novelty value without losing profits due to leaks.[28] The attempt to prevent the leaks eventually failed due to logistic mismanages and details of the plot reached the Internet. But what is more striking is the massive deployment of economic resources, logistics, and physical and legal safeguards around the authorized movement of physical copies of a book. The publisher had declared that the entire legal device surrounding the global release of a product was justified in the guise of protecting readers so nobody would ruin the surprise; in other words, that reading experience was menaced by unauthorized circulation.

The example is also interesting since one of the biggest successes of modern publishing industry appeared in eBook form only in March 2012, and only in the English version. This is also meaningful for these are probably the most digitized books in history (either by typing, OCR, or scanned as an image). None of these digitizations was authorized, of course. Moreover, at first, the author chose to sell the authorized eBook versions directly from a dedicated website instead of the established digital bookstores such as Amazon or Barnes & Noble, and even dared to do so without the DRM technology that limits their circulation, rewriting the rules of the industry from within.[29]

The War of the Clones at the Dawn of the Dead. Digital copies and the widespread idea of free access enhanced the circulation of works as contents adaptable to different unspecific reproduction devices. Free and supposedly identical copies, opposed to leaks, may be defined as *clones*: a copy without its unique identity mark (the number of copy that identifies it) established by legal digital reproducibility technologies. Many of the aspects linked to this type of copy are similar to the ones discussed over the leaks in the preceding sections. The main difference is that clones do seek an identical free copy rather its immediacy. If leaks pay no heed to the increase of noise in the signal in order to put it into circulation as early as possible, clones pursue the greatest possible fidelity to the source copy. The main problem is that while leaks aim to obtain a copy at any given production stage, clones aim to offer, at the very least, a free copy equivalent to the legal circulating copy. That is, to the remediations circulating in a given digital milieu, since, as pure content works can circulate in a variety of formats to be played in different devices. Compression ratio, which involves the inevitable introduction of noise, is perceived as a problem to declare and therefore clone works rely on a series of qualifying labels that are subject to evaluation and tagging by other users. That is why many characteristics of the file are declared: the source of the copy, if there is any compression and the resulting format, the file size, and other technical specifications relating to the quality of the copy, as the amount of frames per second for video, the number of channels for the audio, etc.

Manovich argues that compression and the resulting noise are the norm of social digital circulation and that they unveil what he calls the "myth of the digital," the existence of an identical copy without degradation, that although technically possible, it is not functional. In fact, he suggests that while digital technology theoretically can produce flawless copies, its actual use is characterized by the use of lossy compression, paradoxically producing even more noise and degradation than analog reproduction technologies.[30]

In the case of eBooks, the fixed or flowing text determines the degree of manipulation afforded by the file. A search for the string "do androids dream of electric sheep" on *Pirate Bay* conducted in February 10, 2013, returned three hits. In one, the uploader declared: "As opposed to the 'hard formatted' PDF I could find here, these formats from Sony (LRF/BEBB) and MobiPocket (Mobi) are specifically for reading on e-ink readers and other mobile hardware devices."[31]

From a formal point of view, the division between leaks and clones is shady, as both usually provide low quality copies. This leads to two complementary phenomena worth discussing: first, the persistence of habits inherited from print culture for accurate file management that suggests a (relative) identification of files, and secondly, the persistence of intellectual property laws that have been, since the expansion of printed books, central for the defense of authorship against apocryphal versions. The boom of unauthorized editions was one of the main reasons to argue the distinction of text and book. Likewise, the reasons for a reformulation of the relationship between the works and their storage devices can be traced in the dynamics of pirate digital content circulation. Unforeseen and unwanted by-products of the digital culture industries, these variations defy the aestheticization by abstraction that underpins medial ideology.

Trettien's idea of zombie editions is a powerful metaphor to define idiot automation, but it also suggests other interpretations. Let us leave aside for a moment the image of plague today associated with zombies, the viral proliferation resulting from the return of the dead. Haitian voodoo zombies are closer to golems responding to a master's commands. Zombie, automated, editions are run by the pursuit of profit from people who see a business opportunity in selling eBooks or in providing print-on-demand service of works in the public domain. In reality, the zombie in these cases would not be so much the editing as the editor, i.e., the OCR software that digitalizes the work automatically and without professional review. These copies are not illegal in the strict sense of the term, but share with leaks and clones their derived, precarious condition. They are not uncompleted by urgency, but by withdrawal. To automate the digitization process, the removal of human presence generates copies with errata, wrong titles, and incorrect authors, works that in the rush to generate contents end up lost in the overabundance of files. They cannot be easily identified, as the zombie edition of *Aeropagitica* by Milton wrongly attributed to the editor Edward Arber.

Trettien's finding is eloquent due to the unintentional irony of the careless digitization. Milton's work is a polemical treatise against censorship that advocates for the freedom of printing without a license. At the same time, Milton's acknowledges the need to confirm the name of the editor and, if possible, of the author. In the late nineteenth century, Edward Arber was one of the first editors to provide hitherto unattainable scholarly editions and standardized texts the general public. Extending the zombie metaphor (and the involuntary humor of automatisms), let me conclude this section with a quote of Milton's (not Arber's) *Areopagitica*, rich in allusions to the life of literary works: "For Books are not absolutely dead things, but doe contain a potencie of life in them to be as active as that soule was whose progeny they are; nay they do preserve as in a violl the purest efficacie and extraction of that living intellect that bred them."

Chopping and Sewing: Victor Frankenstein's Dynamic Collages. One of the most widespread kinds of derivative work is the product of remixing. The concept, originating in rock and pop music, implies the result of new mixes using tracks from a master recording. This process has been widely addressed, so I will just point out its most distinctive aspects in relation to the problem of digitization. For the purposes of this book, *remixes* are derived digital works that are composed of one or more existing works along with other elements manipulated in such a way that they result in a work different from the original sources, although the explicit referral to them may be a part of their expressive resources. As Manovich suggests, after decades of media production, today media archives are the "raw data to be processed" by art rather than materials and reality itself.[32]

Remix is commonly associated with the figure of the deejays and veejays but it should not be reduced only to the practice of scratching, the handling of vinyl discs (or devices that enable it in other media such as CD or digital audio files). Remix is a frequent music procedure but has been extended also to video. Its use has also been extended to other cultural practices where there is heavy use of typical functions of the digital milieu such as copy and paste, loops, and insertions of expressive elements alien to the source work. If leaks are mutants, pirate copies are clones, and wacky automated digitization are zombies, then remixes might very well be reanimations. Put differently, they are digital versions of those revived entities embodied by the filmic depictions that have popularized the idea of Frankenstein's monster. (However, it should be duly noted that Mary Shelley's original creature is never described as a limb patchwork.)

The dynamics of remix correspond to other practices in the digital milieu and its logics collide with the notion of intellectual property. The manipulability of digital files and their availability through the vast archive making up the Internet converges with the commodification of the cultural industries that release remasterizations and reversions on an ongoing basis to feed an ever demanding content market. Remix is not just a form of intertextuality but the possibility to manipulate and multiply the materiality of previous works afforded by different analog and digital technologies. The symbolic and economic disputes spurred by remixes highlight the conflictive relationships between the institutionalized notions of art and literature and their material conditions of production and reproduction. Memes, for example, can be a short form of remix.

The most interesting aesthetic aspect of remix resides in the extraction and subsequent embedding of an element in another context. While remixes are almost a native species of the digital milieu, the procedure of creating from the materiality of existing works is still controversial due to the tension between the concept of works as abstract, materiality detached contents subject to copyrights, and works as concretions that may provide raw material for other works; the latter being a wide interpretation of remix and not just new mixture of the tracks in music recording studios. An example of the problems of the tensions between remix and cultural industry is the credits listed since the mid-nineties in the now almost extinct compact disc booklets. Especially in hip-hop, trip-hop, and electronica, in addition to the musicians who participated in the recording of each song, albums produced by major labels usually provided a detailed list of all samples and even of vinyl records used by deejays when scratching.[33] The result looks almost like the "Works Cited" section at the end of a scholarly paper. The fact is that spinning the turntable in the unforeseen direction makes the recordings that serve as raw material unrecognizable. Are they still the same work? The detail of the music albums used to produce a new work, even beyond the possibility to recognize them (neither allographically nor autographically), can be interpreted as a case of excessive zeal by performers to meet the demands of copyright laws; as an artistic genealogical statement;

or even as a parody highlighting the tensions between the changes in the processes of artistic creation in a context strongly mediated by new reproduction technologies and the business model defended by established cultural industries. The open-source documentary film *RIP! A Remix Manifesto* directed by Brett Gaylor makes a strong case for remix and is in itself an eloquent example of remix applied to cinema.[34]

The consolidation of mass culture and the expansion of intellectual property to all types of cultural and intellectual productions in the first half of the twentieth century is challenged by the concurrence of three closely related technical phenomena: (a) *indexability*, the conversion of heritage and works into databases; (b) *manipulability*, the possibility to continue modifying works assumed to be concluded); and (c) *circulability*, the ease of copying and transmitting digital objects. The extension of copyright though the more restrictive form of DRM is an essential aspect in the conversion of works into digital content. Remix and other forms of manipulation of digitized works imply aesthetic, ethical, and political positions that challenge the limits set by static digitization. *RIP! A Remix Manifesto* repeatedly presents the following claims: "1. Culture always builds on the past. 2. The past always tries to control the future. 3. Our future is becoming less free. 4. To build free societies, we must limit the control of the past." In a historical period determined by the possibility of the digitization of everything, the tension between remix and DRM shows the oscillation between two poles, that of static contents and that of dynamics versions. Conclusiveness lays the grounds for the reduction of works to contents that are manageable within a set of controlled parameters, associated with an idea of authorship based on intellectual property. The opposite pole is the idea of inconclusiveness that unfolds the dynamics of permanent re-elaboration and the dissolution of strong authorship.

Benjamin associated the reading of novels by the nineteenth-century bourgeoisie with a loss in people's subjective possibility of making or transmitting experience. This was one of the marks of modernization and industrialization processes, almost contemporary to the decline of the aura of unique objects. In "The Storyteller" Benjamin states that novel writers are isolated compared to previous, mainly oral, forms of storytelling. Stories passing from mouth to mouth were always modified by the different personal variations and ways of narrating. They were also associated with the shared workspace of traders, peasants, and, later on, guild craftsmanship rather than the solitary boredom of the bourgeoisie leisure time.[35] And that shift is bound to a specific storage technology, book printing. What was already in germ in the festive passages of the Homeric epic poems is the decisive feature of the novel, the idea of eternity posed by a definitive stability. The two literary forms, epic poems and oral stories, imply a tension between two opposing forms of interpreting and transmitting the past: the epic "remembrance," dedicated to a hero, event, or battle and the "reminiscence" of many, minor, scattered events.[36] At this point, Benjamin takes on from Lukács' concept of novel as "the form of transcendental homelessness," which is to be understood here as a history uprooted from the tradition that would provide an interpretation of the meaning of the lives of characters for a reader audience already deprived of any other source of community advice, the lonely and silent readers. The interpretation of a novel is conclusive, opposed to the moral of storytelling, which is purposeful.[37] Going back to the idea of technology discussed in the first chapter, I want to suggest that Benjamin's insights on novels, photography, and film actually describe the impact that new forms of exteriorization have on culture when a certain degree of standardization is attained and how they co-constitute new forms of interiorization. That is why print novels are one of the first artistic forms where one can trace the pursuit of conclusiveness detached from previous technical traditions. Novels, inasmuch as conclusive forms, are standardized units, opposed to the more stereotypical reproduction implied in storytelling, which favored changing details and emphasis depending on each particular narrator and his or her adjustments to the audience responses.

Modern printing technology affords the abstraction of a stabilized pure text that can be reproduced in different storage devices. Metaphorically Benjamin described novels as a compensation for the lack of meaning of life in the ever changing landscape of modernization: "What draws the reader to the novel is the hope of warming his shivering life with a death he reads about."[38] In his essay, he is thinking in the new ways to consume culture, the new scenario of solitary readers in the comfort of their living rooms trying to warm up after returning from work, or, paraphrasing Marx, after returning from swimming in the icy waters of selfish calculation.[39] Conclusiveness is the distinctive feature of printed novels that sets them apart from oral storytelling. Such differential relation is also that of the works and their storage devices. Orality implies different voices and variations, dilutes authorship, may be adapted to its audience, while printing establishes limits, stabilizes text, and identifies them to an author as an individual (and intellectual owner).

The defenders of remix claim that creation is a dynamic event necessarily open to appropriation and new versions. Likewise, versions leave traces on each particular realization of the narrated stories. However, it should be always kept in mind that the oppositions presented here are a reduction for the exposition of the argument. Tensions in the works should never be seen as an absolute dichotomy since aspects of each pole do coexist and there have always been oscillations between conclusiveness and inconclusiveness.[40] If the reproduction technology that prevailed during the nineteenth century and most of the twentieth tended towards the first pole, digital reproducibility made it swing towards the second. The challenge to intellectual private property regimes, as the remixer manifesto suggests, signals the existence of tensions within a culture that always builds on the past. A similar conservative role Benjamin saw in tradition is the assertion that the past always tries to control the future. That is the conservative role of settled traditions that technical change uproots or decontextualizes.

The Weight of Things and the Weightless Digits. To discuss early digital culture one must also pay attention to works that reflect on digitization and its relations with materiality. Hybrid works[41] possess material uniqueness, while incorporating some of the affordances of digital technologies. The realization of hybrid works necessarily involves the use of digital technologies. Some examples of hybrid works are *Agrippa*, which will be discussed extensively in the next chapter, the already mentioned Times New Roman 2.1 font size novel *Mucho trabajo* by Katchadjian, or works

as the digitization project *Shoe Box* by experimental photographer
Seba Kurtis.[42] Another example of a hybrid condition may be the
case of artist's book *Humument* by Tom Phillips, a work that has
been ongoing since 1973 and that includes an iPad app.[43] Summarily, the hybrid works discussed in this section imply the use of
digital technologies during their instances of production. In addition, in many cases, they involve interventions on the technical
objects, whether to treat them as a significant materiality or so
that they produce a materiality that exceeds their expected affordances.

Hayles proposes distinctions on literary experimentation by
acknowledging the different uses of technology in the creative
process and its reception. In her book, she establishes differences
between hypertexts, cybertexts, and technotexts.[44] The classification takes into consideration the organization of the materiality
and is not exclusive of digital texts. A hypertext is a print or
digital text with multiple reading paths, chunked text, and an
internal linking mechanism. Some obvious examples are the
hypertext novels produced through the Storyspace software, such
as Michael Joyce's *Afternoon* and Stuart Moulthrop's *Victoria
Garden*. But Hayles' concept also includes books with notes,
journals, and the encyclopedias that could be considered printed
forms of hypertextuality, since they do not follow the linearity of
reading that characterizes conventional novels. Thus, dictionaries,
encyclopedias, Julio Cortázar's *Hopscotch*, or any book from the
Choose Your Own Adventure collection could also be considered
hypertexts, as would an atypical theoretical work such as Benjamin's *Arcades Project*. Due to the scope of the concept, Hayles
notes that there is need to propose others more specific that
describe works in which the technical dimension is determinant
opposed to those in which it is taken for granted.

At a greater degree of artifactual complexity Hayles identifies
cybertexts, printed or digital texts that require a non-trivial effort
by the user to navigate them, associated with an emphasis on
computing or an analytic approximation. The definition takes up
the idea of "ergodic literature" proposed by Aarseth[45] and can be
seen in works such as Shelley Jackson's *Patchwork Girl* or Belén
Gache's *Wordtoys*. The definition exceeds experimental literary

forms and includes video games with a strong narrative presence, for instance graphic adventures such as *Mystery House, Myst,* or the more adult and ambitious LucasArts' series *Maniac Mansion* and *Monkey Island.*

A technotext is a work that foregrounds the social inscription of the technology used to produce it that, by doing so, mobilizes reflective referrals between the world representation it generates and the material devices that embody the work as distinct physical presence. Examples for this are artifactual works as *Agrippa* and *Humument,* but also Hayles' own *Writing Machines* made in collaboration with designer Anne Burdick and that has a web complementation of the printed book realization that takes advantage of the affordances of digital textuality and includes samples of the source material, as well as all the critical apparatus such as notes, errata, index, and lexicon.[46]

Hybrid works are a type of abnormal works, where each example requires a specific conceptualization. Although the double materiality of hybrid works (that of the objects and that of the digital code) would make them examples of technotexts, there is a distinctive feature of the idea of hybrids that is not emphasized by Hayles: their infertility. They do not create standards, not even stereotypes. Each is its own species. Thus innovation accounts for a big part of hybrid works' aesthetics and their artifactual implementation. The dual materiality of hybrid works topicalizes their own technical ontology and therefore each work tends to be exhausted in this gesture and does not transcend as a model for other works: there is no other *Agrippa* although there are many ephemeral works and many visual poems that destroy themselves; Katchadjian's *Mucho trabajo* does not have the same effect if the procedure of printing in a font size illegible to the naked human eye is repeated; *A Humument* is a *work in progress* that finds new life in its iPad app (which is by no means an equivalent to the version of *Alice* seeking to expand the tablet technology tactile affordances exploiting the illustrations by John Tenniel).[47] None of these works creates a new genre or even integrates to any kind of series. Hybridity makes them sterile in terms of reproducibility. But at the same time, these works highlight the limits of literature and art in the age of digitization and resist to be fully integrated into the dynamics of digital contents.

Artworks and the Analog/Digital Divide

> ...El universo (que otros llaman la Biblioteca) se compone de un número indefinido, y tal vez infinito, de galerías hexagonales, con vastos pozos de ventilación en el medio...
> -Jorge Luis Borges, "La Biblioteca de Babel"

The seemingly radical dichotomy between digital and analog, or digital and print in the more specific case of literary works, is false due to the profound intertwinement of their cultural dynamics and mutual conditionings. The concepts on which print and analog culture are based have determined the current orientation of digital culture. But it is a two-way relation, since digital technology also affects how we relate to print and analog technologies.

The utopia of convergence is the integrated position of digital culture based on what I have described as the dynamic of contents, an example of the intertwinement of digital, analog, and print cultures. The prevailing modes of digital circulation, those of *content as a commodity* and of *content access as a service*, are both subject to an intellectual property regime originated in completely different technical contexts. The tensions produced by this phase become evident in the emergence of alternative modes of production and circulation, some of them illegalized, as the ones discussed in the preceding sections.

The illusion of dematerialization concurs with other socioeconomic phenomena where technological change plays a key role such as the effacement of industrial labor, the invisibilization of heavy production by its relocation to underdeveloped and developing countries, the concentration of cultural industries and telecommunications in fewer corporate conglomerates, and the emergence of service based economies. It is in this context that "depicting of information as an essence unto itself, or more properly, as a synthetic (at times even haptic) commodity" that defines medial ideology occurs.[48] As I have discussed earlier, the expansion of digitization to all cultural manifestations establishes an ever-growing Babelian archive, made accessible by indexation. The simplification and acceleration in the manipulation of works causes a crisis in the stability of print and analog cultures and in the very notion of an intellectual property of the digital contents perceived as works. In short, there are overlapping oscillations: between cult and exhibition values, between conclusiveness and inconclusiveness, between material concreteness and intangible abstraction, and, within digital circulation, between works as content and works as part of service catalogs or public archives.

Manhattan Project Physicists and Vatican Theologians. The history of the development of eBooks illustrates these oscillations and underlying cultural and economic disputes. This section presents some milestones, by no means exhaustive, that contributed to a recontextualization of the entities that had preserved (and stabilized) culture during centuries. An interesting fact in this recount is the confluence of scholarly, religious and military institutions along with private companies. Tracing the genesis of digital culture provides fertile insights to understand the actual development of digital technologies and abandon the biased assertions on the neutrality of the technology. My claim is that technology is by no means teleological and it is conditioned by historically specific interests that, in turn, it helps reshape.

An arbitrary event as any for the origins of digital culture is July 1945 when *The Atlantic Monthly* published Vannevar Bush's seminal essay, "As We May Think." There, Bush proposed the creation of a technical device to handle microfilmed archives, the memex. A scientist and an engineer, he had led several military scientific institutions and was one of the early political administrators for the Manhattan Project that conducted research to develop the atomic bomb. The article discussed the role of the archive in the context of the technologies of the time and its possible impact on the production of knowledge from a computational perspective. Despite the technical shortcomings of Bush's memex, the paper anticipated some key concepts for hypertext, the World Wide Web, and the Internet that influenced the later work of Doug Engelbart.

Almost at the same time, in 1949, Jesuit priest Roberto Busa began to collaborate with IBM to produce a computational filing system for the corpus of works of Thomas Aquinas and also of works by sixty-one related authors, under the title of *Index Tho-misticus*. The project is one of the earliest examples in the implementation of digital technologies in the humanities and an eloquent case of digital humanities as a distinct field. The most relevant aspect is that both Bush and Busa sought the automation of textual operations using the devices hitherto conceived mainly for computation. In this quest for text automation hides one possible genesis of digital texts and their current impact on print culture.

The sixties saw the first implementations of hypertext in the NLS (the oNLine System) directed by Doug Engelbart and financed by various United States government agencies such as NASA and the Air Force. Also in this decade Andries van Dam along with Ted Nelson began developing HES (Hypertext Editing System) at Brown University. The system was replaced by the FRESS (File Retrieval and Editing SyStem). In 1971, Michael Hart started *Project Gutenberg*. With the development of digital technology in different areas of education and public administration, similar projects thrived in universities and national libraries. In the seventies, the fifty-six print volumes of the *Index Thomisticus* were produced.

The emergence of an electronic publishing industry took place in the eighties with private enterprises like Voyager Company. This is one of the earliest examples of digital convergence and of the dynamic of contents: they produced digital re-editions of classic film and multimedia CD-ROMs, as well as mostly textual works under the form of "expanded books."[49] The company sold restored classic films on CD and later on DVD and Blu-Ray, and was one of the first to offer content that "expanded" the original reception of the films in the theaters with features such as audio tracks with commentators, behind the scenes takes, alternate endings, and other miscellanea that is the now typical for this type of media. As discussed earlier, these expansions were an attempt by cultural industries to update, or remediate, the value of works that, as content, were becoming obsolete or had exhausted a stage of their commercial exploitation. Eastgate Systems published the hyper-textual novel *Afternoon* by Michael Joyce on floppy disks in 1987. Later it would publish *Victory Garden* by Stuart Moulthrop and *Patchwork Girl* by Shelley Jackson among others, all using the hypertextual narrative software *Storyspace*. In 1989, the CD-ROM version of the *Index Thomisticus* was published.

In 1992, Sony released the DataDisc, a proto eBook reader that had little success outside of Japan. In December 1992, preceded by some buzz in the media and the online bulletin board systems of the day, Kevin Begos, Jr. presented *Agrippa* at the Americas Society of New York. With the emergence of the Internet, the early academic sites devoted to authors or periods as the *Blake Archive* appeared. Amazon, an online bookstore, debuted on the Internet in 1995 and soon became the dominant company in the printed books market.[50] By 1996, *Project Gutenberg* announced the digitization of the then impressive number of a thousand books while setting its goal in a million works. The first eBook reading devices (the Rocket eBook by NuvoMedia, the SoftBook by SoftBook Press, and Cytale's Cybook)[51] were released to the market.[52] In 1999, several online companies such as eReader.com and eReads.com started selling eBooks. In 2000, Microsoft, then the dominant company in the digital world, launched its *Microsoft Reader* software for eBooks that introduced a technology for subpixel display called ClearType; this technology aimed to increase the readability of small fonts on the screens of small devices. Readability was beginning to be a key issue for the digital revolution in order to seriously compete with print culture beyond apocalyptic fears regarding the death of books. Also in that year the best-selling author Stephen King published his *nouvelle Riding the Bullet* exclusively as a digital file, without a paper edition. In 2001, the first site dedicated to Spanish language eBooks appeared, Todoe-Book.com. By 2002, major publishing conglomerates such as Random House and HarperCollins were selling digital versions of their books.

Regarding reading devices, Sony launched Librié in 2004, the first reading device that used the e-ink technology. This was arguably the first serious opportunity for eBooks to dispute the paper book hegemony. In 2007, Amazon launched its own device,

Kindle, associated exclusively with their own online eBook store, a business model that would be followed in 2010 by Apple with *iBooks* for the iPad and by Barnes & Noble bookstores associated with their Nook reading device. Tablets such as the iPad, however have other affordances targeted to multimedia convergence in a single device, while featuring a tactile liquid crystal display instead of e-ink technology. It is in this type of device, with a strong control over the possibilities of copying and manipulation, orientated to the file commodification and the sale of captive associated services, where the dynamic of the contents more clearly develops.[53]

Regarding digitization, in 2004, a new revolution came about when Google began collaborating with some of the most important libraries of American universities to digitize their collections in what was then called *Google Books Library Project,* then *Google Books* and *Google Scholar* and that today is articulated with *Google Play*. In 2005, Google was sued for copyright infringement and that led to a series of reversals and changes to the original digitization project.

In 2010, fifteen years after its irruption as an online retail store for printed books, Amazon reported that their eBooks sales had exceeded those of "physical" books. In that same year Google launched its *Google eBooks* site, which later mutated to *Google Play Books*, an open platform eBook application articulated with *Google Play*). The last decade also saw many important scientific journals abandoning their printed editions to focus on digital ones. To conclude this very brief summary of the history of eBooks, in 2012, U.S. federal prosecutors brought an anti-trust suit against Apple, Simon & Schuster, Hachette Book Group, Penguin Group, Macmillan, and HarperCollins, under the accusation of cartelization to raise the price of books sold by their common competitor Amazon.[54]

Summarizing my very brief history, it all starts with of the unlikely meeting of theological studies, computing technology, and the peer reviewed scientific publishing system based on key words that resulted in the early forms of what would become the eBook and the hypertext (under Busa, IBM, and Bush, respectively). Soon, these developments crossed paths with the American military and aerospace industries, only to end up in a convergence of hardware manufacturers and software companies, content producers (music, film, TV, and publishing industries) and telecommunications services providers (radio, television, telephone, and Internet) in a series of disputes over digital reproducibility. The outcome has also met some resistance by users and grass-roots organizations (manifest in an array of illegalized or borderline practices such as remix or piracy), as well as the attempt of sovereign states, with more or less emphasis, to avoid market concentration and its effects (France being a leading case). Contemporary culture finds itself at a crossroads due to the capacity of cultural industries to extend into the digital milieu the enforcement of a legal regime based on the ownership of ideas and the right to produce copies that originated in a different socio-technical milieu, that of standardized print and analog forms of exteriorization. In order to achieve this extension it is necessary to transform works into contents separated from the materiality of their storage devices.[55]

Paradoxically, many attempts of cultural democratization such as those provided by making available the collections of the Venezuelan *Ayacucho Digital Library* or the more ambitious catalogue of *Project Gutenberg* have not challenged this fact and, arguably, have contributed to the process of transformation of everything into digital content. In an insightful analysis of the challenges digital technologies impose on the humanistic theories, Johanna Drucker notes that during the nineties, on the first online repository building endeavors like to ones for the literary works of William Blake or Dante Gabriel Rosetti, "humanists came into those conversations as relativists and left as positivists out of pragmatic recognition that certain tenets of critical theory could not be sustained in that environment."[56]

What this article explicitly deals with is the problem of discreteness and standardization of digital technologies opposed to the necessarily partial, situated, subjective, and performative nature of humanistic interpretation that precisely for these reasons thrives in ambiguity and does not build on the basis of discrete, calculable certainties, though at times it may take advantage of them. The problem of the unavoidable discreteness and standardized treatment of objects by computing in the field of digital humanities is indicative of this paradox: technical efficiency operates an epistemological reduction, which affords previously impossible (or too expensive, or unforeseen) approaches to the objects of study. Drucker reminds us to keep in mind that digital tools imply such risks and that there are humanistic tools that may compensate them. It is a matter of technical acceleration and how to keep pace without losing much in the pursuit.

The bottom line is that digitization does not necessarily imply contentization, although embracing new technologies uncritically entails that risk, not only in the profit driven cultural industries but also in the digital humanities. The abstraction of materiality afforded by digitization along with the sale of digital objects and/or of access to corporate catalogues (the Apple and Amazon models) or the transformation of collections into services (the Google model) also imply a new phase of what Stiegler identified as the core of technics: anticipation.

Hybrid Manifestations

> ...I'm in the high-fidelity first class traveling set
> -Pink Floyd, "Money"

> ...The Mule spread his hands and laughed again while the First Speaker seemed to find difficulty in absorbing this new state of affairs.
> He said: "The alternative?"
> "Why should there even be an alternative? I can stand to gain no more by any alternative.
> -Isaac Asimov, *Second Foundation*

Throughout this chapter I have resorted to numerous metaphors taken from horror and sci-fi B films to illustrate the illegalized reproduction types according to their marks of origin: zombie editions, clone copies, mutant memes, and Frankenstein's monster-like remixes. Byproducts of the cultural industries, the modes of representation introduced by these forms of digital reproduction allow us to see the limits of the medial ideology sustained by the illusion of container-less contents. If the idealist pole is dominated by the pure, ever transmissible, content akin to the idea of a soul that can leave its corporeal ties, I would like to suggest the existence of another pole, akin to the otherness of B film monsters that provide embodied metaphors for the problematic materiality of works whose reification hides in the ghastly fetishes of retro: these forms that resist full digitization are *cyborgs*, comprising a dual material and digital existence. When something cannot be reduced to content, when its material ties are not digitizable, one of the basic impulses in cultural industries is making them a fetish commodity; for instance, the resurgence of vinyl records due to its specific sound qualities and the subsequent vinyl reissues and expensive collector box sets of rock classics.

However, that implies they can still be technically reproduced, that they are still a standardized, albeit reauratized, industrial product. Cyborg works are something different, their juxtaposed composition is indicative of a hybrid condition, located between digital and material realization, between industrial and craftsmanship manufacture. It also implies the combination of the allegedly homogenous, organic nature of the transparent content with the opaque, heterogeneous, technically originated container. To define cyborg works I need to go back to the concept of technological poetics discussed in the first chapter. Cyborg works can be included in these specific poetics since they reflect on their own technological process of production. They are not technophilic topicalizations of new technologies, but rather technogenic procedures, that is, technology aware interventions on (and with) the devices. What sets them apart is not their subject matter, but how they do so, how they draw attention upon their own formal (i.e., technical) aspects preventing artifactual transparency. It is not only about the content of the works but also about their containers.[57]

Perhaps one of the best takes on the cyborg condition outside of Donna Haraway's widely read "A Cyborg Manifesto" is the soul and body dualism dilemma presented in the Japanese *Ghost in the Shell* franchise. Mamoru Oshii's *anime* filmic versions present cyborgs as networked robotic bodies controlled by "ghosts," a way to refer to human consciousness, or the mind, or the soul, or all of the above. While Haraway's concept of cyborg is focused on the organic and mechanic intertwinements exemplified in the repli-

cants from Ridley Scott's film *Blade Runner*, Oshii's cyborgs are
closer to the original concept presented by Manfred Clynes and
Nathan S. Kline in their famous article "Cyborgs and Space."
Furthermore, networked existence is an element of Clynes and
Kline's first conceptualization of the cyborg: the homeostasis
system they proposed for astronauts was not stand-alone; their
space cyborgs would be integrated to distant operational centers
where other agents would supervise the different indicators and
activate the system functions to preserve homeostasis and let
astronauts free to focus on space exploration tasks.[58]

The most interesting aspect of cyborgness is thus not a flesh
and metal grotesque but an interlocking of individual physical
entities and their technically networked existence. Oshii's cyberpunk informed depiction of cyborgs is also a major change compared to previous *anime* imaginary such as the typical *mecha*
genre that presented humans piloting gigantic robots or heroes
wearing sophisticated technical exoskeletons. Oshii's films replace
the cock pit pilot with the ghost jockey: a human soul inside a
mechanical body with Wi-Fi connection. What makes this iteration
of cyborgs appealing is the ambiguous condition of their disembodied consciousness.[59] Digitized minds are almost a form of digital
content running wild on the Internet, similar to what occurred
with hackers in the first novels by Gibson, while still tied to their
bodily existences, though those ties may be fragile and hazardous.
Something similar occurs with cyborg works such as *Agrippa* or
the iPad version of *A Humument* and its physical counterpart, or
installations such as Proyecto Biopus' *SENSIBLE 2.0 Ecosistema
Textual* that presented an aquatic ecosystem made of textual
fishlike entities that interact with the public and with the mobile
phone network.[60] Eventually a part of them can run wild in the
digital milieu, but at the expense of an ontological loss.

Obviously, the oppositions in this systematization simplify for
analytical purposes the existing nuances between the two extremes. What is interesting in cyborg works is that they incorporate not only formal procedures in the making of the work but also
intervene on the technologies involved, by modifying the affordances of the technical objects. This implies attaining higher
degrees of freedom by trespassing established boundaries set by

the original design and its standards. These works challenge different production processes at the same time: (a) the traditional techniques associated with stabilized artistic procedures of unique objects (paintings, sculptures, music performances, theater plays, and handwriting); (b) those related to crafts and trades (as early printed books and daguerreotypes); (c) the analog industrial processes of technically reproducible products (printed books and scores, photography, phonographic records, films); and (d) the digitization processes that attempt to re-contextualize all of the above by means of codification, as well as born-digital productions (from text, audio, and video files to software programs).

Cyborg works are hybrid due to their dual, digital and material, mode of existence. However, this characterization may be problematic since each work altering the technical device will likely do so in different ways, preventing the presence of common traits that allow the establishment of a series of works or, at least the identification of similar features. They not only defy standards, they also defy stereotypes. Taking on from that, the approach I want to develop incorporates the problem of replication based on the apparatus provided by Stiegler's philosophy of technics.

The existence of pre-industrial works of art and literature was based on stereotypes just as hand-made tools were: books, paintings, statues, and cathedrals may not be standardized but do meet some basic, repeated sets of characteristics that separate them from other objects. Standards are required by the effective technical material conditions that determine the reproducibility of the analog works contained in (and conformed by) negatives, slides, films, discs, magnetic tapes and other media storage. Furthermore, standards ensure digital decodification in the reproduction devices that actualize digitized and digital works. Cyborg works, on the contrary, belong to the realm of prototypes.

There are more differences related to reproduction and replication. Any work is a technical work, but those relying on analog or digital reproduction devices to be experienced imply a key difference with regards to unique or auratic works, and to some reproducible forms such as analog photographic copies and printed books: their need for an energy supply. Let's consider this particular difference before delving into cyborg works. Device mediated reproduction is a problem that transcends the merely mechanical nature of copies because it is, in fact, a case of electrical reproducibility. eBooks introduce an unprecedented need for *sustained realization in time* that was nonexistent in previous print works: they exist as displays on a screen. eBooks entail thus a paradoxical dynamic stillness, a time related mode of existence that brings them closer to cinematographic projections and recorded music than to printed books. Not surprisingly, one of the goals of e-ink technology is to achieve the lowest possible energy consumption along with the longest permanence of text on the screen while complying with increasing requirements for higher resolution in order to meet the perception detail afforded by print technology.

In the context of digital and digitized works, .ePub files are standard formats equivalent to other formats such as .mp3 and .flac for music, or .mpg and .avi for audiovisual. But the convergence of different media in the digital milieu not only dilutes the specificity of the different artistic disciplines (and their storage devices), it also generates a hypertrophy of representations of all the previous artistic forms. For example, the lack of visual aspects in music may be supplemented with the display of album cover art, song lyrics, score, and synthetic images generated by algorithms linked to variables determined by the music output. In the case of literature, the text itself becomes a hypertext: each word opens up to dictionary definitions, encyclopedia entries, images, and even online related publicity. Each written word becomes a link to an entry in a database, the possibility of being reproduced as sound, an indexable value. In short, text itself becomes an interface.

These new affordances producing a new material relation to the works (like sound and tactile features) are compensations for the lack of audiovisual and tactile aspects in digitized works, but not examples of a new hybrid condition. The mode of existence of digitized works depends on electrically powered realizations and keeps no ontological relation with storage means since abstraction has detached them from their material specificity. One of the effects of compensations is to normalize the new formats converging on the devices in which works of different orders are standardized as playable contents with similar affordances. Hybrid works, on the other hand, prevent abstraction, and remain device-specific.

This trait is especially interesting to consider hybrid technological poetics as the polar opposition to the dynamics of the standard convergent digitized content. A cyborg work may not be easily encoded and redistributed, limiting its circulation. And its storage device is also an anomaly, intertwining content and container. But as a hybrid entity it may also be, as biology suggests, sterile. A cyborg will not spawn little cyborgs, just beings that will share with the parents the same organic matrix without their technical matrix, unless they also undergo a similar technification process. In a way, hybrid poetics materially disrupt the idealistic purisms underlying more stabilized poetics at the expense, as noted, of irreplicability.

Throughout this chapter I have presented the different forms in which cultural works exist in the digital milieu. This included how previous works are adapted using the digital technologies and what ontological changes that entails, as well as how the idea of dematerialization establishes a content dynamics in which storage technology seems to lose relevance. Inside that purely digital form of existence I discussed some of the arousing differences between legalized and illegalized contents, different forms of derivation once works are digitized and the disputes emerging from these processes. Finally, this chapter concluded with a definition of hybrid works that, ultimately, allows reconsidering the materiality of the storage devices.

CHAPTER 5
The Book of the Dead
and the Death of Books

...I shall only observe how odd it is, that this
branch of the art has flourished by fits. It never
rains, but it pours. Our own age can boast of
some fine specimens...
-Thomas De Quincey, *On Murder Considered as
One of the Fine Arts*

...Quelle histoire insupportable!
Je ne veux pas la relire dois foix
-Philippe Bootz, *petite brosse à dépoussiérer
la fiction*

...whenever something like this happens, and I
have one of these moments, it ups the face on being a science-fiction writer. It changes the nature
of the game. Another example, maybe a better
one, in a way, was when it was confirmed that
Michael Jackson was going to marry Elvis Pres-
ley's daughter. A good friend of mine in the
States faxed me, and he simply... he said, "This
makes your job more difficult."
-William Gibson, *No Maps for These Territories*

The Nature of the Game

Agrippa has spawned diverging interpretations and they may all
be accurate. Its collaborative and multilayered, multifaceted
material and digital existence affords the most diverse approaches:
a milestone in e-literature history deserving a dedicated and
thorough scholarly site;[1] a milestone in book history deserving its
place in a museum exhibition in the Royal Victoria and Albert
Museum;[2] "the latest golden fleece [...] of the hacking community;"[3] an "Apocalyptic book" evoking the imminent death of

printed storage devices;[4] one of the most successful examples of preservation by redundancy (and of by-passing copyright); an exemplary piece of codework;[5] "the first high-profile electronic poem";[6] one of the earliest tests of controlled content consumerism technologies;[7] an ekphrastic coming of age poem in the tradition of Romantic English poetry;[8] the kind of works that get "canonized before they have been *read*, resisted, and reconsidered among fellow authors within an institutional environment that persists in time and finds outlets in many media";[9] and so on. My contribution to the ongoing discussions surrounding *Agrippa* is the suggestion that the singularity of this work resides in comprising, albeit involuntarily, all the modes of digital existence presented in chapter four of this volume and the modes of digitization introduced in chapter three. But all these modes of existence do not converge, as opposed to what occurs in the content dynamics. On the contrary, *Agrippa* acts as a diffracting crystal, an aleph withholding the fates of analog, print, and digital cultures. My claim is that *Agrippa* contains *in potentia* all forms of digital circulation, both legal and illegalized, restricted content circulation, leaks, clones, memes, zombie editions, and remixes, while at the same time it remains rooted in a peculiar prototypic materiality that simultaneously relates to artisan and industrial craft, as well as print and analog modes of reproduction. Like Oshii's cyborgs, it is a work with a dual ontology pivoting on abstractions and concretions.

This chapter could be considered an application of media-specific analysis as well as a test of its hermeneutical limitations. Ultimately, it may signal the urgent need for the development of a history and a critical theory of technology as necessary complements for critical approaches on digital culture. It may also stress the relevance of philosophy of technics to address its arousing complexities. The reading of *Agrippa* I present here aims not only to consider its internal relations and but also its location in the map of contemporary culture; by this I mean the contemporary artistic and technological practices and products in the digital milieu. More specifically, I trace *Agrippa* in the oeuvre of William Gibson. I also pay attention to lesser works, artifacts, and marginal practices of the period that may shed some light on aspects of the work that have not received much critical attention and suggest new directions to deal with this and other related objects.

Agrippa (A Book of the Dead): **The Book Object**

Over the last years, the legend of *Agrippa*, forged in forums and fan sites, has been contained by thorough documentary sources. First of all, the scholarly project *The Agrippa Files* provides extensive archival material such as photographs, video, floppy-disk images and miscellanea related to the work; but also William Gibson's official website[10] and some relevant academic critical essays.[11] "Text Messaging: The Transformissions of 'Agrippa'"[12] is one of the most comprehensive studies on the circulation of Gibson's poem. As I write this chapter there are also some marginal webpages that still preserve posts from the bulletin board systems of the day[13] and even e-magazines of unclear authorship[14] that provide useful information about the work and its early reception. And there is also an interesting body of scholarly research on the code of this electronic poem and its self-destruction mechanism.[15]

The description of *Agrippa* I present here is based on accounts by James Hodge[16] and Kirschenbaum and corroborated by an inspection of the copy of the work that is in the Rare Books Collection of the New York Public Library carried out by Claudia Kozak. The comments on the software are based on their accounts and the corrections introduced by Quinn DuPont.[17] *Agrippa* is a handmade product that defied the standardization and serialization of industrial printed books, and therefore its publishing history is unusually complex. Two different editions were planned, a "Deluxe" one and another, "Small" or "Regular." The exact number of copies in circulation is uncertain, although in the case of the Deluxe Edition it cannot exceed one hundred copies.[18] There is not much information available on the other version.[19] The Deluxe Edition comprises a dark box made of paper and fiberglass impregnated with resin that simulates a buried relic and, at the same time, an organic product. In the upper right corner of the lid of the box it presents an embedded reproduction of a fragment from the cover of the Agrippa photo album brand sold by Eastman Kodak in the early decades of the twentieth century with the inscription "ALBUM / CA." "AGRIPPA / Order extra leaves by letter and name," which is also quoted in the verses of the poem "Agrippa" (vv. 5–8). The inside of the box is lined with a honeycomb-like material containing a damaged and burned (artificially aged) hardcover book, wrapped in a cheesecloth shroud. The book is large (approximately 15" long by 11" wide). The book itself has eighty-two pages that include: (a) the title page (with the text "AATCA / TACGA / GTTTG / CATAA / CTGAA / TTGGT") hand printed by the editor himself[20] on page 5; (b) eight etchings on pages 4, 6, 11, 21, 31, 41, 51, and 61; and (c) the body of the text repeating part of the genomic sequence of the maternal morphogen bicoid of the Drosophila fly intentionally arranged in two columns similar to the layout of the *Gutenberg Bible* in Sans Gill typography on pages 7–10, 13–20, 22–30, 33–40, 43–50, and 53–60. These copperplate aquatint etchings were printed using uncured toner that erases when touched. Some of these etchings have overprints of old advertisements of products related to photography and other technical devices of the era (the prints of pages 6, 11, 21, and 31). Page 49 presents the genomic sequence, and has an overprint of an early TV set advertisement, although it does not correspond to an etching. The floppy disk buried in the last pages of the book contains an executable file for a Macintosh computer under the System 7 Operative System (compatible with the existing models in 1992, such as the Macintosh Classic II and Macintosh LC II). After running the application program "Agrippa," the screen displayed a black and white low resolution scanned image of the same label that was also on the box for twenty seconds. Then a new window opened and the verses of Gibson's semi-autobiographical poem began to scroll upwards until it finished. After the poem scrolled down to its end there was a visual "encryption effect" (that was not an actual encryption of the file stored in floppy disk)[21] and the file self-destroyed. There were two audio effects during the reproduction of the poem: at 6'05", the sound of camera shutter matching the verse "the shutter falls" (v. 101), and of a gunshot in "I swear I never heard the first shot" (v. 126) at 7'33".[22] The original plan also included the display of Ashbaugh's etchings in the poem file but due to the limited space available on diskettes at the time this was not possible. Similarly, it was claimed that once the book itself was opened, the etchings would slowly fade but this did not occur because of technical limitations. According to the project editor, he opted to use un-cured toner, which would be progressively degraded by the hands of the readers instead.[23]

In 2008, the editors of *The Agrippa Files* received one of the original *Agrippa* floppy disks from collector Allan Chasanoff by intermediation of Begos.[24] From that floppy disk they produced a disk image that is available on the website. They also ran the disk image file on an emulation of System 7 OS, and the procedure was recorded in a video file. This recording provides a full display of the poem on the screen.[25] Since the poem was never cracked in a strictly digital sense, in 2012, Quinn DuPont from the University of Toronto Information Science department encouraged an actual (and scholarly) cracking by issuing the "Cracking the Agrippa Code" contest.[26] His challenge resulted in further digital forensic sources on the work and its technical aspects.[27] In the section "The Body Snatchers" ahead, I discuss the 1992 non-digital cracking of "Agrippa" and its implications from technological and aesthetic perspectives.

The common themes of the poem and the etchings are memory, ephemerality, and recording devices (especially cameras). The poem is an account of the past as it concerns Gibson's family in a rural area of Virginia in the early nineteen-twenties interpolated with events in the life of the poetic persona's childhood and youth. An associated topic is the idea of code, which is more evident in the book object, the etchings, and the software, than in the poem itself. The etchings are "DNA portraits" inspired by the images produced by the gel electrophoresis method used to separate and analyze DNA. Surprisingly (and coherently), as DuPont notes, the self-destruction mechanism of the program that runs the poem uses the DNA sequence letters (C, G, T, and A) to corrupt the file, although this is only visible to those delving into the depths of the code hidden in the floppy disk file.

Although it is not a part of the work there is also a "Promo-tional Prospectus," a press release of sorts, created by Begos and Ashbaugh that was itself a peculiar art object. The prospectus declared the aesthetic intentions animating the project in the style of historical avant-garde manifestoes and made reference to the text layout imitating that of the *Gutenberg Bible*. The only known copy of this item is the one in the Frances Mulhall Achilles Library collection of the Whitney Museum of American Art in New York. The prospectus is a four-page diptych with information on the project and its creators, accompanied by a sample of one of the etchings by Ashbaugh embedded in a 9¼" by 12¼" by ½" honeycomb-like worn object, painted black, with a piece of frayed cord and a cavity containing a black floppy disk, mimicking the *Agrippa* book object. On the surface of the prospectus object and surrounding the cavity there is text apparently printed with uncured toner on a paper with burnt edges.[28]

Perhaps for legal reasons or due to the unusual features of the work, *Agrippa* also included an instruction page for the correct use of the diskette. The directions present detailed technical specifications for running the files and emphasize that the software contained on the disk is not a virus. By that time there had already been several floppy disk–borne viruses that had unleashed some paranoia; the most famous one in 1992 was the now forgotten *Michelangelo*, one of the first digital viruses to receive major media coverage. The symbolic impact of this virus shaped much of the emerging imagery of digital culture. The myth generated around it was that all the information on the infected computers would be deleted if they were turned on March 6, the date of birth of the Renaissance artist, Michelangelo. Although this actually happened to infected computers, its impact was relatively minor.[29] Nevertheless, much of the buzz surrounding *Agrippa* in artistic circles, cultural journalism, and technological specialists was due to a misunderstanding regarding the poem's self-destruction mechanism. This was in addition to the fame of Gibson as the father of cyberpunk and his cult status in hacker subculture.

There seems to be no consensus regarding the title of the work. *The Agrippa Files* suggested the title *Agrippa (a book of the dead)*, the "Prospectus" presented it as "Agrippa (A Book of the Dead)" and the title page of the book object reads "AGRIPPA (A Book of the Dead)". The onscreen display of the poem once the file was executed bore no title, however, and presents only an image of the advertisement for the Eastman Kodak Agrippa albums. There is inconsistency in the title elsewhere: on Gibson's own website the work is referred to as "AGRIPPA: A BOOK OF THE DEAD" and "AGRIPPA, A Book of the Dead" while the online version of the poem posted there goes under the title "AGRIPPA (A Book of The Dead)" using capitalization closer to the title of the printed book. To avoid ambiguity, by *Agrippa* I refer to the work as a whole (the book object with the textual rendering of DNA, Ashbaugh's etchings and the floppy disk with the program that presents Gibson's poem); by "Agrippa," I refer to the digital poem as a stand-alone unit. This chapter focuses mainly on Gibson's poem, and considers its artifactual relationship with the other physical and digital elements of the work. I present an interpretation of the poem in detail because surprisingly there are not many scholarly papers that address it. Scholarly critique has been more drawn by the originality of the presentation and its material history[30] and by the strange cracking, circulation, and survival of the text of the poem,[31] than by the literary aspects of the poem itself and its relationship with the rest of *Agrippa*. This analysis will also allow me to discuss some issues related to the crisis of traditional storage devices and the tendency to reduce all perceptible materiality to digital content that I have commented on in the previous chapters.

Just as printed books were among the most important industrially produced objects that marked the origins of cultural industries, books were also one of the preferred consumer goods at the dawn of digital marketing in the early years of Amazon and eBay. In that particular context, *Agrippa* introduced an original challenge to the growing standardization of cultural consumer goods as pure contents. Due to his tenure in the edition of luxurious collaborative artists' books and his expertise in the artisan handcraft involved in the production of books, Kevin Begos, Jr., mentor to the project, was quite aware of the tensions between the publishing and the art markets as well as the upcoming innovation implied in emerging digitization of literary and artistic works.[32] The political implications of *Agrippa*, a work that self-consumed, were contemplated from the outset. According to Kirschenbaum, ironically an ephemeral work such as is *Agrippa* is today one of the most ubiquitous and persistent digital art and literature works.[33] My claim is that different forms of derivation, as in the ones I discussed earlier in chapter four, have played a decisive role in the life of the work that the following sections address in detail.

The genre of the work is also problematic. From an e-literature studies perspective, it can be considered an example of codework[34] although according to well-recognized criteria, it would not fit into this specific genre.[35] From a formal perspective (and from that of the publishing industry), it would be an eBook of sorts: a text file containing a poem. From an art criticism perspective, it could be considered an ephemeral work and also a collaborative artists' book. With regards to its dual material and digital condition it also has been considered an exponent of artifactual fiction,[36] a genre that builds a fiction around the materiality of the object, although it should be noted that "Agrippa" is not strictly "fiction." In terms of conventional literary criticism, it can be considered as an autobiographical poem with abundant ekphrastic passages. Nevertheless, these passages are descriptions of technically produced images and not of handmade pictures as is the norm in the classical tradition of ekphrasis. And yet, none of these descriptions seems to fully envision all of the elements at stake in *Agrippa*.

Cross-influences and Avant-garde Traditions. *Agrippa* can acknowledge many precursors. The incorporation of digital technology to art as a gesture akin to the twentieth century avant-garde has been pointed out frequently. (Manovich has even expanded the relationship to digital technology as a whole.)[37] Placing an industrial object, the floppy disk, in a niche within a book, which is in turn inside a relic-like box, may be interpreted as a Duchampian readymade gesture. But this particular arrangement may also suggest a *cliché* of the time: the death of books. Materials, textures, and craftsmanship make *Agrippa* also akin to the assemblage and the tactile poetry of artists like Joseph Cornell (whose boxes had already been referred to by Gibson in his novel *Count Zero*), and to the productions of the Fluxus artistic network. Kevin Begos Jr., mentor of the project, has recognized his debts with the French aesthetic and philosophical tradition, from Stéphane Mallarmé to Maurice Blanchot.[38] French postmodernism was also influential in the first scholarly approach to *Agrippa*[39] and in Marshall Blonsky's presentation of the book at the Center for Books Art in 1993. Such claims were flatly rejected by Gibson: "Honest to God, these academics who think it's all some sort of big-time French philosophy – that's a scam. Those guys worship Jerry Lewis, they get our pop culture all wrong."[40] Nevertheless, the divergences between Begos and Gibson are indicative of the tensions underlying the shared authorship of *Agrippa*.

Ashbaugh's etchings included in the work have been compared to the work of other abstract painters such as Mark Rothko and Jackson Pollock. But they can also be related to artists who represent the act of representation, with examples as old as Diego Velázquez' *Las Meninas*. His work is not, strictly speaking, abstract. Instead it represents abstraction by portraying an image of the scientific representation of the components of the genetic code. In the specific case of the *Agrippa* etchings, they are also reminiscent of Surrealist *collage* techniques (the overprints of ads of obsolete technologies) and of Dadaist ephemerality (printing with uncured toner).

Gibson, the most renowned collaborator, and to whom the project owes most of its cult status, has repeatedly and publicly assumed other influences: the beatniks, especially William Burroughs, Allen Ginsberg, and Jack Kerouac, and the meticulous adjective-heavy naturalism of J. G. Ballard.[41] Gibson himself also points out another less obvious influence: Charles Dickens' realistic descriptions of the change in scenery and culture introduced by industrialization during the Victorian period.[42] His own narrative, despite being inscribed in a popular genre and often associated with the more commercial models of cultural industry, had suggested ground-breaking ambitions since his first works.

On Contemporary Art as a MacGuffin. The title of the book that made Gibson a cultural icon in the eighties allowed multiple interpretations: *Neuromancer* may be associated with the figure of the necromancer, establishing relationships between resurrection and technology, while also denoting the neuronalization of technology, typical of cyborg bodies increasingly intervened in and enhanced by prosthesis. But there is another reference enabled by phonetics: New Romancer, a new novelist. With this, his first novel, Gibson became the most prominent figure of cyberpunk, a science fiction subgenre that used a grim future to present an allegory of contemporary late capitalism (and the crisis of the existing socialist world). Like other authors in the genre, his writing moved away from what had become the sci-fi *doxa* from the post-war period until the mid-seventies: stories set in a (frequently shining) future in which the limits of humanity were questioned by either technology or alien life forms, serving as an excuse to present ethical and philosophical debates, with various results. Bukatman has pointed out that the representation of technology and the role that it plays in Gibson's narrative implies an often unnoticed modernist trait because of his apparent affiliation to one "lesser" genre.[43]

Gibson himself can be identified as one of the forerunners of *Agrippa*. The presence of experimental works that challenge the limits of art, technology, and, ultimately, humanity by providing creativity to different technical beings is frequent in his novels. In his plots, which remind of Dashiell Hammet's *noir* and John LeCarré's espionage novels, certain objects linked to the art world often function as what Alfred Hitchcock called the "MacGuffin."[44] A MacGuffin is a looked-for object that moves the plot forward and triggers the action even if it turns out to be irrelevant once it is found. For a spy novel the typical MacGuffin is a manila envelope containing secret papers; for a detective story, a missing girl.

Gibson's MacGuffins are often complex devices involving art and technology in cult or avant-garde works that originate the quest for rare items in order to end up meeting their creators. In *Count Zero*, Marly Krushkova, the owner of a small art gallery in Paris that has fallen into disgrace for selling a fake work is asked to find the creator of a series of boxes similar to those by Joseph Cornell. The boxes apparently hold the key to a "biosoft" that is sought by the CEO of a megacorporation. The relic appeal of these boxes has similarities with the *Agrippa* object, as well as the resonances of a biological software key that can also be compared to the DNA code in the book, the resinous material of the box, and the self-destructing file on the floppy disk. After being presented with one of these boxes containing an arrangement comprising a flute bone, archaic circuit boards, a fragment of lace, and other age-worn things, the character has the impression that the "box was a universe, a poem, frozen on the boundaries of human experience"[45]—very much like the object resulting from the collaboration between Gibson, Ashbaugh, and Begos.

This resource is used similarly in his narrative, both before and after *Agrippa*. In the short-story "Burning Chrome," one of the characters, Slick Henry, creates enormous robotic sculptures, an allusion to the sculptor Mark Pauline of Survival Research Labs. In *Pattern Recognition*, the director of the advertising corporation Blue Ant, Hubertus Bigend, hires Cayce Pollard to discover the identity of the producer of enigmatic short segments of footage that periodically surface online without further explanation, originating a community of highly qualified critical exegetes.[46] In *Spook Country*, Hollis Henry is hired by Bigend to investigate the use of geolocation technology in contemporary art to gain access to Bobby Chombo, a technician with unique tracking abilities in the global logistics and international flow of shipping containers (who in turn is also hunted by rogue intelligence agents and by an obscure post-9/11 government intelligence agency). *Zero History* delves into the relationships between art, fashion, marketing, and big military contracts. Again, Pollard receives a contract to find the origin of Gabriel Hounds, a strange brand of jeans without declared offices, business, or website that has become a cult fetish in the arty rock and design subcultures.

Gibson's MacGuffins repeat some of the tensions surrounding *Agrippa*: among art, technology, and capitalism; and among individuals, governments, and corporations. The history of *Agrippa*, fueled by the various misunderstandings around the project and its digital circulation for over a decade has turned it into a mutable and contemporary myth that articulates the apocalyptic prophecies of the death of books with the integrated emergence of new technologies. Until its recent academic stabilization with *The Agrippa Files*, the work itself was a MacGuffin for digital culture archaeologists, a privileged object to wonder about the ties between works and storage devices.

Between Now and After. Within the context of Gibson oeuvre, "Agrippa" (along with *Agrippa*) is in a strange place. It is not only an anomaly in general terms, it is also is an anomalous work within the author's own writing. Widely regarded as a science fiction writer, Gibson is famous for his narratives, and particularly his novels. These are grouped into three series, each sharing fictional universes and characters. The novels *Neuromancer* published in 1984, *Count Zero* in 1986, and *Mona Lisa Overdrive* in 1988 group together as what is known as the Sprawl trilogy. The series portrays a grim near future dominated by mega-corporations, a pronounced technification of life and growing social inequalities.[47] His characters tend to be antiheroes and outcasts, very much like in hard-boiled detective fiction and spy novels, involved in complex and shady international networks. This group of novels has been inscribed into the core of cyberpunk. A response to the increasing conservatism of science-fiction in the United States, the success of Gibson's first novel brought together other authors of the sci-fi underground such as Neal Stephenson and Bruce Sterling. The dystopian tone and the shift from outer space travels and alien civilizations towards the body and the mind of human subjects turned cyberpunk's *noir* and pulp aesthetics into a powerful cultural allegory of post-industrial capitalism and the then-incipient globalization. Even works originating in other literary traditions have been assimilated into cyberpunk, such as Ridley Scott's 1982 film *Blade Runner*, based on Philip K. Dick's novel *Do Androids Dream of Electric Sheep?*[48] The same thing happened with some films, like the innovative (at least for 1982 visual standards) *Tron* produced by Walt Disney Studios, the 1984 class B horror/action *Terminator* directed by James Cameron, and the ultra-violent (at least by 1987 moral standards) *Robocop* by Paul Verhoeven.[49] Cyberpunk also had a major impact on Japanese *anime* and *manga* as in, for example, the *Ghost in the Shell*, *Cowboy Bebop*, and *Ergo Proxy* narrative universes. The fledgling video game industry also made use of the aesthetics and themes of the cyberpunk.[50]

The second series of books by Gibson, known as the Bridge trilogy, occurs in a very near future in which even though there are new technological advances, the imagination is not as radical as in the previous novels. The common denominators of *Virtual Light* (1993), *Idoru* (1996), and *All Tomorrow's Parties* (1999) are growing class inequalities in a hypercapitalist world; the relationships between technology, transnational capital and organized crime; and the convergence of information and entertainment media known as "infotainment." The series is titled after the large slum that spread underneath the Golden Gate Bridge in San Francisco after it was devastated by a tsunami. While repeating some traits of the previous series, in this case the proximity to the present, the not so sordid plots and a deepening of characters' development have allowed for these novels to be read as postcyberpunk.[51]

The third series, the Blue Ant novels, is named after the Blue Ant Corporation owned by Belgian advertising mogul Hubertus Bigend, a recurrent employer for characters in all the stories, and is located in the immediate present. The novels, *Pattern Recognition* (2003), *Spook Country* (2007), and *Zero History* (2010) are part of this third trilogy. Each novel takes place in the year prior to its publication. Although some characteristic features of Gibson's distinctive prose remain, in these novels the role of art and contemporary fashion, different professions and disciplines related to the information society, the impression of a growing unreality of a world increasingly mediated by digital technologies, industrial espionage, and post-9/11 government surveillance are knitted together to represent a hyper-semiotized present. Following the MacGuffin logic, and based on the ruse of characters pursuing unusual artifacts, these novels describe a world thinned by commodification. Jameson has defined this fictional construction as an "eBay imaginary" and Gibson's descriptive technique as "postmodern nominalism," where what is clear is that the names that accumulate are those of brands, which involves a near-instant obsolescence and a form of neo-exotism since brands originate in a global market ruled by the dynamics of contemporary consumerism.[52] Rather than an allegory of the present set in a dystopian future, the novels of the Bigend trilogy are an attempt to represent the complexity and intertwinements of contemporary society and what Jameson identifies as "an (as yet) unimaginable aesthetic."[53] Postmodern nominalism thrives on arbitrary enumerations in the style of "The Aleph" and "Funes the Memorious," two short stories by Jorge Luis Borges, another of Gibson's declared influences. Although the impact of Borges is not apparent in Gibson's literary style, they do share some recurrent topics: the fragility of memory and the commentary of non-existent works to discuss art and literature.

The rest of Gibson's literary work can be organized in relation to these three trilogies. *Burning Chrome* (1986) brings together stories, some written in collaboration, set in the Sprawl universe, which had appeared before and after the publication of *Neuromancer*. These stories were published originally in science fiction magazines related to cyberpunk. In the impasse between the Sprawl and the Bridge novels, Gibson published two works in collaboration with others: *The Difference Engine* with Bruce Sterling in 1990 and *Agrippa* with Ashbaugh and Begos in 1992. The novel in collaboration with Sterling belongs to a typical subgenre of science fiction: the alternate past. They rewrote Benjamin Disraeli's 1845 *Sybil, or The Two Nations, a roman à thèse* that discussed the motives of the class divide in England (the two "Nations" of the title). *The Difference Engine* provides a grim reinterpretation of the industrial revolution from a retrofuturistic premise: Charles Babbage successfully built his analytical machine, ultimately helping the British to retain their imperial power and prevent the rise of the United States. This alternate Britain is ruled by the liberal industrialist oriented Radical Party, led by the Prime Minister, Lord Byron.[54] Gibson's latest novel, *The Peripheral*, published in 2014, returns to science-fiction in near future small-town U.S. and far future London, involving switching timeline technologies, drugs, and deadly weapons, very much like his early novels.

Finally, in the verge of narrative and close to poetry, is "Thirteen Views of a Cardboard City" (1996). This is a short piece composed of thirteen descriptions of what someone would see on a camera in a script whose still *action* takes place in a series of strange locations. The successive description of images is a journey through an imaginary squatter community located in the Tokyo subway. Using an extreme form of what Jameson termed postmodern nominalism; the descriptions are almost a visual poem and a

form of bitter social criticism, without any action by the characters. This "story" was first published in the anthology *New Worlds*
compiled by David Garnett, and later republished in *Rewired: The
Post-Cyberpunk Anthology* published in 2007 by Tachyon Publications. "Thirteen Views" is of special importance for this chapter
since Gibson deploys a similar method, the ekphrasis that organiz-
es the different verses of "Agrippa," only in this case it is a form of
moving images ekphrasis: the description of camera movements
and cuts in an un-shot film.

Gibson's nonfiction work includes articles and essays for magazines such as *Wired, Time,* and *Rolling Stone* published together in
2012 under the title *Distrust that Particular Flavor.* The book
includes notable pieces such as "Disneyland with a Death Penalty"
on the city state of Singapore, originally published in 1993, which
generated controversy involving influential Dutch architect Rem
Koolhaas and others over modernization in non-Western societies;
and the text "Dead Man Sings," a 1998 essay about recording and
reproduction technologies as a form of modern necromancing.

Gibson has also been a film and television series screenwriter:
the discarded script of *Alien 3,* the adaptation of his short story
"Johnny Mnemonic," and two episodes of *The X-Files* television
series ("Kill Switch" and "First Person Shooter"). He is the main
character of the 2000 experimental film *No Maps for These Territories,* directed by Mark Neale. This film is a long monologue by
Gibson that runs through the central topics of his work and his
impressions of contemporary culture while travelling across the
United States in a limousine. The film includes many embedded
digital images, especially those displayed in the limousine windows including comments from writers Jack Womack and Bruce
Sterling as well as U2's singer Bono.

This very condensed contextualization aims not to historicize
the literary work of Gibson, but to point out two relevant aspects
related to storage devices and digital technologies. First is the
relevance of Gibson's prose (from his early technological baroque to
his later essays and narrative work about the immediate present)
in the development of an aesthetic that challenges technological
sublime. Second, the tension between technology and society
summarized in the use of postmodern nominalism that remains

constant in all of Gibson's works. Gibsonian writing pays special attention to objects and how our relations with them change in different times.

Indeed, nominalism appears in a recurrent manner in *Agrippa*, starting by the title itself (the name of a brand of photo albums that entails deeper connotations), in the text of the poem and in the etchings by Ashbaugh with their overprinted advertisements. But the nominalism also relates to the hardware and software specifics, too; that is, to the problems of compatibility, first and foremost, and obsolescence, shortly afterwards, that it implied.[55] *Agrippa* is an exemplary case of what Bootz has described as the diachronic and synchronic labilities of technically mediated works previously discussed.

Unreadable Works. Some experimental literary works share one key feature with the *Agrippa* project: illegibility. The unreadable DNA code printed in the object-book relates to the tradition of visual poetry, and has been explicitly suggested by Begos,[56] but at this point I want to focus on the illegibility effect produced by the digital poem self-destruction mechanism. The mechanism makes a second reading impossible (or, as DuPont suggests, extremely difficult) and produces a series of effects that challenge both, books as technical devices and writing as codification. Writing provides stability to the text and affords an easy reproduction. This reproducibility technology has been steadily gaining speed since the early stages of the scribes, then the artisan craft at small printing houses, then the industrially produced texts and, finally, the digital texts. By presenting a writing that cannot be read twice, *Agrippa* allows different interpretations. It can be seen as a reauratization from within technological reproducibility due to the anticipated and advertised one-time-only experience: the twenty minutes of the poem scrolling on the screen once the file is executed. In this way, the execution of the file in the floppy disk inside the book *Agrippa* leads to an inverted version of the "reception in a state of distraction" that Benjamin identified as the specific trait of early cinematographic experience. In the first decades of the twentieth century, attending a film for the general public was difficult to repeat given the economic cost and the limited time movies remained on the billboard. Furthermore, the impossibility of introspection imposed by the constantly changing images stressed by Benjamin constitutes the basis of the perception of cinematographic works. Introspected concentration, the visual perceptual habit for the appreciation of paintings (and even for early photographs), yields to a new form of visual stimulus, where there is a primacy of distraction and a perception that cannot stop flow of images.[57] In the case of *Agrippa*, the context is similar, but the restricted possibility of vision encourages a "reception in a state of attention." The example of cinema and its specific technical reproducibility (a shared dark room with projections at prescribed times) provides a larger context to think about the originality of a work as *Agrippa* at a time when content dynamics were being established through the permanent remediations and the digitization of culture was turning works into ubiquitous, always-available content. The self-consuming work demands a "state of attention" that is different from museum introspection but also from the perception imposed by cinematic technical reproducibility analyzed by Benjamin.[58]

The self-destruction mechanism also refers to a phenomenon that had not received much attention at a time dominated by technological enthusiasm: the fragility of digital coding. Digitization does nothing but accelerate the risk of obsolescence of digital and digitized works as well as any other type of files. In doing so, it reveals the dated and located condition of digital code, which the integrated technological form of idealism had hastily assumed as eternal precisely because it had cut the bonds of a materiality subject to physical degradation.

Two later works, in which digital technology is also necessary, demand a comparable effect. In *petite brosse à depoussierer la fiction* by Bootz, one must constantly move the mouse pointer to remove the "dust" that accumulates on the text and impedes reading. In this case it is an entirely digital work; its material existence, although it affects hardware labilities, is not a constitutive part of the work itself. The dust that prevents reading is only made of pixels. The second example of illegibility is the novel *Mucho trabajo* already discussed in chapters two and four in this volume. It is a printed book, but digital technology is necessary in order to key it and then reduce it to print it in a 2.1 pt font size that is illegible to the bare human eye. There are two alternatives to reading this book. The analog way is to use vision assistive devices such as a magnifying glass; the digital way entails scanning the text to obtain a high resolution image and enlarging it to be able to read the text on a screen (or reprint it). In both cases, however, the two works remain intact. There is a challenge, a difficulty in reading them, but without reaching the auratic extreme of an absolute "here and now" imposed on the act of reading that is generated by the self-destroying file in *Agrippa*.

Ephemeral Works. In Western culture, marble sculptures have always been perceived as synonymous with durability. Poetry may very well be the other side of the coin, closely linked to the ephemeral nature of spoken words. The concept of content oscillates between voice and stone, between the fluidity of the rhapsode's verses and to the stillness of the sculpted bust, between abstraction and concretion. Today, the Louvre and the British Museum keep, as testimonies of that ancient durability, the bust of General Marcus Vipsanius Agrippa and the Rosetta stone.

Art of course does not stop its march in the marble sculpture (the paradigm of a durable and concrete representation) nor in writing (the paradigm of reproducible and abstract representation). Ephemerality plays a constant yet elusive part in art history and illustrates some of the recurring tensions between the concept of *work* and that of *storage device*. The importance of time associated with the ephemeral works (and the material difficulty of their serial reproduction) results in cult value prevailing over exhibition value. It should not come to a surprise, then, that there is a strong connection between the various forms of what is today considered ephemeral art and ritual practices such as sand painting in India and Nepal or in pre-Columbian America, or petals or sawdust *Via Crucis* carpets frequently present in popular Latin American Catholic processions, just to mention a few examples.

Another case, more associated with local festivities, is that of ephemeral sculptures, such as those made with sand or ice. This kind of aesthetic practices has been linked frequently to other disciplines that do not produce a durable object: decoration, fashion, makeup and hairstyling, perfume composition, gastronomy, pyrotechnics, graffiti, and others where the storage means have a longer duration, but are also organically bound to deterioration as tattooing and gardening. None of these disciplines would be traditionally regarded as art but it may be argued that they do possess some auratic qualities due to the involved craftsmanship and their distance from the mechanical reproducibility: they produce unique objects. The pages in *Agrippa* with the reproductions of Ashbaugh's etchings whose images erase when touched also bear resemblance with these aesthetic practices.

Avant-garde movements such as Futurism and Dadaism included ephemeral art in their attempts to destabilize the art system. Ephemerality has also been a widely used resource in experimental works such as performances, installations, happenings, or land-art. Without depleting the rich history of the ephemeral in art in this quick enumeration, I want to emphasize that this trait has been always related to the dispute with the stabilization of objects upon which the art market and the market of works as commodities have been built.[59] *Agrippa* explicitly aimed at the same target. It should be noted that it is precisely because of the challenge to traditional art storage means that ephemeral art as well as previous ritual objects have maintained the primacy of the cult pole over the exhibitive one. The importance of materiality is intimately tied to that of ritual temporality (and its rapid degradation or inaccessibility).

Even though not often associated with ephemeral art due to their survival through coding, both music and literature have had moments where ephemerality was their hallmark. It occurred in the musical execution and oral narration before recording, musical notation, or the expansion of written word and literacy.[60] As Gibson points out, after a century of technical archiving and reproduction we tend to naturalize the deep strangeness of hearing dead people singing, the necromantic power of recording technologies:

> I know this because the dead were less of a constant presence, then. Because there was once no Rewind button. Because the soldiers dying in the Somme were black and white, and did not run as the living run. Because the world's attic was still untidy. Because there were old men in

the mountain valleys of my Virginia childhood who remembered a time before recorded music.[61]

The relationship between death and the transmission of experience is at the core of Benjamin's concept of experience. The loss of the ability to make experience and transmit it is associated with the industrial development of technically mediated representations that result in the emergence of information, a pure, decontextualized, fact with no here or now. Or, to put it slightly differently, of disembodied data. That is what Gibson's poetic image of the ghostly voice of the dead men singing for us from the radio summarizes. Recording technologies, the way in which contemporary memory is built, with a digital file always at hand, and the ephemeral nature of that which records seek to turn permanent are recurring themes in his oeuvre. Its obviousness tends to reduce these problems; and the permanence of recordings and registers is naturalized until obsolescence or unfortunate events, such as the destruction of the Library of Alexandria or the Metro-Goldwyn-Mayer vault fire in 1967 remind us that the only permanent thing is the entropic tendency to oblivion, the risk of records being lost forever. Speech and music were the first codifications, the earliest forms of representation to abandon the continuum of the concrete into the abstraction of the discrete, the ephemeral nature of the moment of irruption towards the possibility of repetition offered by the technologies of writing and musical notation. Their technically reproducible descendants, print text and audio recordings, were also at the front line of digital abstraction and its exacerbated ubiquity. But the vertigo of technological development generated a paradox: obsolescence makes technical records increasingly more ephemeral. Some records survive in remediations, in the form of anachronistic and convergent contents, constituting a new canon, the archive of all culture, the "attic of the world" that is still messed up, as Gibson suggests, and that Google wants to "organize."

Ephemeral Commodities. Despite the revolutionary changes introduced by technical reproducibility, twentieth century cultural industries implied a not always noticed continuity with traditional arts: they were both based on the sale of objects. Art as the manufacture of unique objects and art as technically reproducible commodities are both tied to an inescapable materiality. But only in the second case, however, the dynamic of contents arose. Eventually this dynamic produced and updated successive avatars of the works; for instance from film to videotape and then to DVD, and then to online streaming channels. However, at first, each realization of a work was tied to the affordances of a specific storage technology and of the technical objects it was associated with. Once the possibility of digital copying arises, when the storage device becomes non-specific, commodity wobbles. The traffic of identical copies at minimal cost outside industry controlled channels has favored the development of ephemerality in a new direction, of an opposite sign to that sought by the artistic avant-garde: the programmed obsolescence of art as content.

The cultural industries at the end of the twentieth century were not interested in desecrating the art institution or extending its limits as the avant-garde was, they just wanted to assure the survival of an economic model of production of closed works in the age of digital reproduction that threatened to open works up. With digitization, the existence of alternative models of accumulation within the industry becomes evident and the tensions of technical reproducibility resurface. These tensions, however, have been there at least since the nineteen thirties when cultural commodities were industrialized for mass consumption, especially for the emerging middle classes. Even before digital reproducibility appeared the rights of buyers regarding the potential uses of a purchased work were being questioned. Book circulation, for example, was intended to be kept to a minimum, mainly destined to private home collections. In this case, from an extreme approach to intellectual property law, practices such as lending or selling used books and even the existence of free public libraries were attacked under the accusation of causing damages to copyright holders. This dispute escalated with the commercial dissemination of photocopiers in the fifties and their incorporation in university libraries and shops.[62]

Between the end of the nineties and the beginning of the first decade of this century, there were a series of experiments aimed at retaining control over the modes of circulation and reception of objects due to the increasing difficulty of enforcing intellectual property laws. Though such experiments may seem odd, to say the least, from today's perspective, they still underlie many business strategies of cultural industries today. There is a passage from the planned obsolescence of industrial durable goods such as electrical appliances, to what Striphas has called the "controlled obsolescence" of works.[63] This new dynamic implies a shift from the model of private ownership of physical objects towards the controlled access to content in various forms as samples, partial purchases, or limited time access. The novelty here is that the digital technology used in these experiments was meant to retain control over the content even after producers sell it.

One of the first examples was the digital release of Agatha Christie's novel *And Then There Were None* by Rosetta Books as an eBook with a "time limit license" that could be read for ten hours at the price of a dollar. When time expired, DRM software would make it unreadable unless the customer chose to renew the license for an extra dollar or to directly buy the title for five dollars.[64] Against the then-established interpretations, Striphas suggests that the artistic avant-gardist project of *Agrippa*, aimed at both destabilizing the idea of collecting art objects as well as the possession of traditional books, was actually an extreme example of what "controlled consumerism" through DRM software would be, and therefore deeply related to cultural industries: "Little wonder, then, that algorithms akin to those the programmers used to encrypt *Agrippa* have become fairly common among commercial software and hardware developers anxious to regulate the dissemination of digital eBook content."[65]

Today paid access to digital content has become the standard for the case of the eBook as well as audio, image, video, and game files. The trend reached an ominous stage fueling apocalyptic skepticism in the case of the teenager Justin Gawronski to whom Amazon wirelessly erased *his* copy of George Orwell's *1984* from his own Kindle along with the notes he had been taking over the digital text for a school task, due to a suspicion of copyright violation.[66] Thus, works become ephemeral not only due to the time driven obsolescence of technological change but also because of the new dynamics that turn contents into a paradoxical property not owned by the buyer. The concept of "private library" (and, soon after, of music, magazines, and movies collections) is one of the basic bourgeois cultural institutions of the twentieth century, as well as the foundation of the cultural industries business model. Such ideas have yielded to the online account, a form of consumerism controlled by an automated digital panoptic. What becomes ephemeral is not the work itself, which is understood as a secure digital content kept in the servers and the back-ups of the digital stores, but its perceptibility. We *buy* but we do not *possess*, we *access*. Or to put it in Benjaminean terms, the work of art comes to meet us wherever we are... connected. Provided we pay.

Collaborations between Artists and Writers. The multiple storage devices of *Agrippa* also pose the problem of assigning clear authorships, including the participation of programmers, but also, in the book object, of typesetters. As Hodge points out *Agrippa* is "an unusual textual artifact."[67] The poem was written by Gibson, and the etchings were created by Ashbaugh who are most frequently cited as the book's "co-authors." However, the project was conceived by publisher Kevin Begos, Jr., and the self-destructing software that renders the poem inaccessible was written by an anonymous programmer signing as "Brash" with alleged help from John Perry Barlow and John Gilmore from the Electronic Frontier Foundation.[68] The DNA-sequence layout and the book object as a material metaphor for the whole history of books from print to digital were originally Begos' ideas.

There is a long history of collaborations between artists and writers, as well as of works combining text and image. One of the most distinctive traits of these works for the topics being discussed here is the importance of storage in the art piece and literary work interlocking. The most obvious case, although it is not a "collaboration" *stricto sensu* since the artist and the writer are the same person, are the illuminated editions of *Songs of Innocence and of Experience* by William Blake.[69] Another famous example, which I already discussed, is the edition of *Alice in Wonderland* illustrated by Tenniel, or Denis Diderot's *Encyclopédie, ou dictionnaire raisonné des sciences, des arts et des métiers* [*Encyclopaedia, or a*

Systematic Dictionary of the Sciences, Arts, and Crafts]. And all are print culture works. The list will grow exponentially if one looks at the medieval illuminated manuscripts tradition. And there is the case of the renewed fetishization of books in twentieth century editions of canonical works illustrated by renowned artists. Begos himself had been involved in publishing these very expensive books for the Limited Editions Club, such as the numbered and signed copies of *Three Poems* by Mexican poet Octavio Paz accompanied by lithographs by Robert Motherwell.[70]

The most relevant feature of writer and artist collaborations is the relation between text and image (be it complementary or not). But in *Agrippa* this is not so obvious since the pages display an unreadable code, the representation of DNA in letters, in the same way Ashbaugh's etchings *portray* a technical representation of DNA. Gibson and Ashbaugh were fully aware of the risk of the illustrative complementation and wanted to avoid it in order to prevent *Agrippa* from looking pretentious and arty. As Ashbaugh ironically suggests, "art made by collaboration resembles art chosen by committee (L.C.D.) Lowest Common Denominator."[71] Or, as Gibson fears, "'[a]rranged' collaborations [that] are the rule in Hollywood; one only has to look at the overall quality of the resulting product."[72] Kevin Begos has stressed the importance of these problems during the development of the project and has called upon the need of a holistic reading to discuss *Agrippa*, noting that the text and the images were originally planned to coexist in the digital version but that was impossible due to technical constraints. And he even notices that, however, that might have been a risk because it would lose "the whole context of the printed book."[73] That would imply, as it actually occurred, that all eyes would be fixed on the digital part of the project.

Prevailing attention on texts over images is a long standing problem in literary and art criticism in general. It can be blamed both on technical aspects, due to the simplicity of textual reproduction compared to the complexity of image reproduction, but also on the prestige of texts opposed to the idea of images as a deceitful sensory stimulus, reenacting the old bias of written language as the privileged vehicle of abstract reason (or of the word of God) versus the (pagan) ambiguous sensorial icons. It should not come as a surprise, then, that all references to *Agrippa* mention Gibson while only some syndicate Ashbaugh as co-author or collaborator. If at all mentioned, Begos, the project factotum and editor, appears in third place. This brings us to another tradition in which the editorial process, that is, the material making of the object, has a fundamental role: artists' books.

On Edition Considered as One of the Fine Arts. The tradition of artist's books has accompanied the history of the book, but perhaps when they begin to stand out more clearly against the background of the rest of the art and literary works begins after the industrialization of the printing press. By artist's books here I refer to the art of producing works of art deeply related to the book as a device. Artist's books are usually produced in small editions or even one-of-a-kind objects. Not casually, Johanna Drucker, one of the leading scholars in this matter, has noted that artist's books developed especially in the twentieth century and are, she claims, the most distinctive twentieth century art form.[74] In parallel to this very specific art form, the apparition of cheap books and their transformation into popular commodities led to the specialization of a practice linked to the artisan origins of the printing press. This resulted in the emergence of specialized publishing houses dedicated to book editing that preserved (and recovered) the craftsmanship quality related to the production of books in the past, such as handmade sewing, unique types of printing press foundry, printing with manual press, using specific papers and inks, etc. William Blake is again an unavoidable reference for having printed and illuminated his own *Songs of Innocence and of Experience*. In the twentieth century, artist's books, in some cases akin to visual poetry and other forms of artistic experimentation, progressively became an artistic genre in their own right, with deep links to visual arts, and differing markedly from "author editions" that are, basically, books not printed within the system of the publishing industry. In the second half of the twentieth century, artists' books became art objects and drifted away from the realms of literature. However, defining artist's books is still problematic due to the confusion with other terms such as *book art* or *bookworks* in the English-speaking world, or *livre d'artiste* in

French.[75] The distinctive feature of the artists' books to highlight regarding *Agrippa* is the emphasis on the crafts involved in the object production, as opposed the idea of industrial serialization. At this point it is worth noting that the role of Begos, and his experience both in traditional publication and in the edition of collaborations between artists and writers, was a central to a project as peculiar as this and yet it has received little attention.

Finally, it should be noted that *Agrippa* has links both with this experimental tradition that challenges the traditional concept of the book, while it also refers to the history of the standardization of books. This is suggested by the mimicking of a particularly meaningful edition that established not only an aesthetic but also a historical and cultural milestone, the *Gutenberg Bible*. The referral can be perceived in the arrangement of the genetic code in two columns, highlighting the beauty of the object rather than its intelligibility. Thus, *Agrippa* appeals not only to the tradition of artist's books, but also to the history of the book in general by imitating one of its most distinctive realizations. This decision is enhanced not only by the collaborative aspect, but also by its hybrid condition that adds another layer, that of digital elements.

Literature and Electronics. A multilayered work, in its material mode of existence *Agrippa* belongs to several traditions on the borders of established, content centered art: artist's books, experimental works, collaborations, ephemeral and illegible works. But *Agrippa* is even more problematic, since its digital mode of existence also offers many uncertainties: the material/digital constituent hybridity of *Agrippa* separates it from other digital works of the period while drawing it closer to other non-artistic cultural forms.

In an endnote on her extensive text on electronic literature, Hayles points out that a major shift took place in the field in the mid-nineties although overlapping and remediation had always existed; that is, the consolidation of the World Wide Web and the development of more robust browsers that afforded the reproduction of multimedia content.[76] From a concept of electronic literature focused on the hypertext there was an opening towards other forms that include other digital affordances such as randomness or interactivity, together with the possibilities enacted by existing multimedia resources on the web. However, the focus of Hayles in this particular article remains entirely in digital works, where the material aspect is limited to the hardware specifications and aspects relating to its proper execution. These works, perceived as a pure code, are still within the framework of the digital dematerialization, a discourse *Agrippa* and other cultural forms had been challenging even before 1995. It is also curious that the work of Gibson, Ashbaugh, and Begos receives no mention in Hayles' extensive and thorough classification of digital works.

The anomaly of *Agrippa* in the field of e-literature is also due to other factors. Preceding works of greater impact can be identified with the Storyspace School, named after the homonymous software developed by new media theorist Jay David Bolter (creator also of the concept of remediation) and writer Michael Joyce. In 1987 the latter authored the novel *Afternoon: A Story*, written using *Storyspace*, which is based on navigation between textual units known as lexias.[77] Joyce decided to investigate the expressive possibilities of new technologies and collaborated in the creation of a trend that focused on hypertext. Located in the antipodes of the literary field when compared with a best-selling sci-fi author as Gibson, *Afternoon* made of Joyce an inescapable reference in the origins of digital literature. However, as it has been pointed by Hayles, the excessive fascination with the hypertext and the identification with some premises of the American reception of post-structuralism when the novel appeared did not leave much room for critical insight on the specifics of the digital context nor to detect the obvious similarities with print culture, such as indexes, notes, and cross-references. But her most notable objection is to the naïve interpretation of the hypertext technology as an empowerment of readers:

> As a number of critics have pointed out, notably Espen J. Aarseth, the reader/user can only follow the links that the author has already scripted. Moreover, in a work like *afternoon: a story*, looping structures are employed from which there is no escape once the reader has fallen into them, short of closing the program and beginning again. [...] As Aarseth astutely observed, the vaulted freedom supposedly bestowed by interactivity "is a purely ideological term, projecting an unfocused fantasy rather than a concept of any analytical substance."[78]

Innovative aspirations based on a strong theoretical background focused on post-structuralism and the aesthetic ideals of high literature inherited from Modernism were caught up in a fascination that suits what Kirschenbaum has defined as technological sublime, or as an aestheticization of the pure digital form.[79] The case of hypertextual narrative is one of the clearest examples of the transformation of works into tools by the insertion of an artifactual dimension in aesthetic objects that occurs when they become interface. While the self-destruction mechanism designed by "Brash" results in a reauratization directed against utilitarianism, the *Storyspace* software, on the other hand, embraces a purpose, to lay the foundations for the next phase of text technology. Notably, in Europe, the experiments of e-literature did not focus so much on hypertext and were more prone to crossovers with visual arts as well as to the arousing tensions between material and digital realization.[80] It is my impression that *Agrippa* as a collaborative work incorporating (without assimilating) multiple technical and artistic traditions provides an outstanding milestone of contemporary literature and art that challenges the same medial ideology hypermedia fictions celebrated.

Word Games. There are some precedents to *Agrippa* not necessarily related to artistic experimentation, some more integrated to the publishing industry and some others completely alien to the field of literature. The first case is the early trial and error processes with digital texts, from *Project Gutenberg* free eBooks to Voyager Company expanded books, which included in its catalog some books by Gibson. In this section, I want to address other forms, perhaps more akin to Gibsonian motifs: primitive computer games known as interactive fiction. These early digital products start with the first text game *Colossal Cave Adventure*, succeeded by others such as *Mystery House* and later by more elaborate and complex games as *Myst* up to actual studio scale productions such as LucasArts' *Monkey Island, Day of the Tentacle*, and *Indiana Jones* series and Sierra Online's *Leisure Suit Larry, Space Quest*, and *King's Quest* in the late eighties and early nineties.

Games may provide a different insight to analyze *Agrippa* due to their specific modes of digital circulation: the relationship between these *works* (concede me considering games as such), the storage devices (tapes and floppy disks) and networks previous to the advent of modern Internet. *Colossal Cave Adventure* (also known as *ADVENT, Colossal Cave,* or simply *Adventure*) is one of the first digital objects conveying many of the distinctive features of the new medium: mutability, obsolescence, and adaptation to different associated milieus (i.e., the evolving operating systems), as well as the problem of digital conservation. The game was originally developed between 1975 and 1976 by Will Crowther and later expanded in collaboration with Don Woods. The versions of the game multiplied and to date more than twenty have been registered.[81] Running the file on late seventies or early eighties computers would produce the following introduction and instructions of use on the screen:

1 SOMEWHERE NEARBY IS COLOSSAL CAVE, WHERE OTHERS HAVE FOUND
1 FORTUNES IN TREASURE AND GOLD, THOUGH IT IS RUMORED
1 THAT SOME WHO ENTER ARE NEVER SEEN AGAIN. MAGIC IS SAID
1 TO WORK IN THE CAVE. I WILL BE YOUR EYES AND HANDS. DIRECT
1. ME WITH COMMANDS OF 1 OR 2 WORDS.
1 (ERRORS, SUGGESTIONS, COMPLAINTS TO CROWTHER)
1 (IF STUCK TYPE HELP FOR SOME HINTS)[82]

Through a narrow choice of words users could indicate the path to follow and the actions to carry out. The game has become a digital culture legend of the dawn of personal computers, although it has not been considered a work of art or literature or a product apt for cultural industries revenue. This strange object, shared some traits with two other cultural products of the time: role-playing games like *Dungeons & Dragons* and the branched narrative structure of the *Choose Your Own Adventure* books and similar series. Crowther's small program became a milestone in the origins of digital culture and also one of the first lost (and later found) works of the era of the digital reproducibility.[83]

In addition to the complex history of its circulation and code rewriting, there is another aspect that could make it a predecessor of *Agrippa*: its innovative form of relation to texts due to the need for attention in order to solve the problems the game plot presented the reading players with. (The call for attention is, of course, typical of most games.) Although there are other examples in history, the transformation of the act of reading in an act of play is an innovative experience, made possible by the structure of the game: the text is no longer a static representation and it becomes dynamic. Taken to an extreme form, the uniqueness due to the announced self-destruction and the words that are "forever" lost once they reach the top of the screen in "Agrippa" generate a more urgent temporary constraint and therefore create an auratic experience: the condensation of stimuli to the specifically located unrepeatable event of playing the file, a sensory experience that games only insinuate since they can be replayed over and over.

The latter versions of *Adventure* that incorporate very primitive static images, also illustrate the technical problems that conditioned the combination text and image in early digital culture. The inclusion of high-resolution images was difficult in the time of *Agrippa*, and though foreseen in the original plan it was finally discarded.[84] The disparity between what texts say and what images show is a problem that has accompanied the history of books: from the illuminated manuscripts to Blake's *Songs of Innocence and of Experience*, from the printing of the first illustrated science and technology handbooks to the collaborations between artists and writers. In early digital works, these tensions surfaced once again. Television had turned twentieth century culture into an eminently visual one, and the first personal computers that had digitized typewriters (or "simulated" them, in Manovich terms) still could not compete with the affordances of photographic or video cameras. This resulted in a primacy of text until digital images caught up with electronic texts. Though not an ekphrasis as in "Agrippa," the text of *Adventure* is organized as a description of what can be seen, and thus the inclusion of images in later versions was somewhat problematic, due to either redundancy or divergence. The relationship between text and image will be always tensioned by the differences in the forms of representation, and complementation will never be entirely equivalent or corresponding, as it also occurs with Ashbaugh's etchings, Gibson's verses and Begos' typographic layout.

The Technological Context. *Agrippa* was devised just before the universalization of personal computers and the leap in storage capacities that presented an alternative for the physical problems of libraries and archives. It was published and the poem was leaked just before the advent of the web as we know it today. A cultural revolution began on April 30, 1993, when personal computers started connecting via the phone to the Internet, on which the World Wide Web could be accessed. Although the web is a key element in the particular history of *Agrippa*, the immediate previous digital places where the cult around the poem originated were the bulletin board systems. The BBS, which still exist but are a marginal technology nowadays, are online services that enable users to upload and download digital files, read news and newsletters, and exchange messages with other members, by mail or in public or semi-public forums. The interfaces are usually text-based rather than the image based ones we are now used to. The geographic scope of BBS at the time was also associated with local networks hosting specific shared interest communities including electronics enthusiasts but also members of underground collectives. There had been rumors about *Agrippa* in several BBS since May 1992 but also in the media. Kevin Begos Publishing, Inc. announced that it was working on the project in July that year.[85] The work was presented publicly at an event called "The Transmission" in December 9, 1992. The next day, the cracked poem surfaced online in the MindVox BBS. In contrast to a work like *Afternoon* that had circulated in floppy disks and later on CD-ROMs, *Agrippa* appeared in an era in which the digital circulation through digital networks had already begun to be insinuated. Although it failed, the idea of actually performing a "transmission" of the running poem to several points of the world through the Internet announced by Begos in a press release is indicative of this change in the modes of digital circulation.[86] This *Zeitgeist* can also be traced to the clarifications needed by one the first chroniclers that approached the work (and the imprecisions which he incurred). In the already mentioned *New York Times* article, Jonas states that Gibson "was not at all surprised to learn that the international legion of computer hackers had broken the code within a few days of its appearance." Furthermore, he claimed that it was posted in the BBS network that is a precursor of Gibson's cyberspace.[87] The context of emergence of *Agrippa* is even prior to "net.art," although it already shows some traits typical to that kind of work, as mutability and interactivity (hidden in the invitation to be cracked). However, neither does it belong to what has been called "classical period" (establishing a parallel with the references to the establishment of film as an art form), mostly linked to hypertext forms.[88]

Finally, as pointed out by Begos, *Agrippa* also appeared between two economic crises that had a direct relationship with the worlds it was putting into question: the early nineties burst of the Modern Art bubble and the burst of the Dot Com bubble in 2000.[89] Thus, *Agrippa* is not only located in a period of time crossed by a revolution in the storage devices of literature and, not much later, by an unprecedented challenge on the storage devices that had been the privileged art commodities (especially for music and films) throughout the twentieth century; it is also positioned between two very specific economic crises. That of the commodification of art pieces, and that of the exaggerated (and speculative) illusions placed in the digital world.

"Agrippa (A Book of the Dead)": The Poem

There are very few translations of "Agrippa," and all are in Spanish, as far as I am aware. The existing ones are literal fan translations seemingly based on the online versions of the poem without any contextualization whatsoever. Three are, or at least were, available online: (a) by "Saurio" in *La idea fija. Revista bastante literaria* [*The Fixed Idea. A Quite Literary Magazine*], based on the version on Gibson's official website; (b) by "Da5id," uploaded to Scribd.com by "api_user_11797_Francisco Lorin Colorado" and now deleted;[90] and, (c) a fragment (vv. 1–33) in the blog *La tumba del Pardo* [*The Grave of the Mulatto*] posted by "immorfo" that today is only accessible through invitation.[91] As is the norm in this type of digital publications, bibliographic references are quite imprecise. Likewise there is indication on the web of a fourth translation by Sergio Martínez Mourelle, published in the Spanish science fiction magazine *Ad Astra*.[92] Regarding the nationality of translators it is presumable that "Saurio" is Argentinian; "immorfo," Mexican; and Martinez Mourelle, Spanish. I could not find any clues as to the nationality of "api_user_11797_Francisco Lorin Colorado."

All the other existing online versions I retrieved are in English, as is the original. A brief comment about digital versions: Kirschenbaum has pointed out the paradox that the one offered on Gibson's own website presents errata that did not appear in any of the leaked or "unofficial" existing digital copies of the poem.[93] This ultimately endorses his claim that "Agrippa" is one of the best examples of digital preservation by proliferation.

Regarding the importance of experimental and visual aspects in the digital poem, the role of images in "Agrippa" is relatively minor. Its greatest peculiarity is the scroll down movement of the text that is now the *de facto* norm for reading digital texts online. The only image is a very low resolution black and white scan of the label of the original Kodak Agrippa albums at the beginning of the poem. One must also bear in mind that an active attitude for a proper aesthetic experience was encouraged by the awareness that the poem would be irretrievably lost once the scrolling concluded, and that it would be impossible to stop once it started, thus favoring a particularly special predisposition on the reader who decided to play the work.

"Agrippa (A Book of the Dead)" is a long poem consisting of three hundred and three verses, divided into six parts: I (vv. 1–97), II (vv. 98–144), III (vv. 145–181), IV (vv. 182–217), V (vv. 218–262), and VI (vv. 263–303). In sections I, II, and III Gibson's poetic persona opens the album, and describes the old photographs that are in it. The photo album is "the book of the dead," Gibson's elders on the father's side, who in turn died when he was a child. The description of the album focuses on its materiality and physical degradation ("of time-burned / black construction paper," vv. 9–10). The passage of time is associated in the verse progression with the material degradation affecting the photographic images, which are, paradoxically, moments that the camera was meant to preserve. The tension between the alleged eternity of the photographed image and the contingency of the material existence of the photographic copies articulates this and the next two sections. Materiality refers to the inevitable degradation of records that, theoretically, are there to prevent oblivion. The verses present aging photographic copies and deleted handwritten epigraphs. The referral to the particular materiality of various objects and technical products is also recurrent: the "soft graphite" (v. 17) of the pencil, the "eerie Kodak clarity" (v. 41) of the photographic images, and the reminiscence of the "sweet hot reek" (v. 31) caused by the electric saw. As Proust's famous madeleine, childhood is associated with particular moments of involuntary memory triggered by sensory experiences such as sights, sounds, and smells that unwillingly bring dear memories back. But, unlike *In Search of Time Lost*, in this case it is an environment where machines, the "mechanism" that iteratively articulates the poem, are what retrieves the memories, time after time. It is indeed a Stieglerian poem: memory is an external technical phenomenon taking place in the machines; it should not come as surprise then that childhood remembrance is deeply intertwined with the workings of the mechanism. This resource challenges the cliché of technology as progress, in which the future it promised is diluted by presenting it as a past subject to degradation and oblivion, but also as the key to access our most intimate memoirs. This tone is paralleled by a progression that highlights the contrast between a disappearing rural world and an increasingly urban landscape, which goes from the "white big city shoes" (v. 75) opposed to the image of children wearing "broad straw hats" (v. 66); and a photograph showing a steamboat on the Ohio River (v. 154) contrasting with the river bank "overgrown with factories" (vv. 157–158).

Verses 5 to 8 repeat the fragment at the top of the book object, and also the scanned imaged at the beginning of the digital poem. The label is a reproduction of a part of the original Agrippa album found by Gibson around the date that the *Agrippa* project started to take form. Such apparently trivial details actually stress the indexical nature of an unquestionably auratic object, the almost seventy year old photographic family album. The negatives of the photographs have been surely lost, rendering them unique. The auratic traits of this one-off object also establish a personal relation with the biography of the writer. The ekphrasis of "Agrippa" echoes the effect of the "incunabula of photography," as Benjamin refers to the early photographic copies of the mid-nineteenth century. This is important since these pictures come from an age in which photography, in its non-industrial stage, went at a pace that made it possible to be incorporated into tradition. As I will discuss in the following sections, the images described by the poetic persona in "Agrippa" can be identified with the portraits that still possessed an auratic condition in a time of transition from artisan to industrial forms of cultural reproduction. But that aura was not the simple product of a primitive camera. Rather, in those early days the product, the technique, and the technician correlated each other as accurately as they diverged in the following period of industrialization.[94]

Benjamin's take on technology postulates a time of correspondence between technology and culture that is seemingly impossible at an industrial scale (and at an industrial speed, one may add). As Simondon has pointed out, this could be understood as an example of an adequate inclusion of technology in culture due to the mutual understanding of the process and the craftsmanship involved. The time (between 1917 and 1924) and the place in which the photographs were taken (a small town in the rural South of the United States) in the poem, in conjunction with the apparition of cheap small portable cameras in the first decades of the twentieth century that led to the emergence of amateur photographers, has some similarities with the period of the photography pioneers described by Benjamin. This kind of practice, in the particular context of the change from a traditional rural society to an increasingly industrial one, introduces a breakthrough moment analog in some aspects to the intertwinement of technics and culture that Benjamin detected in the early photography in Europe during the second half of the nineteenth century. The correspondence between technics and culture appears again in other "mechanisms" such as the electrical saw that shapes wood; but technical progress modifies that situation at an ever growing speed turning it into a lost time.

The agent of the modernizing drive is the figure of the grandfather, fascinated by modern materials that survive over time but "charmless between mossy stretches of / sweet uneven brick" (vv. 174–175). These verses introduces an opposition between the past that accumulates over traditional materials preserving the passing of time in their own decline, opposed to the modern materials that remain apparently intact but at the price of establishing no bonds with the place and its history. These oscillations reappear in the contrast between the modern Oldsmobile parked on the street and "the dimestore floored with wooden planks" (v. 185). The social dimension of the ideology of progress (and the tensions it implies) can also be seen in the irony of the enlargement of the diner at the bus station that takes down the restroom for black people when it became no longer necessary (v. 234). The conquest of civil rights can also be traced in the changes undergone by that same building: the "colored restroom" is taken down to extend the magazine rack (v. 238) that smells of disinfectant (yet another sign of modernization) but also of the "travelled fears of those dark uncounted others" (vv. 241–242) harassed by the police in the gone restroom. The reference is oblique. It may be alluding to South Carolina small town conservatism, where there was a restroom for blacks, where the sheriff made sure that those who got down from the bus got back up and where, it is suggested, some suffered or not "as the law saw fit" (v. 246).

The ever-growing road network becomes another sign of progress and another manifestation of the ubiquitous "mechanism" that can also be sensed in the traffic lights whose timers are heard a block away in the silence of the night (v. 257); a "mechanism" also resonating in the growl of trucks on the highway. Finally, the station is torn down and replaced by a franchise store (v. 296) but at that point of the poem the poetic persona is already in an absolutely future time in an alien landscape, the District of Chiyoda-ku in Tokyo, where a typhoon wobbles the lanterns. But on this occasion, the poetic persona is in full awareness of the mechanism that in the previous iterations had only been intuited. The image of a swinging electric streetlight over a wire in Wheeling in 1921 "suggesting the way it might pitch in a strong wind" (v. 164) and lanterns that are swaying in a storm in Tokyo in the present of the poem, some seventy years later, along with the opposition of a small rural town and a megalopolis establish contrasts and also coincidences between Tokyo and Wheeling. The opposition organized by the iteration of the mechanism provides a setting for the poetic persona's coming-of-age. My claim is that the poem does not have an "elegiac tone,"[95] or, much less, an "apocalyptic" one.[96] Instead, it establishes a new relation with technology as an co-constitutive trait of humanity, that of the full "awareness" of the technical matrix of the world, that is neither a cry of desperation nor an acritical fascination, but one that finds itself "laughing" (v. 303).

On the other hand, the opposition closes the loop between two objects. The first is a penknife made in Japan, one of the childhood objects recalled by the poetic persona (associated also with the image of eating watermelons, archetypical of American Southern rural childhood). The second is the inverted umbrella in the midst of a storm in Japan, a country that was once the unknown place of origin of the trinkets bought in Wheeling. It is precisely in Japan, where the lanterns are battered, where the "mechanism," the image articulating the poem, comes out as funny (and not ominous) when shaken by the forces of nature. The mechanism appears recurrently in the guise of different objects: the photographic album, the photographic camera, the gun, the traffic lights, the city, the street lighting. The mechanism is also suggested in the road network, the levy office, the migrations booth (in sum, in the State). However, I do not agree that in the poem the "mechanism" appears in a threatening sense. On the contrary, achieving awareness, the possibility of including the mechanism in personal history, in a way it can finally move to laughter, looks more like the possibility of producing an experience rather than a mere inassimilable shock caused by modern technologies in a Benjaminean sense. The iteration of the "mechanism" in the poem corresponds to the different moments of introspection of different ages: remembrance of the father's death when the book is closed, sudden consciousness of mortality when the gun is fired, sexual awakening, once again the fear of mortality when the bullet bounces from the rock, a hint of the world and its complexity when listening to the traffic lights timer returning alone late in the night, the maturity attained in the exile avoiding the draft to go to Vietnam, and an entire retrospective look at personal life from a remote time and place. These memories are deeply related to the moments in which the awareness of the mechanism is glimpsed. The description of very brief fragments of life experiences is parallel to the photographic ekphrasis, assimilating the personal experience to the physical division to what happens inside the mechanism, which is "always / dividing this from that" (vv. 102–103). Such moments are strongly associated with the smell caused by the actions of the mechanism. And, as it is well known, smell is (as of today) the least apprehensible sense by technical means, the less standardized perception. Smell is also the sense more strongly associated with the "involuntary memory" described by Proust (and that is fundamental to the Benjaminean concept of "experience"), "because it deeply drugs the sense of time. A scent may drown years in the odor it recalls."[97]

An example of this is the reek released by the electric saw "biting into decades" (v. 33). Here a very relevant opposition for the study of technology is revealed: the opposition of the organic and mechanic temporalities. The first is perceivable due to the creative violence of the second, a few verses later, in the smell of sawdust in the family sawmill; and finally in the aroma of sap that is brought back to life when an unintended shot pierces the stair railing (vv. 135–141). And here the incidental sounds of the digital poem gain relevance: the only two sounds connote the lens shutter first, and the gunshot later.

Both shots stop life, producing either an image or death. The recurrent relationship between the photographic image and death is stressed in the relation between words and sounds; a relation anticipated in the title, which describes a photo album as a book of the dead.[98] The Benjaminean concept of experience, which includes death as the last and most pregnant moment for its transmission, finds a complement in that of involuntary memory, associated with those memories we cannot control. Technical, controllable memory, discrete as photographs or newspapers' information, is the opposite of this form of unpredictable memory.

Involuntary memory erupts in the order of rational thinking and, in the poem, reveals the passage of time and the action of technology over nature through the smell of wood, that was kept hidden by the forms of the carpentry. The fortuitous moments of awareness of the mechanism irrupt precisely in the unexpected events (those that technics, as I discussed in the first chapter, strives to minimize).

Benjamin indicates a break between the remembrance of involuntary memory and that introduced by technical records. In auratic works the associations of involuntary memory tend to cluster around them; something similar occurs with utilitarian objects upon which "practiced hands" have left a trace. But camera and sound recording technologies imply, on the other hand, an extension of the voluntary memory, a different way to relate with the past,[99] which is discrete, foreseeable, and standardized; in sum, a form of exteriorization.

Benjamin's conceptualization of technical register and recording is echoed in the eternal division of "this and that" (v. 103) caused by the mechanism in the poem. But in "Agrippa," the unintentional use of the technical object can also result in an awareness of the mechanism deeply interlocked with childhood memories. That is, technical memory becomes auratic, as it occurred in the pre-industrial utilitarian objects. With the negatives lost, the old album becomes a unique object, a book of the dead that sets involuntary memory in motion allowing the poetic persona to make experience by reinserting himself and his life history in a particular historical context, where tradition and modernization collide. At this point there is a secondary aspect of concept of aura worth discussing. The photos in the book of the dead are neither postcards nor images for the state records but family photos, pictures whose reference is not effortlessly and efficiently transferable since they fully make sense only in personal and family history.[100] In the poem, the photographic copies trigger involuntary memories, marked by smells, rather than voluntary ones. It is a case in which the separation between the human scale and the technological one is still salvageable, precisely because in the teenager discovery, as in the transitional period during which the grandfather handles the electric saw, the use of the utilitarian objects is more personalized than in later industrial (and adult) stages.

The poetic persona gains awareness of his own history through the images of his dead relatives that are, themselves, in the transition from a rural to an urban world, from a particular to a global culture, from craftsmanship to industrial manufacture. The tensions and the transitions can be seen in how historical events affect local history, such as the brick sidewalks in Wheeling that had known "the iron horseshoes of Yankee horses" (v. 175) in allusion to the American Civil War. Likewise, the year of the father's demise appears contextualized in the history of industry: the poem suggests that before his death he came to know TorqueFlite automatic transmission (v. 182). This introduces a new contrast: the horseshoes linked to blacksmith craftsmanship, *vis-à-vis* the industrial transmission box, and yet both associated with the modes of transportation of their respective times.

In light of these layers of technical traditions, it is worth highlighting the rhythmic dissonance introduced by two passages in prose in verses 160-175 and 178-181, compared to the free verse of the rest of the poem. The first describes the family house in Wheeling and introduces a brief narrative moment in the succession of images (either photographic or remembered); the second is the advertising of a car that is stored in the album or, perhaps, wrapping it. This provides a literal transcription of newspaper ads, with abbreviations and noun juxtaposition listing the features of the product, in this case, a car, and its price. The abrupt change of tone in the middle of the ekphrastic passages is disruptive for three reasons. First of all, it alters the previous versification. Second, it introduces a dated technical object to refer elliptically to the family history of the poetic persona (vv. 182–183). A biographical fact offers a clue to elucidate the sense of these verses: Gibson's father died on a business trip when he, who was born in 1948, was eight years old.[101] The father's death is dated by the appearance of the automatic transmission that began to be used by Chrysler in 1956.[102] This seemingly futile detail in fact points to the profound interweaving between personal life and the history of technical objects. And, finally, the idea of a publicity clip between the verses of the poem, relates to the overprints of ads of innovative technological products from the first half of the twentieth century on Ashbaugh's etchings in *Agrippa*, establishing a multilayered interweaving between life and technology: between depictions of technologically mediated representations of the "code of life" (in the gel electrophoresis) and recording technologies (represented in the overprints); but also between the heterogeneous elements that make up *Agrippa*, namely, the etchings and the poem.

A Critique of Critical Readings. As Henthorne has suggested, the poem "Agrippa" is considered a seminal fact of digital literature and despite this its text has been subject to less critical comments than the technical peculiarities of the project *Agrippa*.[103] There are three academic articles on the poem itself, two that I have already mentioned: "Agrippa, or the Apocalyptic Book" by Schwenger and "Destructive Creativity: The Arts in the Information Age" by Liu. Even though both have a holistic intention, they oscillate between a definition of subject and tone, and a discussion on the concept of the project and the poem itself, as well as its particular digital representation, without clear distinctions of *Agrippa*, "Agrippa" and the digital poem software. The third, "Prosthetic Mnemonics and Prophylactic Politics: William Gibson among the Subjectivity Mechanisms" by Kathryne V. Lindberg,[104] is an interpretation of the subjectivity at stake in Gibson's works that draws heavily in French post-structuralism. While it presents some interesting insights on the resonances of the historical character of Agrippa, some aspects of Wiener cybernetics and Burroughs cut-up techniques, the reading of the poem and the information she presents of *Agrippa* have biased assumptions, clear mistakes, and serious inaccuracies, seemingly based on a single media coverage piece, with no knowledge of the actual work and most notably, of the self-destructing digital poem. (It is also fair to say that the poem and other information regarding *Agrippa* were not easily available at the time Lindberg wrote her paper.) The critic also establishes continuity between Gibson's characters from *Count Zero*, "Johnny Mnemonic," and the autobiographical poetic persona of "Agrippa" that is inconsistent. The essay is ultimately an example of the textual idealism discussed earlier and notoriously unaware of the need for media-specific analysis, more so when discussing a work as *Agrippa*:

> As some of us know, popular culture in print is fast being replaced by electronic impulses on our PC screens. Already interred by its practitioners at various media wakes and academic performances, cyberpunk nevertheless continues to enjoy a profitable half-life. As main authority on yesterday's fad, Gibson continues to mine the matrix, or equation, of mind and body as communication network. Like a properly post-postmodern movement might be expected to do, if literal-mindedly, William Gibson's most computerized text follows new technologies and new textualities from rhizomatic possibility through critical homeostasis to fatally entropic noise. Now that Gibson has failed to produce a self-consuming artifact and/or succeeded in an advertising campaign, we can begin to rethink Gibson's text.[105]

Schwenger's paper declares the influence of Blanchot on the idea of a self-consuming book and discusses the iteration of the poetic image of the mechanism that articulates the poem. While his reading provides a good general context for a first approach to the text, there are inaccuracies regarding the technical aspects and what could actually be made in the object *Agrippa*. Schwenger traces the influences of post-structuralism in the work, without integrating his analysis with a specific discussion regarding the overlapping between the technical aspects of the project *Agrippa* (the materiality of the work, the self-destruction software), the etchings by Ashbaugh, the themes, and the formal and expressive resources of the poem. The apocalypse idea that permeates the article seems to be referring more to discussions about the several "deaths of" (books, history, memory) and the article does not discuss the tension between inaccessibility and free accessibility set in motion by the poem and the project due to its evident challenge to the hacker underworld. Summarizing, it is an approach that focuses on a philosophical aspect of the work and does not take into consideration the interrelationship between the multiple levels of *Agrippa* and the need to consider the technological poetics animating it. For instance, undoubtedly the main topic of the poem, the reference to the absence of dead relatives and their rediscovered presence thanks to a specific technology (i.e., photography), receives just a marginal comment.

Liu's reading proposes a comparison between Gibson's poem and "Lines Written a Few Miles above Tintern Abbey" by William Wordsworth on the premise that the topic of both poems is the question of identity and the discovery of the writer vocation. Liu suggests that there is a tone in Gibson's writing, both in the poem and in his cyberpunk narrative in general, which he considers "elegiac." For the critic, the two poems, Gibson's and Wordsworth's, are articulated around the tension between destruction and creation (and by doing so effectively links the topic with the material storage and the self-destruction software that can be cracked and then, in cyberspace, spread and mutate). However, what is surprising is the attribution of a romantic heritage in Gibson: "Like Wordsworth's poetry, then, 'Agrippa' is a testament to loss that in the end becomes a new testament of recuperation. Gibson's neuromanticism is indeed a disciple of Romanticism."[106] In Liu's interpretation, in the case of Gibson the idea of "mechanism" is equivalent to the idea of "nature" as a source of inspiration for Wordsworth, "What is pen inspiration? Fundamentally, Wordsworth and Gibson answer, it is obeisance to a terrifying, autonomous agency *without* that is somehow also a poetic agency *within*."[107] Besides the rather arbitrary equivalences between the biographies of the authors (the early death of the father, the remembrance of the family home, departure), the idea of an "independent agency" does not, as I have already discussed, correspond with the tensions inherent to the "mechanism," and therein lies a fundamental difference, which again makes such statements disputable. The awareness of the mechanism implies a capacity for action that does not apply to the certainty of the artistic vocation in Wordsworth's verses. The mechanism is a human manufacture and, although it may mold our lives, it can also be molded, assuming that we become aware of its existence along with ours. For this reason a call for intervention on the device in order to regain freedom seems a more accurate exegetic method than the joyful acceptance of a superior force, be it liberating or terrifying. The challenge to crack the code, which was present since the onset of the project, encourages such a quest for freedom: to recover memory, by taking it out of the machine, and not to receive it as a granted grace. The elegiac tone, a singing to things that will soon be lost, cannot be compared with the deep understanding gained with the awareness of the mechanism. The possibility of making experience in the context of the transition to an increasingly industrial culture implies the possibility of political action rather than the maturation of a Heideggerian serene understanding.

The political position is a central element in the stance of Gibson's writing with regards to the sci-fi of his time that he considered had become conservative and deprived of its countercultural potential.[108] In this sense his acknowledged beatnik influences provide a better key than Romanticism to understand the aesthetics of the *Neuromancer*. Instead of a new Romantic, as suggested by Liu, it could be argued that he is a new novelist who, instead of a *Bildungs-Roman,* introduces a joyful deformation process of humanity and technics intertwining. Gibson's writing upsets the rules of a genre that had lost its power to narrate, just as the nineteenth century bourgeois novels that Benjamin harshly criticizes, and retrieves its potential for the transmission of experience, but an experience necessarily interlocked with the mechanisms.

Evidently, Gibson is the polar opposite of Leskov's rural short stories that Benjamin used to exemplify the survival of narration as a model for the transmission of experience, opposed to the mere traffic of information. A *street samurai* that prostitutes herself in order to save enough money to implant retractable knives in her fingernails in order to pursue a successful career as a professional killer or a hacker with a devastated neuronal system do generate an easy empathy that allows readers to understand the sense of the actions of the characters and insert them in the context of the reader's own culture. And, thus, make experience. Leskov's characters referred to a disappearing (and almost idealized) rural world when Benjamin wrote his essay, a context that is radically opposed to the grim allegory of the present in a technified and hypercapitalist future. But, on the other hand, there is a possibility of narration, of the transmission of an experience that reappears in Gibsonian characters precisely in the search for meaning through the cracks of the industrial culture and in the diverse forms of the past crafts surviving in the margins of future society.

His characters do not assume a metaphysical withdrawal from the world. On the contrary, they embody a feet on the ground self-taught relationship with technology developed in order to outlive their expected life spans, a practical relation with technics that recovers, in a twisted way, the Benjaminean idea of experience. Self-education, in the context of contemporary corporate driven technologies, usually departs from the expected usage; it also tends to cross the borders of what is considered correct, safe, and even legal. Such practices highlight some of the tensions between the artisan and industrial cultures (and of other forms of relation to the objects beyond a restrictive form of standardized private property).

An eloquent example of this relationship with materiality is the opening paragraph of the short story "Johnny Mnemonic." Here the use of an obsolete technical knowledge, forgotten but filed under a technical record system (the "microfiche"), allows the title character, Johnny, to get ready for a rough argument with his former employers and provide himself with a loaded shotgun:

> If they think you're crude, go technical: If they think you're technical, go crude. I'm very technical boy. So I decided to get as crude as possible. These days, though, you have to be pretty technical before you can even aspire to crudeness. I'd had to turn both those twelve-gauge shells from brass stock, on the lathe, and then load them myself; I'd had to dig up an old microfiche with instructions for hand-loading cartridges; I'd had to build to lever-action press to seat the primers - all very tricky. But I knew they'd work. [109]

By relating the book object with the poem, Liu retakes Schwenger's figure of the Apocalypse: "[*Agrippa*] is a book whose physically distressed form enacts Gibson's distinctive patina of destructivity. As described by Peter Schwenger in a perceptive article, *Agrippa* is an artifact of catastrophe."[110] My point here is that both critics locate the poem in the context of Gibson's first novels and stories. This implies reducing to dystopia the otherwise complex temporalities that he has created throughout his oeuvre (near future, imminent future, alternate past, extremely recent past) and that, ultimately, seem to be referring to the persistent tensions of the present, instead of crying for things lost. In his interpretation, Liu even identifies Ashbaugh's etchings with "cyberpunk's fetishization of digital, biotech and nanotech fungibility."[111]

The recurring reference to a technically originated apocalypse reduces the text to cyberpunk rather than considering it in relation to the rest of Gibson's production (and to the cultural time in which digital technologies were making their actual breakthrough). The mention of the goals of the original project without considering the material choices that could be realistically carried out (such as the use of uncured toner in the etchings instead of a slowly fading ink), are an idealist approach that ignores what technical decisions do illuminate: the constant negotiations between idea and matter in a historically specific technological context. Liu's interpretation of Gibson as a (new) Romantic maintains the belief in creative genius in the alleged questions of the poetic persona over his vocation as a writer.[112] I disagree. If there actually is a question in the poem, it would be something closer to "What am I?" But there are no questions, just iterations of the mechanism; or put in Stieglerian terms, of the co-constitution of humanity and technics.

Schwenger's analysis (and Liu's to a lesser extent), retake recurrent topics of the apocalyptic view on technology, in the sense of the classical division proposed by Eco. Elegy and apocalypse are interpretations that say a lot about the *Zeitgeist* of the period (akin with the "end of the book" discourses), while, on the opposite in Gibson's works, the future and the past are allegories of the present. The poetics of Gibson repeatedly consist in the paradox of a grim realism, even in science-fiction, made of ethical, political, and social tensions and conflicts, but also of aesthetic disputes that are less a requiem song for a humanist culture in retreat before technical progress than the imagination of new artistic forms and resources. And, also, new effective forms of entertainment, since Gibson is a proven genre writer who draws heavily on pulp fictions. In an excess of biographism, Schwenger reaches the point of referring to the atomic bomb, completely absent from the text, and associates it with the fact that his dead father had worked at a company that for some time was related to the Manhattan Project that developed the bomb. The emphasis on the apocalypse as an overwhelming symbol of the ineffable overshadows the importance of the gradual passing of time in "Agrippa," of the oscillating relationship between oblivion and remembrance, between obsolescence and re-enactment by emulation. The idea of a post-apocalyptic relic is an absolute image that does not match the gradual, nonlinear idea of technical change, with setbacks and unsolved disputes that can be found in all the works by Gibson. The overlapping temporalities challenge the naïve teleology of the progress, as is exemplified by digital courier Johnny Mnemonic, who transports gigabytes of data in his brain, but has to relearn how to load shotgun cartridges and build a lever-action press for them. Quite on the contrary to such apocalyptic approaches, the recurrent aspect of technics in Gibson's stories is its role as a generator of different forms of time that co-exist in the present or survive in its margins. It is a non-teleological reading of technical change, where history never comes to an end but keeps oscillating and resurfacing at the margins of society. Therefore the conflicting representation of memory that is constructed, both in his oeuvre in general as in the poem in particular, is more apprehensible under gradual events that result in the accumulation of multiple layers of past into the present. A clear example of this is the ironic and pedestrian image of "bit rot" that Gibson chooses to describe for the peculiar fate of "Agrippa": "Meanwhile, though, the text escaped to cyberspace and a life of its own, which I found a pleasant enough outcome. But the free-range cyberspace versions are subject to bit-rot."[113]

The abovementioned essays, nevertheless, do illuminate some relevant aspects of the book, which should be considered while disregarding the importance of the apocalyptic leitmotiv, more present in the critical essays than in the work. Liu, in particular, diminishes the apocalyptic stance towards the end of his chapter and highlights another topic not usually associated with "Agrippa": discontinuity, which provides an insightful approach to the problem of technical discreteness. At the end of his interpretation, Liu states that human experience in the twentieth century has been defined by mechanisms that operate based on discrete units, represented by the metaphor of the photographic camera that forever divides "this from that."[114] Liu suggests the camera is a

synecdoche of the modern forms of administration of life, comparable to trench warfare and concentration camps but also to immi-
gration papers and birth certificates. Military organization, state
organized extermination, and state identity validations are opposed to a different form of non-standard discontinuity. And
paradoxically the possession of a family album is untranslatable
and useless for state records, and is bestowed with history and
decay of its own (in a way similar to Kurtis' *Shoe Box* that will be
discussed ahead). In this context Liu suggests that "Agrippa"
belongs to a long tradition of works using destructive creativity
that "fracture themselves in quest of a larger picture of contemporary existence as the survivorship of destructive discontinuity."[115]
Liu's most important contribution to a critical approach of "Agrippa" is thus his discussion of the division of life by technology and
its relations with twentieth century avant-garde artistic procedures. The poem's mechanism works on discrete units and not in
continuous ones, in the same way as state and economic rationali-
ty. And the innovative art proceeds similarly, only that it does so
heading in an opposite direction. Without discontinuities there is
no writing, nor photography, nor digital representation, but
without these discontinuities neither the literary nor the artistic
traditions can be put into question by works like *Agrippa*.

More than a cyberpunk gesture, an omen of grim technological
prophecies, I consider that the ekphrasis of aged photographs from
the twenties is indicative of Gibson's most distinctive trait, Jameson's postmodern nominalism. The procedure deals with the
temporality of the technics (and what its obsolescence brings
about) and is inherent to the detailed brand-conscious, adjective
heavy descriptions. In this way, objects are inscribed into history
and the process of inscription makes Gibson an exponent of a new
literary aesthetic drawing on our current collective unconscious,
suggesting products that may not be real, but might very well be,
in a globalized and market centered world. And that procedure
works precisely because "little by little, in the current universe,
everything is slowly being named [...]. Each of these items is on its
way to the ultimate destination of a name of its own."[116] Adding to
Jameson's accurate description, this can only occur in a time when
not only the Leviathan of the State but also behemoth sized

companies are competing to "organize all the information of the world."

Latin American scholarship provides two critical comments on the work. An example of how the cultural impact of *Agrippa* has been often misinterpreted is that of the Brazilian media arts scholar Arlindo Machado. He inscribes *Agrippa* in a genealogy of interventions on the devices, or as he puts it, in "semiotic machines," along with the works of the video artist Nam June Paik and photographers Frederic Fontenoy and Andrew Davidhazy. Then, he defines it as a "digital novel" that displays on the screen a text that is confusing and is destroyed by computer virus capable of detonating memory conflicts in the device. In Machado's assumption this characteristic of *Agrippa* exceeds the limits of the semiotic machines and radically reinvents their programs and goals.[117] Besides the inaccuracies regarding the "virus" and the intervention on the hardware, Machado forces the interpretation of the work to endorse it to a Flusserian poetic that would answer the call for the active intervention of artists/engineers on the devices. Although Machado seems to understand the relevance of *Agrippa*, his knowledge seems to come from commentary on the work rather than from the work itself.

There is a second contribution by sociologist and philosopher Christian Ferrer, who discusses *Agrippa* in three pages of his long essay *Mal de ojo. El drama de la mirada* [*Eye Curse. The Drama of Sight*]. His text does incorporate some topics that have not been addressed by American criticism on *Agrippa*, despite some inaccuracies.[118] Instead of technophilic or technophobic topics, Ferrer highlights how *Agrippa* has the reader reflecting on the problem of obsolescence by using old ads of already anachronistic technologies. Thus, he wonders if Gibson believes that our contemporary bonds with the machines are seen better when they are left aside by fashion or when they suffer what he calls "the bull of obsolescence." Furthermore, he says, looking at rusty abandoned machines awaiting their final oxidation in warehouses, we come to realize of our own fragility, "we understand that they did not serve us nor did we know how to include them in a spiritual realm that redeemed them. Oxide is not only the virus of the machines, it also is the melancholic patina of history."[119]

For Ferrer, the main topic is the relationship between everyday experience of technology and memory, articulated by the ekphrasis of family photographs. Ferrer also pays attention to a formal aesthetic effect: "The virus in Gibson's book serves as an omen: it purges us from the excess of information and empty words and takes us back to the eloquence of the ragged breath."[120] As it was discussed earlier, the self-destruction process is not a virus, but it does achieve the effect of condensation of attention pointed out by Ferrer. Another distinctive aspect of his critique, perhaps due to the perspective provided by Latin America's peripheral modernity, is noticing the role of obsolescence to approach technology in a poetical way. Thus, the Simondonian call for the inclusion of technical objects in a spiritual (i.e., human) domain gains relevance. This brings us to the relationships of the text with the storage devices, of the codex with the code, of the ghost in the machine with the eerie dead relatives of the pictures, of "Agrippa" with *Agrippa*.

Storage, Containers, Coffins. When Kevin Begos, Jr. donated a copy of *Agrippa* to the Oxford University Bodleian Library, he noted the absence of a comprehensive reading of *Agrippa* even in the best critical approaches such as those by Liu, Kirschenbaum, and *The Agrippa Files* team. That fact, he stated, motivated the donation to a center that he hopes can propose an approach to the totality of the work, including the openness and multiple stages of the work: collaboration; a self-consuming narration that ended up being a poem; the veiling images that ended up being erasable images; the happening of "The Transmission" that did not actually happen; the presentation at the Americas Society; the analog cracking that actually carried out the transmission.... Even when the original motivation declared by Begos was the desire for a wider array of critical and scholarly studies, he acknowledges that Gibson's part in the project would inevitably continue to eclipse the other aspects.[121] Taking into consideration the vacancy note by Begos, this section will discuss aspects related to the multiple storage devices of *Agrippa* and their complex relations with the contents.

Each copy of *Agrippa* is a unique (partly) handmade object, something that is reinforced by the author signatures present in some of the few known copies.[122] The aura of each copy of *Agrippa*, in the Benjaminean sense of the term, is clear and reinforced by the ephemerality of the etchings and the self-destroying digital poem. The peculiar execution of the poem extremes the auratic condition of the work: the certainty of a single chance would make its reception something unique, and unrepeatable (or difficult to repeat), at least in the technical conditions preset by the work, that is by the rules established for its existence. In *Agrippa*, two aspects of storage devices are thus challenged: the auratic, material, concrete, form of existence (which is, in principle, a *closed* work), and the digital, reproducible but erasable, form of existence (which is, again in principle, *open*).

The idea of storage is complex, furthermore in view of the fact that digitization has blurred the *per se* diffuse lines between the inscription of something on a storage device and the storage device as significant surface itself. The imbrications between content and the significant materiality of its container should prevent naïve abstraction (and that is the material basis to postulate the existence of an auratic, unique and unrepeatable condition). The inscription of abstractions, on the other hand, involves a regularized significant surface that is, at least ideally, empty, devoid of meaning, while the traditional works of art are *in themselves* significant. Generally speaking, an art object, as it may be the most obvious case of a marble sculpture, is a form contained on a stone, but it is not an inscription since, inasmuch as storage means, that particular stone has been inevitably attached to a particular work.

The storage devices in which abstractions can be inscribed are based on a different assumption: their meaninglessness (i.e., their transparency), which makes them a neutral container of the stored content. The paradigmatic example of these is paper. However, in the case of texts, the abstraction of the encoding in writing was in fact limited by the changing affordances of the different physical storage devices, as occurred with clay tables, scrolls, and then books. Each inscription is a particular technique that implies specific skills and tools. Their physicality is self evident. With the advent of floppy disks and hard drives afterwards, an affordance until then limited by the physical characteristics of the storage devices emerged: the enhanced erasability of electronic writing (along with its enhanced reproducibility). This effaced the inscription process and turned storage into an abstract notion. But erasability does not imply that information is lost. In fact, digital forensics reveal that, as Kirschenbaum states, every inscription leaves physical marks that can be retrieved.[123] *Agrippa* builds on both forms of inscription and challenges their specific affordances: the reproducibility and preservation of digital texts, the legibility of printed pages, and the permanence of etchings. The different storage devices are part of the work not only in their operation to ensure the transport of the content, but as meaningful containers in themselves.

Regarding digital inscription, in the condensation of attention of the self-erasing poem and the iterative organization around the poetic image of the mechanism, "Agrippa" follows the old three compositional principles established by Edgar Allan Poe in his essay "The Philosophy of Composition": limited length, methodical writing, and unity of effect.[124] Argentine critic and novelist Ricardo Piglia has suggested that literature in the context of digitization has restored the two classic forms of reading: one is isolated reading, the fantasy of the desert island as a symbol of the necessary undisturbed solitude required to read without interruptions; and the second, that of scattered reading, due to the proliferation of signs associated with modern city life.[125] The imposition of a single reading in the digital text contained in *Agrippa* implies a reauratization that send us back to Poe's prescriptions: writing a text whose length depends on the capacity to maintain the attention, a text that cannot be left aside and that can be read at once, in a preset time. For "Agrippa," that is a little bit over twenty minutes.

By contrast, hypertext narratives such as Joyce's *Afternoon* may be associated with the second, scattered reading that Piglia presents as prototypical of Modernism in general and of James Joyce in particular; a reading closer to the sensory experience of urban landscapes rather than isolation propitiated by rural environments. Reading, Piglia notes, is not linear, the reader deviates because he is on a network where the time is fragmented and is multiple. One might associate this position to the movement in a city, where everything seems to be happening at the same time.[126] The contrast between "Agrippa" and *Afternoon* is not arbitrary. The first is an autobiographical poem that imposes a linear and condensed reading, organized around the family past in an isolated rural town, while the second is a hyper-linked novel set in the present in an urban scenario that begins when the narrator sees a traffic accident and thinks that it may have involved his ex-wife and his son. From that premise the possible routes for the text produce a technical twist on a resource as characteristic of Modernism as is the "stream of consciousness."[127] Besides being dated around the same period, just prior to the advent of the web as we know it, these works share another not often mentioned trait: both were stored on floppy disks. The difference was that if *Afternoon*, because of its hypertext structure, favored wandering re-readings through the text, "Agrippa" constrained them to a single moment of reading with no possible distractions.

Both works can also be contrasted on another level. *Afternoon* was produced using *Storyspace* software, developed by Joyce and media theorist Bolter. Created especially for the writing of *After-noon*, this software allows the digital edition of electronic texts based on textual units called "lexias," which can be blocked or enabled according to the ways that the reader has followed in the narration in order to avoid inconsistencies in the multiple readings offered by the hypernovel. Besides being used to write *Afternoon*, *Storyspace* was patented and sold as proprietary software intended for the production of hypertext literature as well as other forms of text production.[128] "Agrippa," on the other hand incorporated a work-specific self-destruction program. In a way, *Afternoon* and *Agrippa* are the opposite sides of the coin of digital reproducibility: in the first case it is planned as part of a series of novels, to be marketed using the same software, a sort of investment in the construction of a hypertext publishing industry; in the second, the project aimed at producing a unique non-transferable experience, while at the same time inviting hackers to free the possibility of its reproducibility.

The works can be seen as polar opposites at several levels: between two literary genres (novel and poem), between two types of program (hypertext and self-destructing text), and two relationships with the objects (the content based commodity logics of proprietary software *vis-a-vis* the disruption of cult value of the work of art and the invitation to be cracked). Benjamin grimly described nineteenth-century novels as one of the earliest products of cultural industry, a desperate consumption of the lives of others due to the impossibility to make experience, to make sense, in the ever shifting context of industrialization.[129] In hypertext fictions this is replaced by a user-guided, though author-oriented, text wandering, allegedly released from the linearity that traditional books enforce. A Modernist gesture of sorts, adapted to the contemporary technological sublime, providing tours (and detours) in a way similar to the word games previously discussed, such as *Colossal Cave Adventure*, though aiming to be included in the field of high literature.[130]

The self-destroying poem, on the other hand, condenses perceptual experience, intertwining it with its topic (the relationship between memory and recording devices). But by silently inviting hackers in, *Agrippa* does not naïvely surrender to teleology of technology; quite the contrary, it encourages subversion. Despite the reauratization caused by the reader's awareness of the self-destruction program and the acquisition of a handmade book object, as a code the digital text encompasses a technical reproducibility contrary to its unique auratic existence. Therefore, if the imposition of self-destruction in some readers might have generated a form of concentrated attention, in others it only spurred the challenge and the expectation of dismantling that single reading chance through the act of cracking.[131] The mere possibility that this would happen (as in fact occurred a day after its public presentation) make the aura of *Agrippa* a partial and provisional one. Partial because only the book object preserves it, and provisional because the self-destruction works as long as the reader does not have access to the online version therefore accepting the rules imposed by the *Agrippa* project.[132]

In the presentation of *Agrippa* at the Americas Society, Begos stated one of the ideas animating the project was that of multiple receptions. It could be read in solitude, read in the projection in the presentation with other people, or cracked, but also told as a story by others, partially forgotten or remembered with errors, inaccuracies, and personal additions.[133] "The Transmission" was originally intended to be an optical fiber broadcast from a barn in the U.S. Midwest backwaters simultaneously played in several places in the world (two cultural centers in New York, a museum in Atlanta, the storefront of a shop in lower Manhattan, a sheep farm in Australia, and other indeterminate locations). Due to the technical limitations of the time this could not be accomplished. The actual event consisted in the execution of the file of the *Agrippa* floppy disk, which was projected on a screen, synchronized with a recording of the reading of the poem performed by actor Penn Jillette. However, the original plans were more ambitious and included an artistic happening that would complement the work. The press release for the event declared:

> Agrippa - transmission aims to go far beyond the previous concep-
> tual global events, and hasten to new form of tribal storytelling. Words
> and images, location, language, and weather will become equal parts of
> the experience. And high technology, built on precision and control, will
> be used in a manner that is certain to go out of control.
> Agrippa - the transmission should in no way to confused with the
> published version of Agrippa. The book is an art object with weight,
> smell, texture, and the charm and weakness of paper, ink, cloth, and
> composite plastics. The transmission will be counterpoint, telling some-
> thing else, another aspect of the story...[134]

The reference to a "new form of tribal storytelling" is worth some attention. Gibson and Ashbaugh did not participate actively in this stage of the *Agrippa* project and it is striking how with their absence some topics typical of technological optimism surfaced. McLuhan's "global village" echoes in the tribes linked to a global transmission that would be facilitated by "high technology," although there is some prevision that this might "go out of control." The writing style of the press release does not seem intimately tied to the project, in contrast with the "Promotional Prospect" that had been created by Ashbaugh and Begos.

Though not in the way it was devised, the control over the poem was indeed lost. How this happened is an urban legend at the dawn of the Internet: the cracking was performed without even attempting to crack the file. The technical team responsible for the projection of the execution of the file that displayed the poem on a screen in the Americas Society videotaped the projection without anyone of the *Agrippa* production noticing and some hours later typed the text and disseminated it through a BBS post. Notably, the presentation of the book, after the idea of transmission by optical fiber failed, can hardly be considered as an artistic happening. The only performative act, ironically crude in the style of the Johnny Mnemonic character of the homonymous short story by Gibson, as Kirschenbaum notes, was that of the analog hackers of the digital file that contained "Agrippa."[135]

Striphas suggests the software of *Agrippa* is one of the first examples of DRM;[136] likewise, the cracking of "Agrippa" might very well be one of the first cases of a digital leak.[137] The technological means used operated the reduction of the work to digital content. In a cultural industry model this might have implied a closing of the work but it derived an opening: "Agrippa" mutated in several parodic versions.

The idea of the *Agrippa* virus is one of the most fertile misunderstandings surrounding the history of this work. In his *Electronic Revolution*, beatnik writer William Burroughs suggests that language is virus.[138] Hayles has observed that, in the context of digital literature, this has been a recurrent topic, noting that Burroughs is cited as a precedence in the "idea that randomization is a way to break the hold of the viral word and liberate resistances latent in language by freeing it from linear syntax and coherent narrative."[139] The misunderstanding regarding the virus was also part of the nineties *Zeitgeist*: in the presentation, Begos refers to the *Morris* virus (which was actually a "worm"[140]) that in 1988 had caused serious problems in the computer networks and that had received media coverage. The worm also resulted in the first conviction of a programmer, the graduate student Robert Tappan Morris, under the American 1986 Computer and Fraud Act. Morris' biography is a somewhat Gibsonian example of life in the digital culture: a student, convicted as a cybercriminal, later on is awarded tenure at MIT and elected fellow at the Association for Computing Machinery, one of the world's most important learned societies for computing. Curiously enough, the *Morris* worm itself has a particular history that relates to the discussion on the auratic condition of storage devices: *the* disk containing the source code of the worm is exhibited at the Computer History Museum of the Boston Museum of Science. The black 3½" disk, looking, of course, just like any other disk, is preserved in a glass box with a sign that reads

The Morris Internet Worm
source code
This disk contains the complete source code of the Morris Internet worm program. This tiny, 99-line program brought large pieces of the Internet to a standstill on November 2nd, 1988.
The worm was the first of many intrusive programs that use the Internet to spread.
        -The Computer History Museum[141]

This is an eloquent case of auratization of an industrially produced storage device, where its contents are inaccessible without the technical objects' associated milieu (the diskette drive, the computer, and the operative system). Placing the specific object in a glass box in a museum prioritizes the cult value of the container over the exhibition (or, better, *circulation*) value of the content.

There is a second aspect of the qualities of code also worth mentioning. In the buzz surrounding *Agrippa* in 1992, there were some comments regarding the encryption technology suggesting it was considered munitions grade material by the U.S. National Security Agency and, allegedly, that resulted in a ban to export *Agrippa* to Japan. The title of a sidebar in an article by Josh Quittner about digital literature meets the topics of Gibson's Bridge trilogy: "When Art Resembles National Security."[142] The rumors surrounding *Agrippa* not only drew attention to the ideas of copyright and of original work upon which the circulation of works in the publishing industry and the art market were based. The technology used for the encryption was said to have called the attention, albeit unintentionally, of State agencies due to national security concerns. This interference and the supposed limitations to the circulation of the work motivated the involvement of cyber-libertarian activist John Perry Barlow, founder of the Electronic

Frontier Foundation.[143] The fact is disputed by DuPont, who suggests that the extremely short 12 bit key-length used in the software would have not been considered as strong cryptography at the time, since the U.S. government allowed RSA cryptosystems using a much more complex modulus of 512 bits, and thus the political involvement of Barlow and the EFF was superfluous.[144]

Summarizing, the events around the publishing project provide new insight into the multidimensionality of *Agrippa*, which transcends the acts of reading and seeing, and poses a challenge in diverse fields. Besides defying hackers and allegorizing on the future of the book, the ephemerality of the work posed also a problem for museum collections. Manovich has noted that this kind of new media work faces some resistance from the logics of the art world based on the Romantic idea of authorship and a controlled distribution in exclusive places such as galleries, museums, and auctions. New media objects such as the digital poems, on the other hand, afford a potential existence of copies and different states of the same work (though it can be argued that it may no longer be the *same* work), as well as network distribution among other features.[145]

Collections are based on the primacy of the cult value over the exhibition value, so it can be expected that some of the collectors who acquired *Agrippa* may have never played the floppy disk in order to preserve it. However, they will possess an intangible something similar to the awkward diskette containing the source code of the *Morris* worm. Furthermore, the simple passing of time has rendered the *Agrippa* disk unusable, since the hardware that can read it and the operating systems that can run its files have become rare specimens. The creators of *Agrippa* were indeed aware of the obsolescence of the technical reproduction devices and also of the work's openness to cracking. This meant that the work would not conclude in the cult object. But, nevertheless, the book object remains and completes *Agrippa*: without the two columns of DNA imitating the *Gutenberg Bible* and the etchings that erase, "Agrippa" would be a rarity, a strange work by Gibson, another example of the nominalism Jameson has acutely described. One of the distinguishing characteristics of *Agrippa* is its double, material and digital, ontology. Steven Jones had proposed that it could be compared with other transplatform cultural forms such as ARGs (Augmented Reality Games), which also show how digital culture unfolds over itself with the expansion of the digital into the physical world.[146] In other posts, he relates the work to other phenomena in contemporary art and technology such as the works by the New Aesthetic artistic movement,[147] or the hardlinking from the physical to the digital world like the one provided by QR codes in which the superposition of material and digital can be detected.[148] In certain ways, these aesthetic forms had been anticipated in fictional geolocated works only visible with virtual reality devices as the ones described by Gibson in *Pattern Recognition*.

In 1992, twenty years before that novel, the juxtaposition of virtuality over reality was only being hinted, an aspect on which I have insisted throughout this book is the artisan manufacture of the *Agrippa* book object. A characteristic element of its making are the small imperfections that confer uniqueness to each copy and that cause small variations. Technophilia is often fascinated with a technological sublime visually and haptically represented in perfect, ideal, surfaces that move away from the contingency of materiality. As mentioned before, Kirschenbaum indicates that the technological imaginary of the eighties was based on an acritical depiction of information as an "essence unto itself."[149] From the luminescent world inside the computer depicted in *Tron* to the design-heavy appealing looks of current gadgets, there is an aspiration to pure forms, devoid of roughness (and of history). Gibson's description of cyberspace in *Neuromancer* is an obvious commonplace for those discussing the digital milieu, a "consensual hallucination" depicted as "city lights, receding."

But medial ideology usually disregards the material counterpart that is present in Gibson's work. For instance, in the case of the oft-quoted description of cyberspace the one that accesses cyberspace is an outcast with a particular physical condition, the hacker Case. At the end of the novel the character undergoes a medical intervention to disable a previous intervention to which he had been forced by his employer. The first intervention had been conducted to make him immune to the effect of cocaine so that he could carry out his contract. Once the job is done, the only thing Case wants is not healing, but to recover the ability to get high at will. This is quite a corporeal, Dionysian, exit, which is the exact opposite of a sublime that shuns from materiality. In its biased interpretation of cyberpunk, medial ideology abandons the outdated smooth shapes, the brightness and luminous surfaces of spacecrafts, only to repeat them in the designed virtual world, similarly bright and perfect. Technological sublime, enhanced by faith in the teleology of the progress, reaches an extreme form of aestheticization in the context of digital technology.

In response to this, the insistence on the materiality and historicity of technology represents an intertwined, complex, and conflicting world that demands a non-idealistic approach to technology. Perhaps one of the best examples to illustrate this opposition is the relative box-office failure of the grim future depicted in *Blade Runner* when compared to the success of the much more elemental, but at the time visually appealing *Tron*. (It is worth noting that the latter has aged to the point of becoming almost a parody of the technological sublime it once represented). The best films of science-fiction usually illustrate a dichotomy involving a material, grounded counterpart: the skyscrapers and aerial avenues of the hedonistic bourgeoisie in 1927 Fritz Lang's *Metropolis* contrast with the squalor of the engine room and the exploitation of workers in the underground; in an inversion of the same motif, the candid and beautiful Eloi in the 1960 film version *The Time Machine* (literally) feed the monstrous Morlocks of the underworld, humans degenerated by technology, who are none other than the descendants of the wealthy classes who managed to hide in underground shelters to survive the nuclear war; the illusory digital world of *The Matrix* hides the reality of humanity in an embryonic dream that is just a power source for the machines; the idyllic realization of small town America embodied by Jim Carrey in *The Truman Show* is a farce, a theater of the world meant for televised mass consumption, a play that everyone is aware of with the sole exception of its leading character; in Duncan Jones' *Moon*, the only employee of Lunar Enterprises at the spotless Sarang base is counting off the days to meet his family only to discover he is nothing more than a clone used as labor force (no longer *cheap*, just *free*), a disposable worker kept hidden on the dark side of the moon while providing cheap and clean energy to Earth, whose inhabitants are happily unaware of his existence.[150] As Žižek has pointed out in his remarkable essay "Welcome to the desert of the real!," it is not so much about the apparent division between real and virtual, instead it is about the dematerialization even of materiality, extending the reach of the technological sublime that medial ideology strives for: "The underlying experience of *The Truman Show* is that late capitalist consumerist Californian paradise is, in its very hyper-reality, in a way *unreal*, substance-less, deprived of material inertia."[151] In Benjaminean terms the phenomenon could be defined as "aestheticization." The dematerialization of the technological sublime is part of a long process by which industrial workers cease to have a full relationship with the produced objects, uprooting both worker and product from the craftsmanship traditions that had given them sense and inscribed them in a local history. In the miniaturization to microscopic scales of the inscriptions on the storage devices, Kirschenbaum finds one of the reasons for the development of a medial ideology. A necessary part of digitization, miniaturization is what turns works into *seemingly* abstract contents, actually concretized in microscopic, invisible inscriptions. Complementarily, Žižek describes a trend towards the invisibilization of manual labor that lays the grounds for the dematerialization of the real. Against these processes, hybrid projects as *Agrippa* introduce a modest yet meaningful symbolic resistance. In relation to the invisibilization of the material labor, Žižek notices that in Hollywood films the only time that we are confronted with a production process is when Bond enters the master criminal's base of operation that agent 007 promptly blows up "allowing us to return to the daily semblance of our existence in a world with a 'disappearing working class.'"[152]

But there is another aspect worth consideration: the loss of indexicality in representations. With the adoption of digital technologies by the film industry, the relatively marginal (and manual) traditions of animation and special effects not only automate but start to coexist on equal terms with the raw audiovisual materials. Opposed to digital synthetic images, analog footage possessed an indexical relation to the *real* world inasmuch they are produced by the reflection of light in matter that has been inscribed in the photosensitive film. The photochemical indexicality of filming yields because a *realistic* (rather than a real) image may be built in the decontextualized chroma-key sets and the animation software. Of course, the real is still there, but in equal conditions with the synthetic digital realities of computer generated images. As Manovich acutely tells us, the specificity of cinema as an artistic tradition was, precisely, its technical specificity.[153] That specificity staggers when, in a general sense, the indexical analog film recording shifts towards the abstraction of the digital simulation of film. And that is a fundamental aspect in the constitution of a medial ideology, such as the one depicted in *Tron*.

Against interpretations that assimilate his writing to a form technological sublime, Gibson has stressed that his interest in the obsolete in his first novels was motivated by his discontent with American exceptionalism and white middle-class "monoculture" that were the rule in a genre that had become militaristic rather than with the consummation of a digital future. He also relates his particular form of gritty realist science-fiction to the poverty of description of previous sci-fi novels:

> The technology depicted was so slick and clean that it was practically invisible. What any given SF would look like if we could crank up the resolution? As it was then, much of it was like video games before the invention of fractal dirt. I wanted to see dirt in the corners.[154]

The emphasis on the need for a "naturalistic" description in science fiction, along with the criticism of a form of militarism associated with a technology so "slick and clean that it was practically invisible" aims directly at the representations of the medial ideology. In addition to the criticism of the monoculture of American exceptionalism and the choice of antiheros (as is the example of the junkie hacker Case), Gibson also ironically notes the problem of taking too literally the world of bright lines by stating his desire to see the filth, the imperfection, before the invention of the "fractal dirt."[155] Some forms of contemporary digital art such as pixel art, where the artificiality of the image meets the eye (by the self-evident pixel size) are also a response to the aestheticization that hides technology behind an idealized perfection.

The multiple kinds of craftsmanship involved in an object as *Agrippa* and all the special features and connotations of its materiality can be inscribed in a Gibsonian poetics present throughout all of his works. The *Agrippa* project is a collaborative work among a writer, an editor, an artist, and a programmer, which is also open to appropriations by the public. But it is also an intertwinement of storage devices, a work of art whose poetics conveys the postmodern nominalism already discussed and that is summarized in the technological naturalism demanded by Gibson. A powerful example of a *poetics of intertwinement*, *Agrippa* illuminates the uncomfortable, material, dysfunctional aspects of technology, allowing to politicize it and to challenge aestheticization. It is not surprising, then, that, in the presentation of the book, Begos talked about the material contingencies of the project and its possible survival within the logics of counterculture. At the Americas Society he suggested that "the best thing that sums up the project are the rough edges;" that "nothing worked right along the way;" and that there had been "astounding problems." In a later exchange, he asserts that Gibson, Ashbaugh, and he had agreed that "rough edges was the way it should be, instead of trying to make something perfect and seamless and flawless."[156] One of the most interesting aspects regarding the foreseen circulation of *Agrippa* is that he expected "Gibson's fans to be selling bootlegs, videotapes of a fuzzy screen, like rock and roll bootlegs."[157] The "rough edges" are precisely the antithesis of the "slick and clean" surfaces that Gibson had criticized in the early eighties science fiction representation of technology. It is almost a statement of artistic principles *from within* the representation storage devices, both against the content dynamics of the cultural industry and the fetishistic collector practices of the art world.[158]

The final version of the poem was cracked and distributed online a few hours after the presentation of the book, as it was expected (and may even have been encouraged) by Begos, Ashbaugh, and Gibson. Such events have generated a reinterpretation of the work: devised as both a paradoxical enduring fetish *and* an ephemeral work, today "Agrippa" is ubiquitous, permanent, and intangible, and is an excellent example of digital conservation by redundancy. The multiplication of versions ensures the survival of the poem whose *original* version can be obtained through the comparison of similarities over the differences of all existing versions. As Kirschenbaum suggests, the poem "Agrippa" shows that preservation is ultimately a social fact rather than just a technical one.[159]

The text in *Agrippa* relates to its storage devices at multiple levels: Agrippa is the name of a line of photo albums produced by Eastman Kodak at first half of the twentieth century. But the subtitle sparks other associations: the family of the author, classical culture, the occultist Cornelius Agrippa von Nettesheim,[160] and the Egyptian *Book of the Dead*. The poetic persona evokes in the verses different photographs of dead relatives preserved in one of those albums. These evocations are permeated by the memory of smells, tastes, and textures that refer to different industrially made objects that have undergone the passage of time (and that are also topicalized to in the overprints in Ashbaugh's etchings in the book object) as well as to a state of nature that has been lost to technical progress. The poetic persona presents: (a) the aging of the album itself (vv. 17–19); (b) the time that has accumulated in the photographed materials (vv. 32–33); and (c) the physical changes in the urban and rural spaces (vv. 148–149; 173–175).

In its storage and content intertwinement, *Agrippa* references the passing of time, the marks it bestows on materials, family memories, and the recording devices that help preserve it (as well as the physical survival of these records). References and evocations are related to the materiality of the book object, of the floppy disk that stores the digital text and of the uncured toner etchings. And both the software in the floppy disk and etchings are peculiar ephemeral storage "mechanisms." Record and memory follow separate, yet related, paths. The result is the separation of life and representation, where photography is a metonymy for all technologically mediated records: the camera shutter that always divides "this from that" (vv. 98–103). The verses suggest a division between what is represented ("this") and the representation ("that"), the product of the photographic machine. Life continues its course after the shot. And the photographic copy, that depicts a still instant from such a lifetime, will also begin a timely existence of its own, in the aging of its materials. As any other recording, the photographs will go on to have their particular history, different from the history of those they portray. The mode of existence of the recordings will be that of their circulation, that is, the history of the decay of the copies and of the preservation (or not) of the master, the unique negative.[161]

Experimentation with the storage devices is also relevant when discussing *Agrippa*, a work comprised of: (a) a book, one of the models of serialized objects, which cannot be read because it holds the encoding of organic matter whose upgrade would entail the creation of life (and that is linked with the digital text once the file has been executed); (b) erasable etchings whose topics are DNA and photography; and, finally, (c) a floppy disk whose files become useless, creating the paradox of a digital text that does not survive its first reading, therefore not preserved from aging and deterioration as digital records were, albeit theoretically, supposed to be. An art object, the *Agrippa* book and its casing consist of many elements (the unusually large volume, the *ad hoc* typography, the cloth surrounding it, the resin case) suggesting the possession of a relic, with a cult value, but also the possession of a key to life, to something organic, encoded in the DNA that is its text, reinforced by the honeycomb, resinous casing. Hodge indicates that "also relevant is the fact that elements of the work were created or finished by hand: each copy of each edition is physically different."[162] The uniqueness introduces one of the most commented aspects of the work, which leads to the subject of the next section, which is also why *Agrippa* is not only an interesting topic for a discussion on contemporary art but also for a debate on digital culture: copying, and copying barriers, and by-passing them.

The Work of Art and the Art of Copying

...Con pocos, pero doctos libros juntos,
vivo en conversación con los difuntos
-Francisco de Quevedo, "Desde la Torre de Juan Abad"

As an artistic device, *Agrippa* generated an aura around the object by altering the reproducibility media existing at the time. The impossible second reading of the poem, the effacement of the images, and the unreadable DNA that imitates the text layout of the *Gutenberg Bible*, result in an oscillation between cult value and exhibition value similar to the one existing in the auratic works of art analyzed by Benjamin, as sacred sculptures that could only be seen during specific rituals, during unordinary, sacred time. Since the poem can only be read once, it propitiates a special preparation in order to ensure reading concentration and prevent interruptions or distractions.

One of the early problems surrounding digital works of art was the question of the object and its uniqueness: How was a digital object bought? How did it fit in a collection? Could a digital work be auratic? This is because the allographic illusion of identicallity in digital art and its apparently immaterial character make its identical and infinite reproduction theoretically possible. What is surprising is that the first auratic digital work was not a visual arts piece, an heir to the cultural traditions of painting or sculpture, but an eminently literary artistic device. By presenting a work that effaces, self-destroys, and whose non-disappearing text is illegible, the project recovers the intensity of aesthetic experience and demands a non-trivial effort in order to survive in the reader's memory without the possibility of relying on a technical recording storage device.

However, Benjamin did not describe an absolute division for auratic phenomena starting with the emergence of automatized reproductive technologies. In his essays, it is presented as a gradual process; hence the idea of "decadence" of what is specific of art rather than its "disappearance" or "death." An *original* traditionally required also a *copy* that referred to the previous existence of the original work, thus making it the first. But, where is the origin to be compared with the copies in technical reproduction? In the realm of art, without an original, there is no possible copy. In previous art reproduction technologies, the inevitable degradation with respect to the master of the old analog recordings still bestowed a quasi auratic condition upon the source. Taking the problem of degradation to the microscopic level, the need for a forensic critique issued by Kirschenbaum, points to the material impossibility of identicallity and suggests that even digital copies may have unique distinctive features. Although relevant for dismantling the medial ideology and the aestheticization it entails, Kirschenbaum's method is not only very difficult to apply without adequate and often inaccessible technical tools, it does not consider much the role of the dominating human sensorium in defining what is identical and what is degraded. My claim is that digital copies are perceived, in the prevailing content dynamics, as *identical* in opposition to other previous modes of reproducibility, in which this degradation was more noticeable. As discussed in chapter four, the norm of digital circulation, that I have also called the ".mp3 paradigm," it is that of compressed formats, due to technical but also economic and legal issues.

Friederich Kittler locates the emergence of identicallity in the invention of Gutenberg's printing press. He considers it the first modern reproducibility technology and interprets it as a breakthrough moment not only in the fields of art and literature, but also in the field of knowledge. But the most salient feature in Kittler's account is that the printing press not only aimed at the standardization of books but to their beautification. That specific feature, the beauty of homogeneity, was the origin of a split in knowledge between "software" and "hardware." Kittler's provocative anachronism is another way of looking at the novelty of the separation of contents (the software) from their containers (the hardware). The most interesting aspect is that he suggests such a change occurred in the context of an increasing secularization of knowledge:

> Universities appeared, on the one hand, whose equally slow and unstoppable nationalization replaced the production of books with that of writers, readers and bureaucrats. On the other hand, that Tower of Babel of books also emerged, whose thousands of identical pages had all the same

page numbers, and whose equally un-falsifiable illustrations put before the eyes that which the pages described.[163]

The idea of a partition between software and hardware that came about with the emergence of the printing press is related to the previously discussed ever-increasing technical abstraction. Although an interesting thought, it is debatable that the goal of the printing press was the embellishment of textbooks and not their identical reproduction. It would be perhaps more prudent to regard it as an effect; though there is a form of beauty in symmetry, of course, one akin to the "slick and clean" surfaces Gibson was targeting in his personal poetics. But the beauty of technical reproduction is derived from the main goal, the enhanced reproducibility of the objects in the automation of the modes of production enabled by standardization. Benjamin defined it as "aestheticization," a phenomenon that can be materially explained as a long process of gradual abstraction from contingency that ultimately decontextualizes the object from the tradition in which it was inserted in preindustrial, stereotypical artisan modes of production. Kittler, however, hints at the possibility of an auratic condition of the hand-copied books. The technically reproducible printed books lay the foundations of an aspiration to identicallity, which, in turn, builds the illusion of the existence of pure, unhistorical, ideal forms. The idea of embellishment in the printed book opposed to the hand-copied one goes in the direction of the decay in the aura of things, usually associated with unique handmade objects, but for the specific case of the materialization of texts. Aestheticization originates, thus, in the concurrence of two phenomena: the automation of the reproduction process and the standardization that affords it.

Agrippa intentionally moves in an opposite direction to that of the standardized textbooks discussed by Kittler. The images, which delete, relate to a text that is unreadable DNA code, and the digital text, the paradigm of standardized code (and that theoretically affords infinite identical reproductions), will be (again theoretically) lost after the first and only reading. The copies of *Agrippa* are handmade, each one different from the others, thus escaping the division that would allow, according to Kittler, the hardware and software split or, in other words, the separation of the work from its storage device that transforms it into pure content. Put differently, the *Agrippa* and "Agrippa" split. But in Gibson, Begos, and Ashbaugh's peculiar work, in the concretion of the book object and the abstraction of the code of the digital poem, such a split implies a mutilation of the work as a whole. That is a partial, either content biased or fetish biased, reading.

Technical Representations. The heterogeneity of *Agrippa* provides an excellent example of the confluence of different technical levels in its aesthetic effect. It could be said that it carries the "everything is text" post-structuralist trope beyond, into a more cyberpunk one, "everything is code." And code, unlike text, entails a form of automated technical or biological agency. In the case of DNA, that involves technical representations: the etchings are an artistic depiction of a scientific representation generated by a specific technology: gel electrophoresis. The same happens with the typographic representation of DNA code. However, it must be noted that these are not two different forms of representation of a single being. The gel electrophoresis that inspired Ashbaugh was extracted from the hair of an anonymous (human) collector.[164] The A, C, G, and T letters repeating in the pages of *Agrippa* correspond to a part of the genomic sequence of the Drosophila fly bicoid maternal morphogen.[165] However, both DNA sequences underpin the visual appeal of the code and the challenge to decode that *Agrippa* presents at all its different levels:

> *Agrippa*, as Gibson and Asbaugh [sic] initially conceived it, would be a futuristic scrapbook, vintage "twenty or thirty years in the future," whose DNA samples would allow one to reconstruct a complete personality—an idea, Begos notes, that Gibson had already been exploring in his fiction.[166]

Just as the encryption can be cracked to "reconstruct" the poem, in the material counterpart of the work, it is also implied that the DNA holds the possibility of "reconstructing" a life form.

In addition, illegibility renders the abstraction of code in a concrete form, drawing attention to its aesthetic, material qualities, in this case with the visual reference to the *Gutenberg Bible* in the two column layout, but also to the purity of forms of the chosen font, *Sans Gill*, also known as *Gill Sans MT*. Begos has declared this was an intended effect: "from typographical standpoint, type is always used to render words and sentences and it was interesting to me to put out a book [where] the typography is really purely visually [*sic*]."[167] Two aspects of the chosen typography illustrate the relationship between technics and storage. The *sans serif* fonts (that is, without lines attached to the end of a stroke in the letter characters) have become the *de facto* standard for on-screen digital text, because the fine details of the horizontal serifs may blink or pixelate, causing them either to disappear or look too thick. Printing on paper using a screen optimized font type is one of the many ironies in the design of *Agrippa*. The function of serifs in fonts is to *guide* the eye though lines of printed texts, while that of those without serif is to avoid eye fatigue on the screen by preventing pixel flickering. Using a letter without serifs on paper is an artistic decision with two different effects: first of all, it strips the letters of a technically and materially oriented conformation drawing them closer to pure forms (*sans serif* tend to simplicity) in order to present a *text* that is unreadable; second, it works as an aesthetic statement rather than as a text, to whose readability the serif would contribute. The "purely visual" typography pursued by Begos is a "signifier" devoid of the "signified" (following the division in the well-known Saussurean definition of "sign") and this is represented using paper, the normalized storage surface used to produce intelligible meaning on the book mechanism.

These details have not received much attention in the scholarly approaches to *Agrippa* and are a key issue to any informed discussion on the material realization of the book object and its auratic condition. In the same interview, Begos reveals that the choice of typography had a very specific connotation due to Gill's dark biography that would complement the sadness of Gibson's biographical poem. The creator of the homonymous type font was a member of the English Arts & Crafts movement[168] led by artist and writer William Morris, a partner of Dante Gabriel Rossetti, and also creator of Kelmscott Press, which was dedicated to luxury editions and artist books. Those hidden biographical references are Begos' veiled allusion to the crafts and trades involved in the production of objects where the community of artist's book makers take personal pride on their products, which had been overshadowed by the industrial modes of production: "The whole community of people, the craftspeople who produce this kind of thing, I think most of them would say there's a spiritual side to it."[169]

The editorial and artistic decisions not only reaffirm the auratic condition of the book object, they also refer to the long history of printed books, from the *Gutenberg Bible*–like two column layout to Eric Gill's *Monotype Sans* font, but stripping them of a readable textuality, the quintessential affordance of books. *Agrippa*, thus, represents pure forms albeit paradoxically, not by an abstraction generated from a technical device but through a conscious and planned referral to its concrete material manifestation, acknowledging the historicity of these forms by associating them to the figures of some of its most representative craftsmen, namely Gutenberg and Gill.

One of the recurrent topics related to technical representation is the tension between accumulation and oblivion, the difference between records and memories. One of the distinctive features of digital technologies is the increased possibility of deletion without destroying the storage devices that contributes to the illusion of the dematerialization of all records. But digital transmissibility and the possibilities of digitization of the various types of recording, as well as the miniaturization of the storage devices lay the grounds for the "myth of the technical register of everything." The threat posed by the overwhelming flow of decontextualized information that cannot be assimilated as experience is a recurrent fear in the age of the multiplication of information through technical reproducibility. This is not new. As Chartier notes, it has been there since the expansion of the printing press and the codex as the main storage device for culture. In fact in the foundational work of modern novels, *Don Quixote*, Cervantes deals with this as fundamental problem of his time.[170]

As discussed earlier, *Agrippa* proposes a return to unique non-transferable experience within a digital and material hybrid that incorporates different forms and periods of technical reproducibility: from hand printing to software programming, from poetry to typography, and from macromolecule analysis to the DNA sequencing. But a particular technical representation device provides conceptual unity to the poem: the photographic camera. And the representation of representation technologies is a recurring procedure common to the entire project. In the book object, Ashbaugh's etchings represent the scientific representation of the DNA. In "Agrippa," the ekphrastic verses represent photographic copies and on a material level, when executed, the software in the floppy disk represents the poem. This introduces a central topic in the work, the necessary technical mediation of art. The fruition of some technically generated works (i.e., music records, films, video games) demands its reproduction from a storage device that is inaccessible without a playing device. It is thus a form of representation that differs from the execution of a score or the staging of a play. In addition, it is also different from traditional storage means that hold the possibility of realization of the work *and* its material existence, as is the case of the canvas for painting or wood or stone for sculpture. In the photographic negative, the film, or the phonogram, there is no original but copies made from the first record (or the final cut, the master, the source). Film edit, code, and audio recording are the paradigms of this technical *mode of existence of works*.

Photographic representation is a key part of modern perception, in which the mediation of technical devices is characteristic. The photographic copy, however, has a fundamental difference. Once the copy is made, there is no need of a playing device. Its material condition places it at the crossroads between the probabilistic existence in the negative (which is also material), the potential execution of scores and dramatic texts, and the material uniqueness of traditional works of art. Photographic copies become objects with material existence whose sensory perception does not require technical execution once they are copied, just like printed books.

The most eloquent artistic examples of the specific materiality of photographic copies can be found in the already mentioned work of Kurtis: *Shoe Box* shows a series of family photos damaged by the passage of time.[171] As in *Agrippa*, family memories, associated with a home that has been left behind, illustrate a reflection on the disputes and negotiations between memory and technical representation. The photographs are the last family heirloom to survive repossessions and exiles caused by the two Argentine economic meltdowns of 1989 and 2001. When the family home and all they owned were seized, the only thing that the Kurtis family saved was a shoe box filled with photographs. The box was stored in the grandparents' house, which in turn, suffered a flood. The *Shoe Box* series comprises images of these photographs, family pictures that have undergone the wear and tear of water and time, but also of the backs of original photographs, in which the emulsions of other pictures have left their traces. Time and crises have turned these technically reproducible images into unique objects: the negatives have been lost and a digital scanning cannot wholly preserve them since in, their own rugged textures, they carry in themselves the marks of worldly existence.

Through deterioration, history is inscribed in the storage device creating a paradoxical auratic object that has been automatically produced. The artistic procedure resides in the curation of the family photos that enhances their auratic condition by placing them in the context of gallery and museum exhibitions. The topics of the images are common to most twentieth century urban middle classes: the parents' wedding, family holidays, religious celebrations, the first family car, newborn children, grandparents with grandchildren, public school events, and the local team championship celebrations. Although the images refer to the past, deterioration marks prevent nostalgia. Opposed to the aestheticization of the past typical of retro aesthetics, the images in *Shoe Box* present the torn images of a happy time. The curation focuses on the materiality of copies. The backs, where parts of other images have adhered, show the object *photographic copy* as signifier in itself and not only as empty surface for the signified to be inscribed. The backs reveal texts and logos signaling the industrial origin of papers ("Made in Buenos Aires by Kodak," "AGFA quality paper made in Germany") but also the traces of a developers trade associated with small family owned shops that has been almost lost today ("Víctor's Photostudio").

Technically reproducible copies are inscribed in the context of family history: the memory is not only what the photos depict but also the invocation of the textures of different photographic papers, the logos on the back of the copies and photo development as a traditional practice linked to small shops. The gesture of displaying the back of the copies provides the objects with a historical dimension that otherwise might be considered just frozen moments of the past, memories saved by technology. And being stained by other images bestows them a specific historicity absent in the *normal* copies where the back would not be a meaningful topic possible to represent. Time passing turns technically reproduced records into auratic objects. By becoming unique, their negatives long lost or destroyed, these photographs speak not only of the immortalized moments (the content), but of their own physical existence (the container), such as the book of Gibson's dead relatives.

The "fall" of the shutter that divides this from that is a metaphor of a three part division. Although in the poem the shutter "falls," shutters actually do not, and diaphragms "close."[172] But the guillotinesque idea of a mechanical cut, definitive as death, is strengthened by Gibson's choice of words. What matters is, in any case, the idea of a three part division caused by the act of taking a picture. First, the depicted materiality that continues to exist in the world; second, the captured instant; and, third, the photographic copy (which is only a potential existence inscribed in the negative) that, once it is copied, begins to exist (and age) as an object. We can thus recognize three different times at stake: the *moment* that has been frozen; the *future* that came after that past moment, which is known or can be known (that is to say, that can be dated and inserted in a chronology); and the time that sediments on the photographic copy as an object, in which memory moves from personal experience towards the physical degradation of the storage device. This kind of organized matter is what Stiegler calls exteriorization and it is ultimately responsible for the very idea of "time" as I discussed extensively in chapter one. Benjamin did not think much of the problem of the physical existence of copies (the eventual auratization process by becoming unforeseen unique objects), but he did notice the particular temporality that the act of capturing an instant with technical automated devices created, the "tiny spark of contingency, of Here and Now,"[173] the interlocking of location and time. As he noted, the nature that speaks to the camera is different from that speaking to the eye because through the mediation of the photographic device the unconsciously constituted space is replaced by one created by human consciousness. John Berger has also discussed this discontinuity in the relationship between memory and photography:

> A photograph preserves a moment of time and prevents it from being effaced by the supersession of moments. In this respect photographs might be compared with the images stored in the memory. Yet there is a fundamental difference: whereas the remembered images are the *residue* of continuous experience, a photograph isolates the appearances of a disconnected instant.[174]

However, with digitization, the image of an instant is released from its indexical ties of fidelity to reality, which is trapped in the materiality of the storage device, escaping to the afterlife of code mutations and purely synthetic images.

Indexicality is thus another feature that photographs share with other analog technical records such as film or pre-digital phonography. In analog reproduction technologies, that which is represented derives from an index, the trace of a material existence captured by the inscription on the storage device. Through the development of simulation and synthesizing, digital images and sounds can be entirely artificial with no indexical relation to things existing in reality. While mechanical reproducibility was fundamentally indexical during the nineteenth century and most of the twentieth, digital reproducibility does not need to be. In addition, today there are no more family albums whose negatives are lost but inscriptions on a hard drive that obsolescence may render inaccessible except for media archaeologists. Furthermore, deep down in the hard drive, there will be only image and video files each *belonging* in multiple albums based on what their metadata specifies. The images do not exist in a given location but rather they are realized in different locations by means of their tags. Put technically, the same file can be retrieved from different contexts. Put ghastly, images can be summoned at will.

Digital Reproducibility and Circulation. Benjamin did not foresee the development of digital technologies and, especially, one of its most groundbreaking implications: the aspiration to over-coming the materiality of storage. Book, phonograms, photograph-ic copies and film reels are all exposed to existence in time due to their unavoidable material nature that reproduction seeks to preserve. There are two ways of differentiation for identical works under industrial technical reproduction regimes: (a) *particular wear* (i.e., stains or scratches) that sets the copy apart from the series as a material entity bearing in itself the marks of the passage of time, but at the expense of limiting or eliminating the possibility of an adequate reproduction; or (b) *fetishization*, either through the signature of the author, a process that had already occurred with books, or by the process of auratic degradation as exemplified by Kurtis' *Shoe Box*.

Digital technology is a different stage in reproduction since the degradation regarding the original is minimal and imperceptible due to the detachment of contents from media specific material storage devices (at least in the ideal conditions of fidelity that are not the current *de facto* lossy compression standards for digital circulation). The renewed cult of collections is thus encouraged by cultural industries as a response to pirate circulation of copies (a trend also foreseen in the design of the *Agrippa* project). Since the popularization of digital technologies, piracy has enhanced, rather than undermined, the distinctive feature that previous technical reproduction industries (the publishing houses, the record labels and the film companies) had introduced. Digital piracy not only has works meeting the audience wherever it may be as in early analog reproducibility, it has them doing so for free (or at least with enhanced accessibility). And that has game-changing implica-tions for art as a technically reproducible commodity.

The material-digital hybridity of *Agrippa* staged a novel form of oscillation between exhibition and cult values in its various modes of circulation: as an artistic object, exposed in cultural centers, galleries and museums, emphasizing its auratic condition, but also as code in the early BBS, and then on the World Wide Web. *Agrippa* oscillates between the book object, a unique artisan-al product, and as pure text, non-established and subject to the dispersion and instability of digital existence. But both modes of existence are dynamic: (a) the object due to its uniqueness and artifactual disposition devised for degradation, and (b) the code due to its mutability.

Family Crypts. There are only four copies of *Agrippa* available for consultation on special collections: the Bodleian at Oxford University, the Rare Books Division in the New York Public Library, the University of Western Michigan Library, and the collection of the Victoria and Albert Museum. The Frances Mulhall Achilles Library of the Whitney Museum of American Art has a copy of the promotional "Prospectus" of *Agrippa*. Also there is mention of copies in the hands of private collectors such as Peter Schwenger[175] and Allan Chasanoff.[176] The object *Agrippa* has also been exhibited in cultural centers and museums: at the Center for Book Arts in New York in a presentation on April 23, 1993; at the Gallery and Museum of Florida State University between March 5 and April 10, 1994; as a part of the exhibition "The Book and Beyond" in 1995 at the Victoria and Albert Museum in London; at an exhibition for the launching of *The Agrippa Files* website at the University of California Santa Barbara on December 1, 2005;[177] and in a retrospective of Ashbaugh's work in the Instituto Valenciano de Arte Moderno between September 24 and November 18, 2007.[178] An unknown number of copies, but less than a hundred, are supposed to exist in private collections, actual crypts where it lies, perhaps with other works as peculiar as this.

The first presentation of *Agrippa* at the Americas Society of New York on December 9, 1992, which replaced the failed artistic happening planned for "The Transmission," stands apart from the others. The presentation was not only a projection of the execution of the file in the floppy disk that performed the auratization through technical means; it was also where the cracking of the poem (but not of the code) occurred. The succession of events related to *Agrippa* between December 9 and 10, 1992, are a rare example of how a handcrafted auratic object, one of the first e-literature works, the logics of museum exhibition, and those of digital circulation may converge. The presentation of *Agrippa* in the context of the art world was followed, almost immediately, by the digital dissemination of "Agrippa."

As I have noted in the previous chapters, the self-destruction process of "Agrippa" implies a new form of auratization from within technical reproduction technologies. The photographs and gel electrophoresis are visual representations. The DNA sequencing and the software are, on the other hand, codifications. The code is a central issue in the work, both in *Agrippa* and "Agrippa," that is, in its digital and material manifestations. The digital part also highlights the role of a fourth participant in the project who is not widely considered as an author in most of the literature or bibliographic descriptions, the anonymous programmer "Brash." In the case of the digital poem, the code is of special importance not solely for what it denotes but for its agency, for the generation of an unusually limited reproducibility. The self-destruction mechanism has several aspects worth addressing. As said earlier, it inscribes *Agrippa* in a long tradition of ephemeral works, thus generating a new auratization and dismantling the implicit content dynamics stimulated by cultural industries. But, within the hacker subculture spurred by the participation of Gibson in the project, the limitation of the digital circulation was an incentive to "release" it.

In reality, the process of self-destruction implies concealment rather than effacement. The interpretations of Liu and Kirschenbaum, later rebutted by DuPont, along with some misunderstandings regarding the software of the digital poem disseminated the idea that "Agrippa" was a self-encrypting poem. Though inaccurate, that interpretation has come to be a significant part of how *Agrippa* has been received. The idea of encrypting a book "of the dead" is suggestive, to say the least, since it literally means placing it in a crypt. If the photographic image preserves still images of the past, familiar faces of those who are no more, the encryption works in a similar way, as the presence of an absence. Both book and file need to be "open," as is announced in the hesitation of the first lines of the poem ("before untying the bow / that bound this book together," vv. 2–3). The imbrications between topic and code are summarized in the first reaction to the object in the poem, the poetic persona before the Kodak Agrippa photo album that is a book of the dead. The hesitation before opening the album corresponds to that of the readers before executing the file, knowing that it will be the only time that they will be able to read the poem. In the original project, the creators of *Agrippa* also envisaged the slow pressure of obsolescence, the ephemeral condition of the technological storage itself, the disk, which depended on associated devices and contexts that would inevitably become increasingly scarce. "Agrippa" was meant to disappear, either by file corruption if the file was executed or by obsolescence if it was not, by the changes in the digital milieu in which the digital object existed (the operating system for which it was programmed) but also by the changes in the technical milieu (the hardware that could read the disk).

The Body Snatchers. The foreseeable destiny of digital degradation was overshadowed by the swift cracking of "Agrippa"[179] and the almost immediate dissemination of the poem in the BBS of the time. The book was presented on December 9 at the Americas Society and on December 10 it was already posted in the MindVox BBS. If, as discussed previously, the alleged "Agrippa" encryption algorithms were interpreted as the onset of DRM, devised to limit digital circulation,[180] the cracking of the program by "Brash" that displayed Gibson's poem, can also be thought of as a milestone in the history of digital piracy. Obviously there were other examples of digital piracy at the time, mostly associated with commercial software and video games. However, the circulation of unauthorized copies associated with the *works as contents* described in chapter four did not exist at the time. The .mp3 audio compression format was released in 1993 and its massive use for the circulation of music would take five more years, with the advent of Napster in 1999. However, the 1992 cracking of *Agrippa* included several forms that would later be prototypical of illegalized digital circulation. What is more striking is that these forms are not only linked to the unauthorized circulation of texts, but that they anticipate other forms as well, especially those associated with the film industry. No vault was open to break "Agrippa." Instead, an analog cracking was performed. A pair of technicians was hired to capture the computer monitor where the floppy disk was executed and project it on a drop-down screen so that the public at the Americas Society could read the verses of the poem. While at it, they introduced a videotape in the camera used to capture the monitor and pressed the REC button. With this analog audiovisual recording, after the presentation of *Agrippa*, they went home, played the tape, typed the text of the poem from the TV screen to a computer and then uploaded it to MindVox BBS under the alias of Templar, Rosehammer, and Pseudophred.

The above mentioned *perception in a state of attention* is not, thus, the only aspect linking "Agrippa" with early cinematic experiences. Its cracking is probably the first example of camrip such as the ones that thrived on *Pirate Bay* and other pages that distribute unauthorized digital contents, by providing movie footage just a few hours after a movie premieres (sometimes with the shadowed figures of a few actual spectators sitting in front).[181] Strange by-products of the cultural industries, these extremely information lossy rips, in formats like .avi or .mp4, are one of the typical forms of viral dissemination of works on the web.

The redigitization of "Agrippa" is also peculiar when compared to text digitization discussed in chapter three. It is the only digitization by typing of a digital text that I am aware of (besides the fact that the text has been copied from a screen rather than from a book or manuscript). The typing also explains another important feature of the circulation of "Agrippa." In the technological context of the day, bandwidth did not allow the traffic of large files. As a text file in ASCII format, "Agrippa" spread easily through the BBS, mailing lists, newsgroups, and other network services of the time.[182]

In a BBS post immediately after "Agrippa" surfaced online, Anthony Garcia suggested that the cracking encouraged by the creators project was not actually an intervention on the device but the exact opposite, the fulfillment of the role foreseen for the hackers by the project creators, and therefore *Agrippa* should be understood as performance art rather than an art object.[183] Garcia's interpretation is very interesting, not only because it was posted immediately after "Agrippa" disseminated, but because of some aspects he takes into consideration that have not been further pursued in later commentaries of the work. The text was published in the *Future Culture* mailing list on December 16, 1992, seven days after the presentation of *Agrippa* at the Americas Society and six after the digital circulation of the poem began. This text is not a consolidated reference in relation to the work, and for this reason it deserves to be quoted extensively:

> However, I do not think that "the impermanence of memories" is the true theme of "Agrippa".
>
> I believe the real purpose of "Agrippa" is to be a dynamic, "performance art" demonstration of the "Information wants to be free" concept, performed by 1.) Gibson & company, 2.) crackers (who do not necessarily understand that they are "performing" in the piece!), and 3) The Net.
>
> The "objet" [*sic*] which the disk is encased in is a reference to the copy-protection "dongles" that accompany some software packages, and the "dongle effect" provided by traditional publishing of paper books: every "official" copy of the information is tied to a physical piece of "hardware". Thus, the entire "Agrippa" package represents the concept of pure information, buoyed upwards by its (supposed) innate "desire to be free", yet "chained down" by archaic and ultimately-ineffective hardware and software-based attempts to assert ownership and control-of-access over it.
>
> "Agrippa" is not officially a cracker-challenge, yet it obviously is one: the goal is to successfully capture the text of the poem (written by one of your favorite authors, mind you.) in unprotected/freely-copyable electronic form. Extra points if you actually defeat the software mechanisms on the disk, as opposed to merely transcribing (crude & styleless, possibly information-lossy, but effective) the text as it scrolls past.
>
> By implicitly issuing this cracker-challenge (and arranging the "protection" scheme so that it's not *too* hard to defeat), Gibson ensures that his cracker fans will take the text and "wideband" it through their favorite Net hangouts: bulletin boards, mailing lists, Usenet newsgroups, FTP sites, gopherspaces, IRC channels, etc.
>
> Thus, the performance art aspect: "Agrippa" is released, and just like predictable clockwork automatons (no offense, crackers; how could you have restrained yourselves? I couldn't have.) one or more crackers goes to work, defeating the "protection" and uploading the unprotected text to one or more points on the Net. Maybe the cracker realizes that Gibson *wants* him to do this; it's more sweet, though (and more style points for Gibson), if the cracker actually believes that he is "breaking" the author's supposed intention to keep the information under control.[184]

Even without knowing the specific details of the self-destruction program, Begos' tenure in the editorial trade and all the documentation on the project that exists today, Garcia detected fundamental aspects that set the work apart from other cultural production in the digital context of the time. He suggests that the main topic of *Agrippa* is not so much memory as information and its impulse towards freedom, much in tone with the hacker subculture. While print or photographic records are associated with death by their static and permanent nature, codified records are more akin to living entities, due to their mutable, ephemeral, and reproductive conditions. One of the most innovative features of digital abstraction is precisely its capacity to be manipulated and the instability that this introduces in cultural entities. In response to this, DRM systems were the first attempts to constrain digital circulation using software.[185]

Secondly, Garcia emphasizes the performative aspect of the project. The role played by the hackers in *Agrippa* would not be a Flusserian intervention on the device; instead it would have been foreseen by "Gibson and Cia," turning to so-called free agents in hacker culture into "predictable clockwork automatons." From this perspective, the book presentation event that replaced "The Transmission" was not a performance in itself, but a part of a broader performance that is the project *Agrippa* as a whole, including the anticipation of the file cracking.

Finally, in relation to the cracking, Garcia indicates the existence of different levels regarding what I have called modes of digitization and digital derivations. Typing as text scrolls over the screen is effective but information lossy, rudimentary, and "styleless"; on the other hand, introducing a playful dimension, the deciphering of the code will be a more valuable cracking. In the first type of cracking, misprints are to be expected, as well as incorrect tabulation and line breaks, and this last aspect does have special importance regarding the typographic representation of a poem, especially a free verse one. The anticipation of this fact is a key element for *Agrippa* to become a milestone in digital art and literature: the network. Once it has been cracked it is expected that *Agrippa* will circulate as a plain text file precisely in the net "hangouts." This playful dimension has been reintroduced by DuPont when noting the positive impact "gamification" may have on digital humanities.[186] The challenge of cracking is also the polar opposite to the distracted labor generated by Google's reCAPTCHA program, an immediate input devoid of meaning.

Viral dissemination would have been impossible in the case of *Afternoon* in the same technological context due to the complexity of the work and the size of the files it involved. The hypernovel was remedied for newer operating systems and for a web version, but always contained within the parameters of the authorized circulation.[187]

Another distinctive feature of *Agrippa* setting it apart from the rest of digital literature is its storage and code interlocking, the transit that goes from the self-destruction software on a diskette to the online text file. Self-destruction is a paradoxical resource: it generates a recovery of the aura in a "print" work while referring both to the history of the book as well as the discourses about its disappearance in the digital context. In addition, in the same movement it also issues a challenge to the established circulation of works as mere reproducible goods presenting it as a fetish for the hacker subculture that was the avant-garde of the then nascent digitization of culture. These seemingly contradictory effects introduce a political dimension in the work that is not a mere declamatory position but the realization of an unprecedented mechanism of self-destruction *and* dissemination. The mechanism challenges two cultural logics: that of the object as a commodity that had organized the cultural industry of the twentieth century, but also that of the content idealism of the medial ideology governing the authorized circulation of works in the digital context.

The material-digital imbrications of *Agrippa* possess a double meaning: on the one hand, the process of data ciphering; on the other, the book as a tomb in whose niche the disk lies. And in the file within the disk, the photo album of the poem as a book of the dead reappears. The connotations are reinforced by the genetic allusions. Both the serialization of DNA and the gel electrophoresis are representations of life. As Chartier points out paraphrasing Quevedo, books allow us to "listen to the dead with our eyes."[188] In the same way, Benjamin claimed, photographic portraits are the last refuge of humanity, where the eyes of the dead still hold an aura at the time of photography as a fair trade. *Agrippa* restages, thus, a metaphor that has crossed the history of Western culture: the book and the photographic copy (text and image) as retentions of the past that preserve the voice and the look of the dead, or, in other words the inevitable relationship between death and memory storage devices.[189] According to Kirschenbaum, data preservation devices are ultimately related to death, or at least to the suspension of life, and therefore associated with the "the uncanny, the unconscious, the dead."[190] In contrast to the storage of information, its transmission involves life, by allowing multiplication, but also, mutation.

Digital Hronirs. Jorge Luis Borges' fantastic short story "Tlön, Uqbar, Orbis Tertius"[191] tells the amazing discovery of a fictional world that starts pervading the real world. In the story, a character named Borges realizes that for centuries a secret society of intellectual conspirators has developed a fictional world, Tlön, with its own history and philosophy and they are slowly instilling it into our real world. This is carefully executed by subtle means as the insertion of mentions to parts of Tlön in encyclopedia entries and scattered articles in popular magazines. Eventually the character comes by an apocryphal book, *A First Cyclopedia of Tlön. Vol. XI. Hlaer to Jangr.* One of its entries discusses the peculiar idealism that rules Tlön and introduces the following situation, typical of the duplication of lost objects: Two persons are looking for a pencil. The first finds it and does not say anything, and then the second person also finds a second pencil that is as real as the other, but closer to the second person's expectations. Such secondary, derived, objects, in the imaginary world of Tlön are called *hronir* and are "a little longer." The short story ends with the character Borges retreating from daily life slightly troubled before the increasing intrusion of imaginary objects of Tlön into the physical world, and the imaginary languages of Tlön slowly taking over the real languages. The story could be read as a metaphor of the reproduction of things and thoughts, or, as Stiegler would put it, of the exteriorizations that co-constitute humans and technics. In the short story, a fellow writer of the character misquotes the apocryphal words of one of the heresiarchs of Uqbar, an ancient realm of Tlön, claiming he had stated that copulation and mirrors are abominable because they multiply the number of men. Digital culture implies a somewhat similar form of replication and slow pervasion. And as Ferrer acutely noted, one of the most distinctive effects of *Agrippa* is that it purges us from the excess of information.[192] Or, if I may rephrase it, from the ever accelerating replication of things.

Digital reproducibility of literary and artistic works was slowly gaining speed when *Agrippa* was published. But this stage of digital culture did not yet involve the reappropriation and dissemination practices that would expand since the mid-nineties with P2P networks, filesharing, social networks, and other forms of file downloading. However, the text of the poem "Agrippa" was one of the first cases of an online meme, although it did not come to be very successful in terms of fertility, as I will discuss later. I will follow here the concept of meme according to the classification proposed by Knobel and Lankshear, presented in chapter four, to deal with new literary forms in digital culture.

As I noted in the previous section, the book object *Agrippa* was released on December 9, 1992. The surfacing of the cracked text in the MindVox BBS occurred a day later (although it was detected by a user on December 11) and finally "Templar" claimed in a brief post the action in the following day.[193] In the following weeks some parodic copies, which could be considered proto online memes, surfaced. There were different versions on how the text of the poem "Agrippa" was "freed," and there were extensive debates on whether it was an analog cracking or leak in the sense discussed earlier. As for "Agrippa" as a meme, it should be noted that it was subject of discussion in other BBS such as ECHO BBS in New York months before its online appearance. In part it may have been caused by the influence of the previous narrative work of Gibson in the conformation of the hacker subculture imaginary and the concept of cyberspace, as well as by the expectation generated by a digital approach to his writing, an approach perceived as formally more akin to his poetics than the traditional publication of his novels and stories in printed books and magazines. The BBS of that time often constituted a local phenomenon, and since many of their members lived in the same area, face-to-face meetings occurred, partly coinciding, in this case, with the editorial and artistic scenes in which the project *Agrippa* was created.

Perhaps unwillingly, and beyond having anticipated the cracking, *Agrippa* was an artistic event that encouraged its memes, some of which are still online. The nature of the work, with the multiple possible readings of the concept of DNA as metaphor for encoding life and of experience mediated by technical devices, as well as the predicament of Gibson in the hacker subculture, implicitly spurred the breaking of the misunderstood "self-encryption code" that would make the work inaccessible after its first reading. The first meme appears in a series of postings attributed to "Scotto" as part of a discussion with an alleged "William Gibson"[194]:

> AGRIPPA
> (A Book of The Dead)
> Text by William Gibson and Scotto
> All Rights Reserved At 7 PM tomorrow night; we have your favorite table...
>
> I hesitated
> before untying the bow
> that bound this book together.
>
> Then I decided,
> why the hell not,
> it cost me a couple hundred dollars.
>
> A Kodak album of time-burned
> black construction paper
>
> Like the stuff I used
> to do in kindergarten art
> only without all the Elmer's glue
>
> ---->
>
> Ah, skip it, it sure ain't worth it now. Anyhow, I hear *Kroupa* (trumpet fanfare) beat me to it...[195]

Almost simultaneously, a second parodic version titled "AGR1PPA (A Book of The Mentally Disturbed)" was posted, remitting to the typos of the first filtered version and proposing an alternative version of the full text. It was written by , a hacker and one of the administrators of MindVox, under the pseudonym "US@phantom.com." This version referred to the origins of data processing and other products of the cultural industry:

> I waited
> before unlocking the clasp,
> that bound my mind together

a black box:

VOICES
(in the mInd)
To create greater order
rhyme or reason,
        take 2 Haldol & call me in the morning. [196]

There is notice of another meme posted by "Zorgo" in the Future Culture BBS on December 21 that went "1 HESiTated / bEf0Re tHe B0w unty1ng / tHAt B0uNd th1s B () 0 K t0g3th3r"[197] but that today is unavailable on the web. Unlike the parodic versions of "Scotto" and Kroupa, this version suggests a challenge to intellectual property using a typographic reformulation that mimics the text based on visual similarities, while also questioning standardization. In sum, an unaware form of what I have called *unaddressability*. This was a practice typical of the hacker subculture in the early nineties often used later on to circumvent automated copyright enforcement in file sharing programs such as Napster by changing the music album titles, making them recognizable to humans but undetectable to early crawler bots.

"Agrippa" did not generate a successful meme, following the fertility criteria assumed by Knobel and Lankshear.[198] But in the case of *Agrippa*, its memes do present the characteristics of fidelity to the original, and of longevity, due in part to digital conservation by organizations that were involved in some way with the project, as in the case of the Electronic Frontier Foundation, which had allegedly provided Begos with legal advice. Because of its length and complexity "Agrippa" is not easily memorable and therefore it did not generate many variants, but the mutability implicit in the commented versions shows a rapid initial dissemination. Undoubtedly, part of its longevity may have been caused by the documentary work carried out by the existent scholarly research, something not usually present in the majority of memes. Furthermore, this might have also limited its memetic dissemination potential by establishing the text and debugging the versions with variations or errata.

The presence of *Agrippa* in the media is an element considered by Knobel and Lankshear in their definition of "successful" memes; that is, those that achieve wide dissemination, transcending their original context, something that did not finally occur in this case. The originality of the initial project and the fame of the author of the poem motivated mentions of *Agrippa* in the media; but the cracking and the memes of the text were not reported by the media (or it cannot be corroborated today on the web through search engines). However, the memes of "Scotto," Kroupa, and "Zorgo" give us a glimpse of the special cultural context in which "Agrippa" was produced and its role within the nascent scene of digital literature.

The medium where these particular memes were disseminated, the BBS, was a too narrow affinity group for the "Agrippa" memes to spread massively. However, the "self-destructive book" as the idea has permeated many discussions since the universalization of digital reproduction. The poem was coded in ASCII, thus its replicability was simple although media-general techniques such as "copy and paste" were not yet a common affordance of the operative systems of the time. There is, however, a fourth non-textual meme, the experimental video *re:Agrippa* produced by those that accomplished the cracking.[199] Originally intended to mimic *Agrippa*'s self-destructive feature using malfunctioning playback devices,[200] the video is actually more a meme from the project *Agrippa* rather than a meme from the poem. As an audiovisual product it is closer to the music video-clips of the day and some elementary experimental video resources. Its little transcendence as a meme might also be related to the technological conditions of the time, when mass digital video file circulation was yet to be invented.

Summarizing the debates regarding *Agrippa*, this chapter discussed the different technical and artistic traditions it questioned, its place in the oeuvre of Gibson, the trajectories of the other collaborators, the critical and social reception of the work. I also argued against some assertions made by the existing scholarly research on the work based on the need for a holistic approach in order to provide an informed interpretation of the work, its technical dimension, and its relations with other cultural phenomena and some possible genealogies. The aesthetics of *Agrippa* can be traced in the intertwinement of contents and containers, the negotiations between abstraction and concretion, and the referrals to "high" and "popular" cultures, in the implication of digital, industrial, and artisan production, ultimately allowing an interpretation of its underlying politics. I expect this recontextualization will provide a deeper understanding of Gibson, Ashbaugh, and Begos' strange artifact, its importance for digital culture and how it was an early example of the many (and conflicting) forms of existence in the digital milieu.

EPILOGUE
Hybrid Genealogies in Digital Culture

Negotiations between Matter and Digits

...Teu orgulho parece o rapa
não olha me do jeito que sou.
-Edilson Moreno, "Camelô"

The reproduction of art as a commodity has been at the heart of discussions around cultural industries since their origins. From Benjamin's insight on the deep cultural meaning of the nineteenth century Parisian arcades to what can be thought of the blankets where street vendors used to exhibit their "counterfeited" CDs at the beginnings of the twenty-first, one problem remains: the evasive ontology of copies. And it is not only about works (of literature or art), it is about, as I argued in the introduction to this book, that the very dynamics of replication is the central aspect of technics, and therefore, of humanity. Humankind begins when replicable exteriorization begins. Perhaps among those things occurring outside ourselves, a portrait or a poem, appear to be of a different kind than, say, a horseshoe or a transmission box. My claim is that these are all signs of our technical ontology, and that as reproduction technologies accelerate, so does humanity. And one of the key elements to understand the importance of *Agrippa* for digital culture, a culture based on the reproducibility of abstractions but also on the agency such abstractions possess, are the artifactual aspects of the work. That *Agrippa* is, among many other things, a *device* links it with traditions other than literature or the arts, establishing some relations with tools and games.

The fact that *Agrippa* came with "instructions for use" inserts it into a long tradition of pre-digital experimental works that require a number of very specific conditions for their actual perception.[1] Or, in the terms of philosophy of technology, it places *Agrippa* in the demand that technical objects have for a specific associated milieu in order to exist as such. Instructions for use draw attention to the *deviceness*, whether of the book or the floppy disk, breaking the illusion of transparent storage devices and the idealism of pure contents. The need for instructions is also indicative of a rupture with the operational standards that rule the established technical reproducibility and products of the cultural industries. After a short time no one needed to be told which the upper side of a compact disc was. Once incorporated in the usual and expected procedures, storage devices lose their opacity.

Instructions for use were a constitutive element of specific digital works such as complex video games during the eighties and early nineties. With time, game play became more transparent: novelty was assimilated by the gradual introduction of innovations in the game narrative itself, under the form of a progressively increasing difficulty, and by the so-called in game tutorials. Computer game buyers in the early nineties would usually buy a box with one or several diskettes, some key sets to secure intellectual property and limit unauthorized copying, a handbook, and other sundries.[2] Today all this is digitized and included within the same work, similarly to what has happened with books or DVDs. This makes the affordances of the storage devices obsolete, and the instructions become transparent, a part of the work itself.

Something *a priori* trivial as the instructions for use shows the tensions between storage devices and contents that determine the material and artifactual condition of early digital works. Now outdated, the different material anticopy protections were a dynamic example of the disputes for the access and property of culture that digital reproducibility introduced in the realms of cultural industries. But these protections also signal some continuity between digital representation and representation on a print storage device.

As the gaming industry and digital piracy developed (the later would grow exponentially with the .mp3 format), software protections became one of the most common ways to enforce the use of certified copies (or "originals," in the marketing and collectors jargon). At the beginning a simple serial number or key that came in the product box sufficed. Then this was bypassed by the practice of including that information in separate files in pirate copies. To avoid it, and in tune with the games' growing complexity, packages evolved to include extra information in the manuals and ask the user to look there to gain access to the game. Subsequently, such information began to be requested at different stages, integrating into the game narrative, generating a remission to the materiality of the handbook from the digital code. Scanning images took up too much storage space (i.e., extra floppy disks), it was it not a widespread hardware, and multitasking was not usually afforded by the computers of the time. The obvious response was, as Gibson's Johnny Mnemonic would put it, "going crude": crackers started photocopying. The gaming industry countermove was producing manuals on dark papers that prevented black and white photocopying. Another option was the creation of artifacts that hid the keys, such as the code wheels of the first installments of the *Monkey Island* graphic adventure series. In turn the wheels would be reproduced by taking the trouble of disarming them, photocopying, clipping, cutting, and joining the copies using a butterfly clip.[3] Discussing this seemingly trivial history regarding *Agrippa* is not arbitrary, as evidenced by some discussions in the BBS in the days just after the cracking. User "citrus!vector0!jon@csusac.ecs.csus. edu" suggested that "[IBM warez k00l dudes seem to like "cracking" games these days which don't even have so much as codewheel protection!] [Anyone remember Spiradisk, and all the fakesync nasties of "the good ol' days"?]."[4] The constant negotiations between matter and digits to prevent unauthorized reproduction have led to extreme cases, almost absurd, such as the *lenslok*, a plastic device with a prism that allowed users to see a code on the screen. The device obviously enough did not work well on all screens (it did not make a standard) and it was discontinued, but still offers an eloquent example of the overlapping between storage devices, content, and reproduction devices.[5]

There were also other peculiar devices that allowed displaying the keys to access the programs, or to continue to use them after a certain point in the game narrative, such as a red slide viewer of the *Indiana Jones and the Last Crusade* game that allowed the player to read a code printed in blue ink to avoid photocopying. In addition to these objects, the packages of authorized copies added other objects, for instance, an abridged version of the *Diary* of Henry Jones, Sr., the MacGuffin in the homonymous film. The *Diary* was also necessary to solve some of the riddles presented by the game.[6] The inclusion of such non-digital objects also entailed an accessory low level fetishization of the "original" copies, that were, of course, a cultural industry reproducible commodity. "Original" copies gained a collectable and cult object status, enhanced by the sensation of dematerialization that digital copying introduced. Any kid can tell you the difference of appeal between a glossy hard-cardboard box containing the disk and other fancy-looking miscellanea *vis-à-vis* a black disk with hand-written labels and a clipped bunch of blurry xeroxed pages.

Another example of the attempts to limit the unauthorized digital circulation of code is the so-called dongles, hardware plug-in pieces that allow authorized software execution. In that context, dongles operate as material anchors to the sea bottom of the intellectual property against the menacing tides of dematerialization by drifting into free code. While these devices still exist as USB pendrives, they are now more associated with specialized and very expensive commercial software. Video game companies, on the other hand, have thrived in a model of integration with the hardware. That is the case of the gaming consoles (such as Nintendo's Wii, Sony's PlayStation, or Microsoft's Xbox) sometimes combined with an authorization of use of the copy via authentication over the Internet, a model similar to the one chosen by Amazon with the Kindle eBook reader. This kind of practice is relevant since it was the background from which a project as *Agrippa* emerged. (And in doing so it generated a controversy regarding ownership, preservation, and use of the works.)[7]

There is another significant affordance of the digital copy restriction technologies. In some games, when the program detected that it was an illegal copy it executed a limited version or "demo mode." What drives technical decisions like this is the interest for profit, assuming that the main interest of the player is to reach the end of the game: conclusiveness is one of the most decisive features of video games as a narrative, the teleological nature of their overwhelming majority. But there was also a variant of the "demo mode" that resembles the self-destruction process of "Agrippa": games that executed an unplayable version when illegal copying was detected. It was the case of *Starflight* that sent invincible police ships to destroy the ship controlled by the player, or *Superior Soccer* that turned the ball invisible for the human players, making it impossible to win.[8] The invisible ball and self-destroying text can be considered extreme digital representations of DRM and other ways to retain the property over copies. However, the self-destruction mechanism in *Agrippa* can also be interpreted more as a challenge and an aesthetic decision than as a business strategy in a cultural industry that was reacting to the crisis introduced by digitization.

Using literal "hands-on" procedures and physical tools over the materiality of storage devices in unauthorized reproduction was frequent in the hacker subculture in the period (and in culture in general as evidenced by practices such as using adhesive tape to allow re-recording over an pre-recorded cassette storage, rewinding tapes with a pen to avoid eating batteries, perforating 5¼-inch floppy disks to afford data inscription on both sides, etc.). This becomes evident in the analog cracking of "Agrippa" that released it for digital circulation, but also in the dual nature and the material counterpart that completes *Agrippa*.

Works, Storage, and Code

Summarizing the discussions developed throughout this book, I hope the detours and back roads I have taken to *Agrippa* provide new insight on the hybrid nature of digital culture and the materiality inherent to digital products.

The idea of "work" has always been slippery. This book cannot (nor expects to) close that debate. I would only like to note that it has ties to several overlapping technologies and temporalities. A form of exteriorization and one of the earliest examples of humanity, from the first sketches on a cave wall onwards, artistic productions have stood apart or made stand apart. (Take your pick based on the concepts of technics and aesthetics you may ascribe to). My claim is that artistic works that exist as inscriptions on a materiality oscillate between growing levels of abstraction and the affordances of the material storage devices. As already pointed out in the first chapter, reproducible exteriorization deters death and preserves works beyond the life of its creators; exteriorization creates time, evading the tyranny of now by placing a bet in the *tomorrowness* of things. Digital culture takes the bet further by detaching inscriptions from the historical existence of storage devices, and making them multiply realizable abstractions. This is, by no means, innocuous. All technologies are opaque, more or less explicitly all bear the marks of their own materiality, and none is substanceless.

Digital culture studies should, therefore, consider the technical genealogies at stake in order to produce a form of cultural criticism that acknowledges the specificities of each technology in particular cultural products and phenomena, and also of the general dynamics of technics. That is, a form of criticism that incorporates the political dimension of any technology and challenges the notion of digital forms as neutral and transparent. The debates over the ownership and use of copies are just one of the many examples of the politics of technics. As exemplified by the axial work in this book, such critical and historical approaches to technology are necessarily linked to personal biographies, suggesting, ultimately, that the constitution of *new subjectivities* is deeply intertwined with technical change; or put differently, of *new objectivities*. Cultural products, from something as apparently unbound as the verses of a poem to something as bound as the printed pages in a book, are oscillations indicative of the co-constitution of humanity and technics. Ontological oscillations between inscription and circulation, cult and exhibition, autography and allography, or abstraction and concretion; but also historical oscillations between auratic prototypes and standardized products, obsolete and cutting edge, rough edges and slick clean surfaces.... In its defectively self-destroying yet successfully self-preserving digital existence along with the numbered copies existing in personal and library collections, *Agrippa* stands out as an involuntary and privileged example of the early hybrids of digital culture.

NOTES

PREFACE: Pirate Havens and Digital Coyotes

1   Its first and most famous English translation can be found in Walter Benjamin, *Illuminations* (New York: Schocken Books, 2007), 217–252.
2   Fredric Jameson, *Postmodernism, Or, The Cultural Logic of Late Capitalism* (Durham, NC: Duke University Press, 1991), ix.
3   Ibid., 419.
4   Jorge Luis Borges, *Labyrinths: Selected Stories & Other Writings*, trans. Donald A. Yates and James East Irby (New York: New Directions, 2007).
5   Indulge me a minor observation. In his groundbreaking book *Mechanisms: New Media and the Forensic Imagination* (Cambridge, MA: MIT Press, 2008), Kirschenbaum suggests that "Cortézar" [*sic*] was an important influence on the first hypernovel, Michael Joyce's *Afternoon: A Story*. The notorious typo shows how pregnant ideas can be, when commentary of the work precedes the actual knowledge of the work, extending the Borgesian preference for commenting on nonexistent works rather than taking the trouble to write them. This, by no means, affects in any way the deep impact Kirschenbaum's book has had on digital studies and related fields.

CHAPTER I: Introduction: Milestones between Matter and Digits

1   My claim is by no means groundbreaking. It has been a topic of scholarly debate since the origins of new media studies but has gained relevance in the last years and today is an obvious fact in fields ranging from platform studies to media archeology. It is also one of the most important contributions to digital studies coming from philosophy of technology.
2   This book was written in Argentina. While it may sound irrelevant to some, when talking about technology, location does matter. A common mistake is that places where there is no cutting edge technology being developed or where the social digital gap is evident are not the best sites to conduct research on such topics. That perspective is as naïve as the idea of the neutrality of technology, or its universality. Particular locations force particular insights.
3   There is an ongoing research project on the subject by Diego Lawler and Jesús Vega Encabo. An introduction to their ideas can be found in "Creating Artifac-

tual Kinds," in Maarten Franssen, *Artefact Kinds: Ontology and the Human-Made World* (Cham: Springer, 2014).

4   I will use the concept of "milieu" to refer to the environment in which any given technical object works and interacts. When using the term "media" I will be referring to the cultural aspect of technology and its social and institutional organization. For a broader discussion on the concept of "milieu" see Gilbert Simondon, *Du mode d'existence des objets techniques* [*On the Mode of Existence of Technical Objects*] (Aubier: Editions Montaigne, 1958).

5   Nick Montfort, "Continuous Paper: The Early Materiality and Workings of Electronic Literature," nickm.com, (January 2005), http://nickm.com/writing/essays/continuous_paper_mla.html. This and the following hyperlinks in this book were accessed in March 2015, unless specified otherwise.

6   Kirschenbaum, *Mechanisms*, 33–45. I believe this observation is accurate, although it sidelines the relevance of the speakers' output. Quite early in computing history, it complemented that of screens. It is the visual and auditory output (and its combinations) that has biased most reflections on digital culture, rather than just the screen.

7   Ibid., 38.

8   Simondon, *Du mode d'existence des objets techniques*.

9   Throughout this book I will use "technics" to refer to a general sphere of human thinking (akin to epistemology, ethics, politics, and aesthetics). The term "technique" will be reserved for a specific set of procedures regarding a technical outcome (i.e., fly fishing, pot cooking, or etching), whereas the term "technology" will be used in a broader sense to an integrated group of technical objects and procedures (i.e., steam-engine technology or digital technology). The suffix -logy, from Greek λόγος, suggests the existence of a formalization of the practical lore at stake. In other words, there is a rational discourse on the technique that brings it closer to modern science. Of course, some "technologies" are more formalized than others; the cases of photography and the printing press are eloquent of the transition from craft to industry, from technique to technology, which will be discussed later.

10 The prosthetic conception of technics is an ongoing debate. However, for this introduction's sake, I will not discuss it. I would like to suggest that digital technologies are a new phase in the history of exteriorization that is the history of humanity (and of technology). For a summary of the different positions, see Diego Parente, *Del órgano al artefacto: Acerca de la dimensión biocultural de la técnica* [*From Organ to Artifact: On the Biocultural Dimension of Technics*] (La Plata: Edulp, Editorial de la Universidad de La Plata, 2010), 35–87.

11 Bernard Stiegler, *Technics and Time, 1: The Fault of Epimetheus* (Stanford, CA: Stanford University Press, 1994).

12 In a complementary development to Stiegler, Gilbert Simondon proposes the existence of "technical lineages." See *Du mode d'existence des objets techniques*.

13 Ibid. Scaling takes the idea of technics as a prosthesis to a limit that is determined by the complexity of modern technical systems.

14 The question that Stiegler does not answer is who invents standards. I suspect that the answer may be to approach standards from a Stieglerian

perspective, considering them as the emerging feature of a specific co-constitution: the one of modern science and of modern industry.

15   For an introduction to this see T. J. Pinch and W. E. Bijker, "The Social Construction of Facts and Artefacts: Or How the Sociology of Science and the Sociology of Technology Might Benefit Each Other," *Social Studies of Science Social Studies of Science* 14, no. 3 (1984): 399–441.

16   For this and other very interesting stories on the history of technics, see Pablo Capanna, *Maquinaciones. El otro lado de la tecnología.* [*Machinations. The Other Side of Technology*] (Buenos Aires: Paidos, 2011).

17   For a history of these interactions and negotiations see Bruno Latour, *We Have Never Been Modern* (Cambridge, MA: Harvard University Press, 1993).

18   Bernard Stiegler, *Symbolic Misery*, vol. 1 (Cambridge: Polity Press, 2014).

19   Lev Manovich, *Software Takes Command: Extending the Language of New Media* (New York: Bloomsbury, 2013). It is not casual that the Russian scholar paraphrases the title of a 1948 book by historian of the architecture and technics Sigfried Giedion, *Mechanization Takes Command*, to indicate the magnitude of the change.

20   Yuk Hui, "What Is a Digital Object?," *Metaphilosophy* 43, no. 4 (2012): 380–395.

21   The possibility of *loss* in the human condition has been refuted by Donna Haraway's critique of essentialisms and by the critique of the myths of origin carried out by Stiegler, among others.

22   Google's declared goal of "organizing the world's information and make it universally accessible and useful" is an example of this. For an insight on the ambitions and scope of the digitization enterprise, see Barbara Cassin, *Google-moi: La deuxième mission de l'Amérique* [*Google me: The Second Mission of the United States*] (Paris: Albin Michel, 2006).

23   William Gibson, *Neuromancer*, 1984, 51.

CHAPTER 2: Bit Rot

1   In the digital context, Apple's iTunes and the Institute Fraunhofer IIS' .mp3 codification protocol *de facto* settled the discussion choosing the song as the universal unit over others such as, for instance, the long-play disc. What prevails here is a constructivist definition of the limits of the object in its digital form.

2   There is, of course, the idea of an infinite loop, a recurrent *da capo* on the score, but that would be more an *avant-garde* conceptual resolution than an effective accomplishable instruction. Eventually, players would cramp.

3   Available at https://elearning.unipd.it/cab/mod/glossary/showentry.php?course id=4&eid=41&displayformat=dictionary.

4   Ray Jackendoff, *Consciousness and the Computational Mind* (Cambridge, MA; London: MIT Press, 1994), 30.

5   Hui, "What Is a Digital Object?"

6   Manovich, *Software Takes Command*, 70.

7   Hui, "What Is a Digital Object?," 389.

8   Trevor Owens, "The Is of the Digital Object and the Is of the Artifact," *The Signal: Digital Preservation*, October 25, 2012, http://blogs.loc.gov/digitalpre servation/2012/10/the-is-of-the-digital-object-and-the-is-of-the-artifact/. In this book I refer to what Owens calls an "artifact" as a "storage device."

9   Benjamin, *Illuminations*, 223.

10 Something similar occurs with film, another example of discrete linear arrangement, but of frames instead of words. Think, for instance, of the multiple versions of Fritz Lang's classic film *Metropolis*.

11 "Cyclic Redundancy Check," *Wikipedia, the Free Encyclopedia*, http://en.wiki pedia.org/wiki/Cyclic_redundancy_check.

12 Owens, "The Is of the Digital Object and the Is of the Artifact."

13 TrueType is a font standard format developed by Apple to compete with Adobe's format "Type 1." Microsoft bought the TrueType license from Apple and turned it into one of the most extended typesetting standards in the digital milieu.

14 The idea of a "crisis of the book as a storage" or more dramatically a "death of books" has lost force compared to the mass media outcries between 1990 and 2000. Some interesting readings on the impact of digital technologies in book culture are Milad Doueihi, *Digital Cultures* (Cambridge, MA: Harvard University Press, 2011), Jean-Claude Carrière, Umberto Eco, and Jean-Philippe de Tonnac, *This Is Not the End of the Book: A Conversation* (Evanston, IL: Northwestern University Press, 2012), and the deeply informed book by Theodore G. Striphas, *The Late Age of Print: Everyday Book Culture from Consumerism to Control* (New York: Columbia University Press, 2009).

15 N. Katherine Hayles, "Electronic Literature: What Is It?," *The Electronic Literature Organization*, January 2, 2007, http://eliterature.org/pad/elp.html.

16 N. Katherine Hayles, *Writing Machines* (Cambridge, MA: MIT Press, 2002), 25.

17 Claudia Kozak, ed., *Tecnopoéticas argentinas: Archivo blando de arte y tecnología* [*Argentine Technopoetics: Soft Archive of Art and Technology*] (Buenos Aires: Caja Negra, 2012), 224–226. All translations for this and other quotes from sources unpublished in English are mine.

18 Ibid., 182–183.

19 For a broader discussion see Michael Witmore, "Text: A Massively Addressable Object" in Matthew K. Gold, ed., *Debates in the Digital Humanities* (Minneapolis: University of Minnesota Press, 2012), 324–326. There is also an open-access on-line version that affords scholarly debate at http://dhdebates. gc.cuny.edu/ debates/text/28.

20 For an example of Césari's works see http://thenewpostliterate.blogspot.com. ar/2013/04/3-books-from-mauro-cesari.html.

21 To access the recreations of the work and a vast related documentary archive see the exhaustive website *The Agrippa Files* at http://agrippa.english. ucsb.edu/.

22 The piece can be "read" in http://www.bootz.fr/brosse/brosse.html. Bootz is also an important scholar in digital arts and literature.

23 This work favors an aesthetic experience akin to *Agrippa*. One may wonder if this novel will eventually circulate on the Internet in a *reader friendly* version

of the text that involves less work and dilutes its materiality in the abstraction of the code in a way similar to what happened with Gibson's digital poem. For an excerpt of *Mucho Trabajo* and a critical commentary see Tomás Vera Barros, ed., *Escrituras objeto: Antología de literatura experimental [Object Writings: Anthology of Experimental Literature]* (Buenos Aires: Interzona, 2013), 10; 139–148.

24 For a detailed discussion of this work see *"A Humument* as Technotext: Layered topographies" in Hayles, *Writing Machines,* 76–99.

25 By digital culture I refer to all those manifestations framed in the practices and cultural productions originated in the use of digital technologies, in forms akin to the use of "print culture" by Chartier and others. As he has stressed, it should always be kept in mind that there are multiple print cultures, the world of print is not a homogenous or monolithic unit. That same observation applies to the current context where many digital cultures coexist and dispute over the legitimacy of different forms of digital existence. However, to avoid confusion I will preserve the more extended singular denomination while maintaining the implicit heterogeneity and its inherent conflict.

26 Roger Chartier, *Escuchar a los muertos con los ojos: Lección inaugural en el Collège de France [Hearing the Dead with the Eyes: Opening Lesson in the Collège de France]* (Buenos Aires: Katz, 2008), 48.

27 Kirschenbaum, *Mechanisms: New Media and the Forensic Imagination,* 25–71.

28 Hayles, *Writing Machines,* 30–31.

29 Striphas, *The Late Age of Print,* 41.

CHAPTER 3: Crossing Borders

1 Hayles, "Electronic Literature: What Is It?"

2 Chartier, *Escuchar a los muertos,* 11.

3 Roger Chartier, "Hay una tendencia a transformar los textos en bases de datos," ["There is a Tendency to Transform All Texts in Databases"] interview by Horacio González et al., *La Biblioteca.* N° 6, 2007. For a broader discussion on the problem of the mutual influence between different media in the context of information and communication technologies see Jay David Bolter and Richard Grusin, *Remediation: Understanding New Media* (Cambridge, MA: MIT Press, 2000).

4 *Phaedrus,* 274e–275b.

5 Lev Manovich, "New Media from Borges to HTML," in Nick Montfort and Noah Wardrip-Fruin, *The New Media Reader* (Cambridge, MA: MIT Press, 2003), 11.

6 Manovich, *Software Takes Command.*

7 Manovich, "New Media from Borges to HTML," 17.

8 *The Language of New Media* (Cambridge, MA: MIT Press, 2002).

9 Ibid., 36.

10 Ibid. Hayles has pointed out that Manovich's proposal indicates a crucial aspect: computers have become an extremely powerful medium. Therefore, the

basic assumptions of culture move from the traditional vehicles of transmission (such as political and religious rhetorics and gestualities, or scientific, philosophical, literary, and historical narratives) to the material operations of computing devices. Cfr. "Electronic Literature: What Is It?" Manovich's idea of transcoding also shares some features with the concept of "remediation" proposed by Bolter and Grusin in *Remediation*.

11 The equivalent group for pre-digital works of art is that of works produced in an "analog culture" paradigm: music recordings and films, but also pre-industrial auratic art pieces. This last case may be subject of debate; I will locate it here in an opposition with the digital mode of existence of works, considering its material, storage-specific features.

12 The anachronism implied in the simulation of a previous specific storage as context for the digital realization of a work is a study in itself that exceeds this research. Let me suggest that these kinds of simulation are examples of "remediated" texts as mere content. Although this matter is not considered by Bolter and Grusin, it should be noted that the emergence of tablets and other reading devices that can compete with the book more efficiently than the computer screen were still not settled technologies when *Remediation* was published. Equivalents from other arts here are all encodings of previous media objects, such as image, music, and video files that afford reproducing pre-digital contents in a computer.

13 There are broader definitions for digital work than the one I propose here, for example one provided by the Electronic Literature Organization: "work with an important literary aspect that takes advantage of the capabilities and contexts provided by the stand-alone or networked computer." Quoted by Hayles, "Electronic Literature: What Is It?"

14 This effort is evident in Google's declared goal: "Google's mission is to organize the world's information and make it universally accessible and useful." Note that the ambition of the company is global and points to universal usefulness and accessibility. The organization of information is equivalent to an administered world: the abstraction of entities into representations, subject to indexation.

15 Extending the problem of technical reproducibility to printed texts, Kaufman says: "Let us consider the book in the age of technical reproduction. There is no such thing as a divergence between reading and contemplation of images, or between paper and screen. The dichotomy is not only sterile, it is entirely fallacious. The book is digital and there is no book that is not digital since the widespread use of computer typesetting. In the mechanical printing press era, the material condition of the existence of a book occurred in the relationship between the metal types and printing on the paper. The book had no other existence than on that material storage. It was written by the same procedure using a typewriter—that came after hand writing and copying—and printing was limited to copying the originally settled text with the addition of a special format called book. For several years now, the book has reached its existence in digital form, stored on the hard disk of a computer." Alejandro Kaufman, "Imaginarios, lecturas, prácticas," ["Imaginaries, Readings, Practices"] *La Biblioteca* 6 (2007): 76–83. Hayles points out that the distinction between

print and digital works to discuss the specificity of electronic literature is indiscernible: "In the contemporary era, both print and electronic texts are deeply interpenetrated by code. Digital technologies are now so thoroughly integrated with commercial printing processes that print is more properly considered a particular output form of electronic text than an entirely separate medium. Nevertheless, electronic text remains distinct from print in that it literally cannot be accessed until it is performed by properly executed code." Hayles, "Electronic Literature: What Is It?" In fact, the idea of the circulation of texts that are not bound to their bookish materiality reduces printed books to just one among the many possible outputs of the pure (or electronic) form of the texts.

16 For a very detailed discussion on the transition from analog to digital see "'Every Contact Leaves Its Trace': Storage, Inscriptions, and Computer Forensics" and "Extreme Inscription: A Grammatology of the Hard Drive" in Kirschenbaum, *Mechanisms*, 25–72; 73–110. Both chapters identify the invisibilization of the material inscription process in the context of digital technologies that occurs inside hard drives. This contributes to the illusion of text, image, sound, and video as immaterial entities, whether they are born digital or digitized.

17 Ibid., 90.

18 Ibid., 133–140.

19 Chartier, *Escuchar a los muertos*, 25.

20 Unaware of the scale and scope that digital reproduction would provide, in "A Small History of Photography," Benjamin foresaw at the beginning of the twentieth century that technical reproduction had started a process of abstraction that allowed a new form of assimilable perception. He noted that since paintings, sculptures, and architectural works can be apprehended in a photograph better than in reality, methods of technical reproduction are also a reductive technology that provides a degree of domination over the works otherwise unattainable by direct, unmediated, contact. Cfr. *One-Way Street and Other Writings* (London: Verso, 1985), 240–257. Digital reproducibility builds on from that early analog dominion over works.

21 Cfr. Benjamin, *Illuminations*, 220–221.

22 Kirschenbaum has argued this assertion with his call for a digital forensics methodology. But the degree similarity of digital copies perceptible for untrained human senses is far higher than the verifiable degradation of copies of copies of copies (and so on) in analog reproduction technologies. Or at least, in what makes for the visual and aural perception, which account for most of the contemporary reproduction technologies. The tactile developments are still focused on the input of the interfaces to the tactile stimuli (whose most obvious examples are tablets and cell phones featuring touch screens, GPS, gyroscopes and other sensors to register the input of hand and, to a lesser extent, body movements). The olfactory and gustatory developments are not very established or standardized features of contemporary reproduction technologies.

23 And this is without taking into consideration derivative works, the illegally originated copies that are discussed in chapter four.

24 I would like to insist on the difference between pre-digital literary works, digitized ones, and those specifically digital. For a discussion on the code as a form of creative writing, as well as the legal ramifications that this implies see Doueihi, *Digital Cultures*. For the genre of electronic literature known as codework, see Hayles, *Writing Machines*, 51.

25 Vilém Flusser, *Towards a Philosophy of Photography* (London: Reaktion, 2005).

26 Kirschenbaum, *Mechanisms*, 80–81.

27 Chartier, *Escuchar a los muertos*, 13.

28 This phenomenon is parallel to those occurring in other arts and disciplines as is the case in cinema. To a lesser extent the phenomenon can also be seen in architecture in the process of projection and layout; simulations of scientific experimentation, or the production, editing, and circulation of the images anachronistically referred to as "photographic." For a very informed discussion of these changes see Manovich, *Software Takes Command.*

29 There are other marginal practices such as digitization though speech recognition, also known as ASR (Automatic Speech Recognition) or STT (Speech to Text) whose incidence in the multiplication of digitized texts is negligible. This is not to be confused with voice recognition technologies, aimed to verify the identity of a person. Although it exceeds the goals of this book, it should be noted that speech recognition technology can be thought of as a novel relationship between oral and digital cultures. Beyond the obvious Orwellian nightmare of every phone or recorded conversation being registered and indexed by search engines, this technology is also related to the convergence of discursive genres in devices: a single device simultaneously affords sending text messages and voice (that is, sound), as well as producing still and moving images.

30 Pre-industrial printing implied a plurality of trades. In digital culture, these trades converge in fewer roles. I will discuss this issue later.

31 Vauhini Vara, "Project Gutenberg Fears No Google," *The Wall Street Journal Online*, December 10, 2005, http://www.wsj.com/articles/SB1134154031132186 20.

32 For an informed discussion of the problem of the errors in the digital milieu see Paul Fyfe, "Electronic Errata: Digital Publishing, Open Review, and the Futures of Correction," in *Debates in the Digital Humanities*, ed. Matthew K. Gold (Minneapolis: University of Minnesota Press, 2012), 259–280. There is an open-access link at http://dhdebates.gc.cuny.edu/debates/text/4. This essay provides a historic background on the problem of the error proofing considering different textual storages and the technologies associated with them. This is a relevant issue indeed because, "ignoring the particulars or correction ironically threatens to replicate a conservative notion of textuality that digital publishing was supposed to displace." Ibid., 261.

33 One of the clearest examples of Hart's positions on the matter is the post "A Graceful Exit," originally posted at the *The World Public Library Blog Newsletter Volume 1, Number 25* that is now unavailable. A copy of it has been reposted in an obituary by Gregory B. Newby, "Michael Hart of Project Gu-

tenberg Passes," available at http://brewster.kahle.org/2011/09/07/michael-hart-of-project-guten berg-passes/.

34 Michael Hart, "The History and Philosophy of Project Gutenberg," *Project Gutenberg*, August 1992, https://www.gutenberg.org/wiki/Gutenberg:The_History_and_Philosophy_of_Project_Gutenberg_by_Michael_Hart.

35 For an example, see the above mentioned post "A Graceful Exit," fully reproduced by Newby.

36 "France has adopted this invention, and from the first moment it has shown pride of being able to generously benefit the whole world with it." For a detailed discussion on the personal and political motivations behind this legislative decision see R. Derek Wood, "A State Pension for Daguerre," *Annals of Science*, 54, no. 5 (1997): 489–506.

37 For a critical analysis of Google's digitization and indexing project see Cassin, *Google-moi*.

38 For an analysis of the disputes in the publishing market see Chimo Soler, "eBooks: La guerra digital global por el dominio del libro," ["eBooks: The Global Digital War over the Dominion of Books"] *Real Instituto Elcano*, September 6, 2010, http://www.realinstitutoelcano.org/wps/portal/rielcano/conteni do?WCM_GLOBAL_CONTEXT=/elcano/elcano_es/zonas_es/lengua+y+cultura/ari92-2010. Despite focusing on the economic aspect of electronic publishing, the article introduces the competing business models and the convergence of bookstores, publishing companies, telecommunications, entertainment, as well as electronic and software companies involved in the processes of production and distribution of texts in the context of digitization. In *The Late Age of Print*, Striphas introduces a dispute of models between "consumer capitalism" favoring the possession of material storages, such as books, and "controlled consumerism" managing the access to symbolic commodities, that is, "contents" governed by intellectual property under the form of digital objects. Although focused on the English speaking publishing industry, Striphas incorporates in his argument the effects of political and cultural imperialism and the inequalities existing in the rest of the world to explain the alternatives that challenge both models.

39 Chartier, *Escuchar a los muertos*, 25. Similarly, Hayles stressed to the political and economic dimension that enables the treatment of works as private property, the impact it has had on modern literary criticism, and the stabilization of the concept of literature that disregards the materiality involved in the production of texts: "the long reign of print made it easy for literary criticism to ignore the specifications of the codex book when discussing literary text. With significant exceptions, print literature was widely regarded as not having a body, only a speaking mind," Hayles, *Writing Machines*, 31–32.

40 See http://shakespeare.mit.edu/.

41 The Arden edition is named after Shakespeare's mother. Started in 1899, it required twenty-five years to be completed. After World War II, there was a second edition that included forewords by editors, introductory studies, and detailed critical notes. In 1995, a third editorial project started. For a brief history of the Arden editions see Richard Wray, "Bloomsbury Buys Arden

Shakespeare," *The Guardian*, January 6, 2009, http://www.theguardian.com/business/2009/jan/06/bloomsbury-buys-arden-shakespeare.

42 See http://www.quartos.org/.

43 See http://commons.wikimedia.org/wiki/File:NBSFirstScanImage.jpg.

44 For a discussion on addressability and the affordances of digital texts see Michael Witmore, "Text: A Massively Addressable Object," in *Debates in the Digital Humanities* (Minneapolis: University of Minnesota Press, 2012), 324–327, http://dhdebates.gc.cuny.edu/debates/text/28.

45 See www.blakearchive.org.

46 For a discussion of editorial policies and digitization in the case of the *Blake Archive* see Kirschenbaum, *Mechanisms*, 149–155, and Johanna Drucker, "Humanistic Theory and Digital Scholarship," in *Debates in the Digital Humanities* (Minneapolis: University of Minnesota Press, 2012), 85–95.

47 This type of referral to the bookish materiality of texts also appears in complex simulations of the book that frame the visual representation of the eBooks on Apple's iPad's reading software, for example. This effect is also enhanced by the tactility of the screen and the simulation of the text of the folded page accompanying the movement of the fingers to "turn" the page.

48 This difference will be important to discuss the anomalies in order to reconstruct the materiality of digital and hybrid works. The *Agrippa* project planned on printing changing or ephemeral images, which encompass the risk that there will be nothing left to digitize, as opposed to what remains in the case of Blake's etchings, a stable cultural object. If the images change, veil, or are erased, there is no stable reference to digitize and one must resort to an emulation that represents the process (in fast motion to make it perceivable). I will discuss the problem of stability ahead.

49 Whitney Trettien, "Zombie Editions: An Archaeology of POD Areopagiticas," Blog, *DIaPSaLMaTa*, http://blog.whitneyannetrettien.com/2010/12/zombieeditions-archaeology-of-pod.html. In her post, Trettien tracks the history of a particular digitalized version of Milton's *Areopagitica*, which in turn comes from a popular edition of the nineteenth century, to discuss the modes of circulation of digitized texts in the context of its commodification as digital contents. She has further pursued the intuitions of her post and systematized them leaving aside the idea of "zombie edition" in Whitney Trettien, "A Deep History of Electronic Textuality: The Case of English Reprints Jhon Milton Areopagitica," *DHQ: Digital Humanities Quarterly:* 7, no. 1 (2013), http://digitalhumanities.org/dhq/vol/7/1/000150/000150.html.

50 For a thorough discussion of Google's digitization project, the obstacles that have delayed its implementation, and its cultural implications see Cassin's above mentioned long essay *Google-moi*.

51 It should be noted that (ro)bots and zombies are kindred metaphors, based on the idea of an automated non-intelligent agency, eventually guided by a master (either the machine maker, the voodoo witch doctor, or the necromancer). The golem as a metaphor for automated idiocy also meets these criteria. What is more, there are no ghosts or souls in these machines and bodies. I will return to this in the following sections.

52 Since bots evolve, so does the system to prevent their access. For the latest state of CAPTCHA technology at the time of the writing of this chapter see http://googleonlinesecurity.blogspot.com.ar/2014/12/are-you-robot-introducing-no-captcha.html.

53 Benjamin, *Illuminations*, 84.

54 Fyfe, "Electronic Errata: Digital Publishing, Open Review, and the Futures of Correction," 262.

55 Chartier, *Escuchar a los muertos*, 25.

56 Benjamin, *Illuminations*, 85.

57 Fyfe, "Electronic Errata: Digital Publishing, Open Review, and the Futures of Correction," 263.

58 The first prototypes date from the seventeenth century and Remington began producing its famous typewriter in 1873 although there were previous models that had had some commercial success.

59 Benjamin, *Illuminations*, 87.

60 Susan Buck-Morss has stressed the importance of the body sensorium as a whole (taste, hearing, touch, smell, and sight) at the origins of the concept of aesthetics as a philosophical discipline and how the changes brought about by industrialization progressively narrowed the scope to focus on the primacy of sight (and the relevance of this phenomenon in Benjamin's philosophical work). Cfr. "Aesthetics and Anaesthetics: Walter Benjamin's Artwork Essay Reconsidered," *October*, no. 62 (1992): 3–41. Scott Bukatman suggests that true industrialization of the printing press occurred at the confluence with typewriting technology. Cfr. Scott Bukatman, "Gibson's Typewriter," in *Flame Wars: The Discourse of Cyberculture*, ed. Mark Dery (Durham, NC: Duke University Press, 1994), 74–75.

61 Benjamin, *Illuminations*, 237–241.

62 Buck-Morss suggests that the base of the shock as the dominant aesthetic (i.e., perceptual) phenomenon in modernity is a mimetic defense, the reflex movement of the operator to accommodate the body to the rhythm set by the automation of machines so as to avoid being hurt. That same automation, without the risk of limb amputation, underlies the reCAPTCHA. Reading becomes automated; it follows the pace set by the machine without any understanding, just a reflex, although not defensive as the operator's, to validate access. There is no meaning but instead mere perception output, isolated word recognition, and a mindless urgent input, hastened by the countdown time of the reCAPTCHA. That this rationalization of the work of the human eye can occur outside working times is an example of the blurring lines between work and private life posed by the expansion of digital technologies.

63 Luis von Ahn et al., "reCAPTCHA: Human-Based Character Recognition via Web Security Measures," *Science* 321 (2008): 1467.

64 Let me note that the term derives from outsourcing, one of the forms of effacement of industrial labor in late capitalist Western societies. I will discuss the erasure of labor in the digital milieu in the following chapters since it is also a very relevant aspect of what Monfort called screen essentialism and is also at the very basis of the notion of continent-less contents.

65 Cassin, *Google-moi*, 189.

66 https://archive.org/details/texts.

67 Leonid Taycher, "Inside Google Books: Books of the World, Stand Up and Be Counted! All 129,864,880 of You," *Google Books Search*, August 5, 2010, http://booksearch.blogspot.com.ar/2010/08/books-of-world-stand-up-and-be-cou nted.html. As it can be seen in the post, Google's definition of "book" was determined by the practical issues of the project, the selection criteria, and the affordances of its software implementation as well as by the complex legal disputes project stirred. For a history of this dispute, see the already mentioned works by Cassin and Striphas. The history of the project presented on the *Google Books* site is also worth reading: http://books.google.com/google books/about/history.html. Complementarily, *Wikipedia* provides a detailed history of the obstacles that the project faced and the agreements, lawsuits, and settlements generated over almost a decade of existence: http://en.wiki pedia.org/wiki/Google_ Books#Timeline.

CHAPTER 4: Illegalized Aliens in the Land of the Copyrighted

1 *Mechanisms*, 11–15.

2 Philippe Bootz, "La poesía digital programada: Una poesía del dispositivo" ["Programmed Digital Poetry: A Device Poetry"] In *Poéticas Tecnológicas, Transdisciplina y Sociedad: Actas del Seminario Internacional Ludión-Paragraphe*, ed. Claudia Kozak [*Technological Poetics, Transdiscipline and Society: Proceedings of the International Seminar Ludión/Paragraphe*] (Buenos Aires: Ludión, 2011), 31, http://ludion.com.ar/archivos/articulo/2012_Lu dion_Actas-1.pdf.

3 As explained on *Wikipedia*'s dedicated page, a "Wikipedia Book is a collection of Wikipedia articles that can be easily saved, rendered electronically in PDF, ZIM or OpenDocument format, or ordered as a printed book." This kind of eBook is an eloquent example of the conclusiveness-inconclusiveness negotiations regarding digital works. For more information see http://en.wikipedia. org/wiki/ Wikipedia:Books.

4 For a discussion on fanfictions see Angela Thomas, "Blurring and Breaking through the Boundaries of Narrative, Literacy, and Identity in Adolescent Fan Fiction," in *A New Literacies Sampler*, ed. Michele Knobel and Colin Lankshear (New York: Peter Lang, 2007), 137–166.

5 For a detailed description with examples of each of these genres see Hayles, "Electronic Literature: What Is It?"

6 A digitalized version of the *Odyssey* can be found at http://www.gutenberg.org/ catalog/world/readfile?fk_files=1329237&pageno=2. Note that this copy has most likely been typed, since OCR optimization for Greek language was barely at the level of the Latin alphabet.

7 Arlindo Machado, *Máquina e imaginário: O desafio das poéticas tecnológicas* [*Machine and Imaginary: The Challenge of Technological Poetics*] (São Paulo, SP, Brasil: Edusp, 1993), 28.

8 Bolter and Grusin, *Remediation*, 17.

9   Consider for instance the reengineering that has resurrected cassettes, although for new uses: Mike Lata, "Return of the Tape: Sony 185TB Cassette Tape Packs a Wallop but for What Purpose?," *Tech Times*, May 6, 2014, http://www.techtimes.com/articles/6556/20140506/cassette-tape-tape-sony-185tb.htm.

10 *The Language of New Media*, 61. For an introduction to the dynamics of remediation inside franchises see Espen Aarseth, "The Culture and Business of Cross-Media Productions," *Popular Communication* 4, no. 3 (2006): 203–211. Aarseth's article pays special attention to what extent a narrative may be preserved in different media, operating with different associated milieus and exploiting different affordances.

11 Laura Testoni, "E-Book italiani: Quale bibliodiversità? Lo stato dell'arte 2011," ["Italian E-Books: Which Bibliodiversity? 2011 State of the Art"] *Bollettino AIB: Rivista italiana di biblioteconomia e scienze dell'informazione* 51, no. 4 (2011): 348.

12 Striphas, *The Late Age of Print*, 11.

13 Ibid.

14 Federico Heinz, "De libros electrónicos, agua seca y otras quimeras," ["On Electronic Books, Dry Water and Other Chimeras"] in *Argentina Copyleft*, ed. Beatriz Busaniche (Villa Allende: Fundacíon Vía Libre, 2010), 96.

15 Michele Knobel and Colin Lankshear, *A New Literacies Sampler* (New York: Peter Lang, 2007), 201–202.

16 Ibid.

17 An unprecedented case combining the characteristics of both kinds of leaks (of corporate information and of a work of art) is the case of the cyber attack on Sony Pictures Entertainment. The hack suffered by the company disclosed company documents, such as private e-mails from company executives and company employees' information along with at least four unreleased DVD screener copies of Sony movies, some of which were still in theaters and others that had not even been released, and the script of a James Bond film still in production, *Spectre*. An Internet search for "Sony Pictures Hack" provides countless of articles on the story, but the bottom line for the matters discussed here is the fact that this case exemplifies the challenges imposed on hegemonic cultural industries by the works of art (and entertainment) in the age of digital reproducibility.

18 For discussion of the early crisis in the cultural industry triggered by the emergence of new technologies see the detailed study by Juan C. Calvi, *¿Reproducción de la cultura o cultura de la reproducción?: Análisis económico, político y social de la distribución y el consumo de productos audiovisuales en internet* [*Reproduction of Culture or Reproduction Culture?: Economic, Political, and Social Analysis of Distribution and Consumption of Audiovisual Products in the Internet*] (Madrid: Universidad Rey Juan Carlos I, 2008). The research may have grown a bit outdated due to the fast rate of changes occurring in digital technologies but the analysis of the peer-to-peer file exchange is still acute and accurate.

19 The obverse of leaks are cultural industry derivative products associated with the creation process, increasingly marketed to extend the revenue life of a particular work under forms such as "found notebook," "drafts," "sketches,"

"making of," "behind the cameras," "B-sides," "B-takes," etc. The creative genius fetishism emerges here next to content idealism under the drive of profit
maximization.

20   Hito Steyerl, *The Wretched of the Screen* (Berlin: Sternberg Press, 2012), 44. I
only became aware of her book at the end of my research and she presents
similar interpretations of digital culture. The quoted essay, "In Defense of the
Poor Image," is an appropriate complementation to the discussion presented
in this chapter, although Steyerl has a different appraisal of the impact of
compression lossy formats.

21   For a detailed history see the above mentioned Calvi, *¿Reproducción de la
cultura o cultura de la reproducción?*

22   For a brief history of the disputes over photocopying in the United States see
Striphas, *The Late Age of Print*, 31–39.

23   Julie Bosman, "Romance Books Are Hot in the E-Reading Market," *New York
Times*, December 8, 2010, sec. Books, http://www.nytimes.com/2010/12/09/
books/09romance.html?_r=0.

24   For a discussion of aesthetic experience in the nineteenth and twentieth
centuries in relation to socially controlled environments, see Buck-Morss,
"Aesthetics and Anaesthetics," 22–23.

25   Benjamin, *Illuminations*, 220.

26   Mariana Enriquez, "Charly García: Cuando me empiece a quedar solo,"
["Charly García: When I Begin Being Left Alone"] *Rolling Stone Argentina*,
June 11, 2008, http://www.rollingstone.com.ar/1020573. The disk remained
unpublished until it was released by Sony Music on December 22, 2010 in the
wake of García's public resurgence. The leaked version dates from 2007.

27   A brief account of the story behind the film can be read in Marcelo Cajueiro,
"'Elite' Stirs Controversy, Box Office," *Variety*, October 19, 2007, http://variety.
com/2007/biz/news/elite-stirs-controversy-box-office-1117974360/.

28   For a detailed analysis of the case see "Harry Potter and the Culture of the
Copy," Striphas, *The Late Age of Print*, 141–173. The author incorporates the
political dimension of the unauthorized circulation of copies and the social
reactions to abusive exercise of the copyrights by the developed countries'
cultural industries: "Whether intented or not, the ubiquity of Western products within the context of foreign manufacture helps to stimulate a demand—even an expectation—among those charged with producing them. This
isn't a problem in itself, but it becomes one when Western and local rights
holders are unwilling to make their goods available at prices consistent with
the manifest economic conditions." Ibid., 169. Striphas research also provides
some hilarious examples of printed illegal derivative works such as the Chi-
nese versions *Harry Potter and Leopard Walk Up to Dragon* or *Harry Potter's
Sister*; the Indian derivation *Harry Potter in Calcutta*, or the unusual Russian
plagiarism *Tanya Grotter i Magicheskii Kontrabas* [*Tanya Grotter and the
Magical Double Bass*] and *Porri Gatter I Kolor Filosof* [*Porri Gatter and the
Stone Philosopher*], together with their histories and the legal reactions they
faced.

29 Peter Svensson, "Harry Potter Breaks E-Book Lockdown," *Yahoo News*, March 27, 2012, http://news.yahoo.com/harry-potter-breaks-e-book-lockdown-2053436 80. html.

30 Manovich, *The Language of New Media*, 36. For a discussion on these matters see also the already quoted book by Steyerl, *The Wretched of the Screen*.

31 Since December 9, 2014, when police raided the *Pirate Bay* premises and seized servers due to copyright infringement claims, the site has been offline.

32 Manovich, "New Media from Borges to HTML," 22.

33 One of the best examples of this is the booklet of Portishead's album *Dummy* (New York: Go Discs/London Records, 1994).

34 The film is available at http://ripremix.com/.

35 *Illuminations*, 83–85.

36 Ibid., 98.

37 Ibid., 99.

38 Ibid., 101.

39 Karl Marx and Frederik Engels, *The Communist Manifesto: A Modern Edition* (London: Verso, 2012), 37.

40 For instance, Benjamin builds his argument on storytelling exemplifying from the work of the Russian short story writer Leskov, and to a lesser extent Edgar Allan Poe and Robert Louis Stevenson, among other authors, whose works have circulated basically under the form of printed books.

41 The concept of hybrid that I want to discuss here has no relationship with that proposed by Manovich in "Understanding Hybrid Media," Hertz (Ed.), *Animated Paintings*. San Diego: San Diego Museum of Art, 2007. This essay describes the language of the contemporary moving images media rather than the constitutive materiality of works, even though the author does address the material conditions of production in these languages. Nor does my idea of hybrid works refer to the hybrids described by Bruno Latour that deal with the social, natural, and discursive aspects of phenomena, a hybrid condition derived from the oscillation between the subject and the object poles. Cfr. *We Have Never Been Modern*, 25. My concept of hybrid works is narrower, aimed at the specific materiality of storages and their combination with digital code. Since all text (print or digital) is now ultimately digital, I will consider here as hybrids those works that manifest such duplicity.

42 *Shoe Box* is available at http://www.sebakurtis.com/index.php?/in-deep-water/fronts/.

43 See http://humument.com/. For a critical discussion see "*A Humument* as Technotext: Layered Topographies," in Hayles, *Writing Machines*, 76–99.

44 Ibid., 24–25.

45 *Cybertext: Perspectives on Ergodic Literature* (Baltimore, MD: Johns Hopkins University Press, 1997).

46 The web supplement is available at http://mitpress.mit.edu/sites/default/files/titles/content/mediawork/titles/writing/sup/sup_index.html.

47 For an example of this form of remediation see the YouTube commercial at https://www.youtube.com/watch?v=gew68Qj5kxw.

48 Kirschenbaum, *Mechanisms*, 38.

49   Expanded books provided some affordances now considered standard as in-text search, changeable font size, non-intrusive forms of navigation, and the possibility to annotate in the margins and some interactive notes. It is also worth noting that the titles published by Voyager included the first three novels by William Gibson that had laid the foundations of the cyberpunk: *Neuromancer, Count Zero* and *Mona Lisa Overdrive*. They were published in a one digital "volume," that is, on a single CD-ROM.

50   Speculating a bit one could suggest that what allowed the development of the e-commerce and the low incidence of piracy in Amazon's business was precisely the combination of three events. First of all, the storage and mailing possibilities of the object book versus other goods; second, the existence of stocks distributed in libraries with digitalized databases; and, finally, the difficulty of the reproduction of their specific content (i.e., the text and images) compared to the crisis that soon would loom over the music and film industries with the popularization of sound and image information-lossy compression formats.

51   At this early stage of the development of e-reading devices, corporate concentration of device manufacturers, content producers and service providers was still a few years ahead. For a discussion of the process see the previously mentioned Calvi, *¿Reproducción de la cultura o cultura de la reproducción?*

52   Surprisingly one of the first prototypes for an actual e-reading device was not produced in the United States, Germany, or France, then the technology research cutting edge countries besides Japan, but in Milan's Polytechnic School in 1993 as part of a bachelor thesis on design by architects Franco Crugnola and Isabella Rigamonti. Without ties to the major electronic corporations or the publishing industry, this invention never exceeded the handmade prototype instance. For some curious images see http://milano.repubblica.it /cronaca/2011/06/24/foto/franco_l_uomo_che_invento_l_e-book_ma_nel_1993_ nessuno_ci_diede_retta-1813 7331/1/.

53   In Western countries and outside of the United States, which has been the decisive market during the consolidation in the eBook as a commodity, there were other devices such as the French CyBook and the BeBook from the Dutch company Endless Ideas BV, the Kobo eReader of the eponymous Canadian company and the Spanish reader Cervantes produced by BQ company. All of these electronic companies operate in partnerships with large publishing houses and bookshops from their countries of origin as well as telephone and Internet providers. In the case of tablets, they usually make alliances with audiovisual and musical content producers and providers. In all these countries oligopolistic concentration rules the legal circulation of digital and digitized works.

54   In "re Electronic Books Antitrust Litigation," 859 671 (Dist. Court, SD New York 2012).

55   For a historical tour of the different types of eBook, storages, and reading devices of this period see the online catalogue for the museum exhibition *The Book and Beyond. Electronic Publishing and the Art of the Book* (Victoria and Albert Museum, 1995).

56   Drucker, "Humanistic Theory and Digital Scholarship," 88.

57 These concepts are inspired by Rubén Gallo's *Mexican Modernity: The Avant-Garde and the Technological Revolution* (Cambridge, MA; London: MIT, 2005). In his book Gallo describes "mechanophilic" and "mechanogenic" poetics in the wake of Mexico's modernization in the first half of the twentieth century to differentiate works representing technology in the already stabilized forms from experimental ones. An example of the first case is Diego Rivera's technological utopianism in his ill-fated and uncompleted fresco *Man at the Crossroads Looking with Hope and High Vision to the Choosing of a New and Better Future.* An example of the second are works that self-reflectively incorporate technology drawing attention to their own technical conditions, such as the "Stridentist" radio poems incorporating interference and sound as a constitutive part of the pieces.

58 Manfred Clynes and Nathan S. Kline, "Cyborgs and Space," *Astronautics* 13 (September 1960): 26–27; 74–76.

59 Oshii's is also a major shift from the elementary previous *anime* cyborgs such as *Cobra*'s homonymous character whose distinctive trait was a "psychogun" that replaced his forearm.

60 For description of the work (in Spanish), videos, and pictures see http://www.biopus.com.ar/sensible2/.

CHAPTER 5: The Book of the Dead and the Death of Books

1 Alan Liu et al., "The Agrippa Files," http://agrippa.english.ucsb.edu.
2 Douglas Dodds, *The Book and Beyond.*
3 According to the first uploader of the cracked version, as quoted in http://agrippa.english.ucsb.edu/templars-introduction-to-the-first-online-copy-of-gibsons-agrippa-poem-1992item-d44-transcription.
4 Peter Schwenger, "Agrippa or The Apocalyptic Book," *South Atlantic Quarterly* 92, no. 4 (1993): 617–626.
5 Kirschenbaum, *Mechanisms*, 235.
6 Leonardo Flores, "Reading Agrippa: A 4-Part Series," *I ♥ E-Poetry. Short-Form Scholarship on Born-Digital Poetry and Poetics,* July 14–23, 2012, http://iloveepoe try.com/?page_id=7913.
7 Striphas, *The Late Age of Print*, 40–44.
8 Alan Liu, *The Laws of Cool: Knowledge Work and the Culture of Information* (Chicago, IL: University of Chicago Press, 2004), 345.
9 Joseph Tabbi, "Locating the Literary in New Media," *Electronic Book Review,* http://www.electronicbookreview.com/thread/criticaleco logies/interpretive.
10 See http://www.williamgibsonbooks.com/.
11 Liu, *The Laws of Cool: Knowledge Work and the Culture of Information*; Schwenger, "Agrippa or The Apocalyptic Book"; Flores, "Reading Agrippa: A 4-Part Series."
12 Kirschenbaum, *Mechanisms*, 213–248.
13 See https://w2.eff.org/Misc/Publications/William_Gibson/agr1ppa.parody.
14 See http://www.quut.com/berlin/scream/5.txt.
15 See http://www.crackingagrippa.net/.

16 "Bibliographic Description of Agrippa (Commissioned for The Agrippa Files)," *The Agrippa Files*, November 6, 2005, http://agrippa.english.ucsb.edu/hodge-james-bibliographic-description-of-agrippa-commissioned-for-the-agrippa-files.

17 Quinn DuPont, "Cracking the Agrippa Code: Cryptography for the Digital Humanities," *Scholarly and Research Communication* 4, no. 3 (2013).

18 Although critical studies have not established a definitive number, in a newspaper article, Gerald Jonas claims that there were 95 [De Luxe] copies, "The Disappearing $2,000 Book," *NYTimes.com*, August 29, 1993, http://www.nytimes.com/1993/08/29/books/the-disappearing-2000-book.html.

19 There used to be a description as part of a programmed exhibition at the Center for Book Arts that now retrieves a 404 error message. The description was at http://www.centerforbookarts.org/exhibits/archive/showdetail.asp?showID=62. Today the Center for the Book Arts has the 35ᵗʰ copy of *Agrippa* in its collection: http://www.centerforbookarts.dreamhosters.com/index.php/Detail/Object/Show/object_id/1189. The idea of the Small Edition was apparently abandoned and there are no known copies in existence. The Deluxe Edition has been established as the basic reference in critical studies. One of the reasons for this may be that due to the commercial failure of the project Begos closed his publishing house. See Kevin Begos, Jr., "On Agrippa (A Book of the Dead)," October 26, 2002, *The Agrippa Files*, http://oldsite.english.ucsb.edu/faculty/ayliu/unlocked/begos/letter. html. The only declared Small Edition copy is apparently that of the Waldo Library of the University of Michigan: https://catalog.library.wmich.edu/vufind/Record/1106657. In this chapter I will focus on the Deluxe Edition.

20 Kevin Begos, Jr., "Interview with Kevin Begos, Jr.," interview by Paxton Hehmeyer, February 19, 2006, *The Agrippa Files*, http://agrippa.english.ucsb.edu/hehmeyer-paxton-interview-with-kevin-begos-jr.

21 DuPont, "Cracking the Agrippa Code: Cryptography for the Digital Humanities."

22 According to the time of execution displayed in the audiovisual recording of the running poem presented in *The Agrippa Files* website.

23 Begos, Jr., "Interview with Kevin Begos, Jr."

24 Matthew Kirschenbaum, Doug Reside, and Alan Liu, "No Round Trip: Two New Primary Sources for Agrippa," *The Agrippa Files*, December 5, 2008, http://agrippa.english.ucsb.edu/kirschenbaum-matthew-g-with-doug-reside-and-alan-liu-no-round-trip-two-new-primary-sources-for-agrippa.

25 The video of the poem file running in the emulation can be seen on *Google Video* at http://agrippa.english.ucsb.edu/category/theBook-subcategories/the-poem-running-in-emulation.

26 See www.crackingagrippa.net.

27 See www.crackingagrippa.net/submissions-toc.html.

28 A more detailed description of the "Promotional Prospectus" can be found at http://agrippa.english.ucsb.edu/hodge-james-bibliographic-description-of-agrippa-commissioned-for-the-agrippa-files#14.

29 Steve R. White, Jeffrey O. Kephart, and David M. Chess, "Computer Viruses: A Global Perspective," in *Proceedings of the Fifth International Virus Bulletin Conference, Boston*, 1995, 185–191.

30 Liu, *The Laws of Cool: Knowledge Work and the Culture of Information*; Schwenger, "Agrippa or The Apocalyptic Book"; Flores, "Reading Agrippa: A 4-Part Series."
31 Kirschenbaum, Reside, and Liu, "No Round Trip: Two New Primary Sources for Agrippa"; Kirschenbaum, *Mechanisms*; DuPont, "Cracking the Agrippa Code: Cryptography for the Digital Humanities."
32 Begos, Jr., "On Agrippa (A Book of the Dead)"; Begos, Jr., "Interview with Kevin Begos, Jr."
33 Kirschenbaum, *Mechanisms*, 218.
34 Ibid., 235.
35 Hayles, "Electronic Literature: What Is It?"
36 Kirschenbaum, *Mechanisms*, 221.
37 Manovich, "New Media from Borges to HTML," 22.
38 Begos, Jr., "On Agrippa (A Book of the Dead)."
39 Schwenger, "Agrippa or The Apocalyptic Book," 62–65.
40 Jonas, "The Disappearing $2,000 Book."
41 Frederic Jameson also identifies Hunter Thompson's *gonzo* journalism and Thomas Pynchon's paranoid conspiracy novels as other notable influences in Gibsonian prose. Cfr. "Fear and Loathing in Globalization," *New Left Review* 23 (October 2003): 107–111.
42 William Gibson, "The Art of Fiction No. 211," interview by David Wallace-Wells *Paris Review*, 197, Summer 2011, www.theparisreview.org/interviews/6089/the-art-of-fiction-no-211-william-gibson. It is not a coincidence that Dickens describes the period in which Benjamin set the processes of industrialization and the decline of the arts and craft traditions. Benjamin also stressed its links with the phenomenon of urbanization, discussing a text that had great impact in literary circles both in London and in Paris in the second half of the nineteenth century: "The Man of the Crowd" by Edgar Allan Poe. In the interview, Gibson says that today we find ourselves in a cultural context similar to that: "I think the popular perception that we're a lot like the Victorians is in large part correct. One way is that we're all constantly in a state of ongoing technoshock, without really being aware of it—it's just become where we live. The Victorians were the first people to experience that, and I think it made them crazy in new ways. We're still riding that wave of craziness." Ibid.
43 "Gibson's Typewriter," 84–85. It should also be noted that Gibson has expressed his discomfort with the cyberpunk label, since it was quickly assimilated by the same cultural industry that he had attempted to undermine. Gibson, "The Art of Fiction No. 211."
44 William Gibson, "William Gibson: The Father of Cyberpunk," interview by Alex Dueben, *California Literary Review*, October 2007, http://calitreview.com/263/william-gibson-the-father-of-cyberpunk/.
45 William Gibson, *Count Zero* (New York: Ace Books, 1987), 31.
46 For a discussion on the enigmatic footage and its relationship to contemporary aesthetics see the thorough analysis in the already mentioned article by Jameson, "Fear and Loathing in Globalization."
47 In the fictional world of the novel, "The Sprawl" refers to a vast urban layout resulting in a megalopolis extending from Boston to Atlanta on the East coast

of what was once the United States and that has been split after a world war
that did not reach the stage of nuclear annihilation.

48 However, the very title of the novel indicates its affiliation to an electronic
world rather than to a cybernetic one.

49 Even the sequels of films such as 1979 Ridley Scott's *Alien*, took a cyberpunk
twist by emphasizing the subordination of life (and of genetics) to corporate
capitalism, as occurred in *Aliens* (1986) directed by James Cameron, *Alien 3*
(1992) directed by David Fincher, and Jean-Pierre Jeunet's *Alien Resurrection*
(1997). Gibson even wrote a script, that was discarded, for the third film in
the series which now circulates online (see http://www.awesomefilm.
com/script/Alien3.txt), in a similar fashion to what happened with "Agrippa."

50 The effective cyberpunk portmanteau has since spawned endless derivatives
and retrospective qualifications ranging from steampunk to group novels
portraying a Victorian form of alternate past, or dieselpunk for fifties themed
alternate timelines, to more wild and far-fetched iterations such as stonepunk
(to describe *The Flintstones!*) and even elfpunk for urban themed fantasy
novels.

51 Lawrence Person, "Notes toward a Postcyberpunk Manifesto," *Nova Express*,
1998.

52 Jameson, "Fear and Loathing in Globalization," 108–109.

53 Ibid., 110.

54 For a discussion on Gibson and Sterling's rewriting experiment see Elisabeth
Kraus, "Gibson and Sterling's Alternative History: The Difference Engine as
Radical Rewriting of Disraeli's Sybil," *Node9*, December 1997,
http://web.archive.org/web/20020214220820/http://node9.phil3.uni-freiburg.de/
1997/Kraus.html. Gibson and Sterling's novel also kick started the already
mentioned retrofuturistic steampunk.

55 Regarding the recurrence of brands, the role that Macintosh computers play
here as an associated milieu, in the Simondonian sense, is very relevant under
the light of media-specific analysis.

56 "Interview with Kevin Begos, Jr."

57 Benjamin, *Illuminations*, 238–240.

58 From this point of view, the poem could also be included in what Aarseth has
called "ergodic literature," due to the required effort for apprehension, making
it an experience somewhat closer to that of video games although the auratic
traits of the project demand a more holistic approach to the work in its double
digital and material mode of existence. Cfr. Espen Aarseth, *Cybertext: Perspectives on Ergodic Literature*. Baltimore, MD: Johns Hopkins University
Press, 1997, 1.

59 For a discussion on the avant-garde attempt to liquidate the concept of work
and its relative failure, see Peter Bürger, *Theory of the Avant-garde* (Minneapolis: University of Minnesota Press, 1984). However, it should also be noted
that the tensions around the stability of works come not only from artistic
experimentation but also from emerging and traditional practices that nou-
rish (and often also feed from) established artistic works.

60 For an acute take on the role of the phonograph and other recording devices in
the constitution of a new Western sensorium and its impact on the rest of the

colonized world see Michael T. Taussig, *Mimesis and Alterity: A Particular History of the Senses* (New York: Routledge, 1993).

61 William Gibson, *Distrust That Particular Flavor* (New York: Berkley, 2012), 63.

62 Striphas, *The Late Age of Print*, 31–40.

63 Ibid., 181–182.

64 Ibid., 42. For an early example of how experiments with DRM as a business model for digital content were received, the specific technical problems presented by the emergence of new reading devices, and also the idea of *Agrippa* as pioneer see Jeff Kirvin, "Gone in 10 Hours," *Writing On Your Palm*, http://web.archive.org/web/20011222005912/http://www.writingonyourpalm.ne t/column010827.htm.

65 Striphas, *The Late Age of Print*, 41.

66 Brad Stone, "Amazon Erases Orwell Books from Kindle Devices," *New York Times*, July 17, 2009, http://www.nytimes.com/2009/07/18/technology/compa nies/18amazon.html?_r=0.

67 Hodge, "Bibliographic Description of Agrippa."

68 The Electronic Frontier Foundation (EEF) is a non-profit organization founded in 1990 that provides legal support to individuals and organizations and its goal is to defend civil rights in the field of telecommunications and digital technologies. Its web site hosts some files related to *Agrippa*: http://w2.eff.org/Misc/ Publications/William_Gibson/. The reasons for the anonymity of the programmer may be due to a practice typical of the hacker subculture, although in an interview published on the EEF site Gibson suggests there were US national security issues at stake and legal aspects linked to the kind of algorithm used for encryption. Cfr. "Interview with William Gibson," interview by Mike Rogers, *Electronic Frontier Foundation*, https://w2.eff.org/Misc/Publications/William_Gibson/rogers_ gibson.interview. The assertions regarding the encryption used in *Agrippa* as a munitions grade restricted export in the US have been rejected by DuPont, "Cracking the Agrippa Code: Cryptography for the Digital Humanities."

69 It is no coincidence that this work was one of the first being digitized and made available by a scholarly site as already discussed. The difficulty, if not sheer impossibility, for the technical reproduction of this work makes it an eloquent example of the reductionism of considering literary works as a mere texts devoid of any materiality.

70 These and other collaborations can be seen at http://limitededitionsclub.com/ three-poems-by-octavio-paz/.

71 Dennis Ashbaugh and William Gibson, "Dennis Ashbaugh and William Gibson," *Art Journal*, 1993, 79.

72 Ibid.

73 Begos, Jr., "Interview with Kevin Begos, Jr."

74 *The Century of Artists' Books* (New York: Granary Books, 2004).

75 Besides the already mentioned influential book by Drucker, for a discussion on the artifactuality of artists' books, see "Experiencing Artists' Books" in Hayles, *Writing Machines*, 65–99. Hayles states these works are true techno-texts that refer to the artifactual dimension of works thus showing that mate-

rials are also content, extending the idea established in the literary criticism that form is also content. The problem of the artifactuality in *Agrippa* will be addressed in the following sections.

76 "Electronic Literature: What Is It?," n8.

77 In a similar way to what occurs with *Agrippa*, there is no critical consensus on the established title of this novel: *afternoon, a story*; *Afternoon, A Story*; *Afternoon: A Story* and other variations around the capital letters and the use of a comma or colon. In this book I will follow Kirschenbaum's normalization, *Afternoon: A Story*. Cfr. *Mechanisms*, xvii.

78 Hayles, "Electronic Literature: What Is It?" For a critique of the overly optimistic approaches to the aesthetic possibilities of hypertext and its ties with more traditional literary theory see also Hayles, *Writing Machines*, 25–28. The underlying idea of multiple fictions that animated Michael Joyce's project reminds of Cortázar's *Hopscotch* multiple reading paths or the resource of narrating the same events under the perspective of four different characters as in Lawrence Durrell's *Alexandria Quartet* novels. The mention of Borges' short story "The Garden of Forking Paths" is recurrent in critical approaches to the hypertext. Kirschenbaum has referred to Cortázar as one of the acknowledged influences on Jay David Bolter and Michael Joyce for the creation of the *Storyspace* software, along with those of Lawrence Sterne and James Joyce. Cfr. *Mechanisms*, 172.

79 For an informed discussion about the production context of *Afternoon*, its different editions, and the *Storyspace* software see "Save as: Michael Joyce's *Afternoon*," *Mechanisms*, 159–212.

80 For a discussion on the importance of art institutions and the technological factors that may explain this difference see Manovich, "New Media from Borges to HTML," 13–16.

81 For a genealogy of the game, see Russel Dalenberg, "Adventure Family Tree," *Mipmip*, March 20, 2004, http://www.mipmip.org/adv/advfamily.shtml.

82 Quoted in Dennis G. Jerz, "Somewhere Nearby Is Colossal Cave: Examining Will Crowther's Original Adventure in Code and in Kentucky," *DHQ: Digital Humanities Quarterly* 1, no. 2 (2007), http://www.digitalhumanities.org/dhq/vol/001/2/000009/000009.html.

83 The *Fortran* source code for the first version of *Colossal Cave Adventure* was made available online in http://jerz.setonhill.edu/if/crowther/ in 2007 by Jerz.

84 Begos, Jr., "Interview with Kevin Begos, Jr."

85 Kirschenbaum, *Mechanisms*, 221, 224.

86 The text of the press release is available at http://agrippa.english.ucsb.edu/transmission-press-release-item-d11-transcription.

87 Jonas, "The Disappearing $2,000 Book."

88 Hayles, "Electronic Literature: What Is It?"

89 Begos, Jr., "On Agrippa (A Book of the Dead)."

90 See http://es.scribd.com/doc/6732324/Gibson-William-Agrippa-Un-Libro-de-Los- Muertos.

91 See https://immorfo.wordpress.com/2008/04/22/agrippaun-libro-de-los-muertos/.

92 The circulation of *Ad Astra* magazine is limited to Spain. On the other hand it should be noted that it is not a leading publication in the genre as *El Péndulo*

[*The Pendulum*] or *Minotauro* [*Minotaur*], both published by Minotauro, which, moreover, holds the rights for William Gibson's work in Spanish.
93 *Mechanisms*, 239.
94 Benjamin, *One-Way Street and Other Writings*, 240–257.
95 Liu, *The Laws of Cool: Knowledge Work and the Culture of Information*.
96 Schwenger, "Agrippa or The Apocalyptic Book." I will discuss both critical readings in the following sections.
97 Benjamin, *Illuminations*, 184.
98 The title also affords two interpretations: it could refer to the owner of the book, that is, Gibson's father, or those portrayed in it, the family.
99 Benjamin, *Illuminations*, 186.
100 For a very detailed discussion on family albums in the twentieth century, see Martha Langford, *Suspended Conversations: The Afterlife of Memory in Photographic Albums* (Montreal, Que.: McGill-Queen's Press-MQUP, 2001). For a discussion and illustrative examples of photographic prints becoming auratic objects see Geoffrey Batchen, *Forget Me Not: Photography and Remembrance*, New York (Princeton Architectural Press, 2004).
101 Tim Adams, "Space to Think," *The Guardian*, August 12, 2007, sec. Books, http://www.theguardian.com/books/2007/aug/12/sciencefictionfantasyandhorror.features.
102 A history of the Torqueflite transmission can be found at http://www.allpar.com/mopar/torqueflite.html.
103 Tom Henthorne, *William Gibson: A Literary Companion* (Jefferson, NC: McFarland, 2011), 19.
104 Kathryne V. Lindberg, "Prosthetic Mnemonics and Prophylactic Politics: William Gibson among the Subjectivity Mechanisms," *Boundary 2* 23, no. 2 (Summer 1996): 47–83. This article is an interesting example of the American academia reception of French philosophers (Derrida, Guattari, Deleuze, Paul de Man, Barthes) that Gibson dismissed in a quotation worth repeating: "Honest to God, these academics who think it's all some sort of big-time French philosophy – that's a scam," in Jonas, "The Disappearing $2,000 Book."
105 Lindberg, "Prosthetic Mnemonics and Prophylactic Politics: William Gibson among the Subjectivity Mechanisms," 62.
106 Liu, *The Laws of Cool: Knowledge Work and the Culture of Information*, 345.
107 Ibid., 346.
108 Adams, "Space to Think."
109 William Gibson, *Burning Chrome* (New York: HarperCollins Publishers, 2003), 20.
110 Liu, *The Laws of Cool: Knowledge Work and the Culture of Information*, 339.
111 Ibid., 440.
112 Ibid., 341.
113 William Gibson, "Introduction to Agrippa: A Book of the Dead," *Official Website*, http://www.williamgibsonbooks.com/source/source.asp.
114 And upon the consideration of photography as a synecdoche of technics it is inevitable to note that two of the most influential thinkers about the relation-

ship between technics and aesthetics, Benjamin and Flusser, focus precisely on the photographic camera and its cultural and political effects.

115 Liu, *The Laws of Cool: Knowledge Work and the Culture of Information*, 348.
116 Jameson, "Fear and Loathing in Globalization," 108–109.
117 Arlindo Machado, *Arte e mídia* [*Art and media*] (Rio de Janeiro: Jorge Zahar Editor, 2007), 14.
118 Ferrer states that "Agrippa" is a poem in prose when it is free verse; the process of scroll down display and subsequent encryption by a virus is not correct; the DNA repeated in the printed pages is not human but the DNA from a Drosophila fruit fly; finally, he repeatedly talks about "Gibson's book" without any references to Ashbaugh or Begos. It should be noted that making the text an essential feature of the work, without any mention of Ashbaugh, Begos or the engineers who wrote the poem software could be considered a form of textual idealism. Only the text of the poem "Agrippa," which is precisely what was leaked and is publicly accessible, seems to be relevant to Ferrer when discussing *Agrippa*.
119 Christian Ferrer, *Mal de Ojo* (Buenos Aires: Colihue, 2005), 135.
120 Ibid.
121 Kevin Begos, Jr., "An Interview with Kevin Begos, Jr.," interview by Courtney Traub, *The Oxonian Review*, April 23, 2012, http://www.oxonianreview.org/wp/an-interview-with-kevin-begos-jr/. Ironically, the Bodleian catalogue presents several mistakes in the physical description of the object that do not meet Begos' declared hopes: it states that the disk has a virus that produces self-encryption and that the DNA sequence represented on the pages is from human genetic profiles. See the library item description at http://solo.bodleian.ox.ac.uk/primo_library/libweb/action/dlDisplay.do?vid=OX VU1&docId=oxfaleph019300382.
122 Hodge, "Bibliographic Description of Agrippa."
123 *Mechanisms*, 25–71.
124 Edgar Allan Poe, *The Works of Edgar Allan Poe*, vol. 2 (New York: Widdleton, 1871), 259–270.
125 Ricardo Piglia, "Las bibliotecas no sólo acumulan libros, modifican el modo de leer" ["Libraries not only Acumulate Books, they Modify the Ways of Reading,"] interview by Horacio González and Sebastián Scolnik, *La Biblioteca*. N° 6, 2007, 31–32.
126 Ibid., 31.
127 For a detailed and illustrative description of "stream of consciousness" and "interior monologue" narrative resources, see the classic essay "The Brown Stocking" by Erich Auerbach, *Mimesis: The Representation of Reality in Western Literature* (Princeton: Princeton University Press, 1953).
128 For a discussion on the aesthetic and ideological aspects of early hypertext fictions see Hayles, *Writing Machines*, 27–28; Kirschenbaum, *Mechanisms*, 171–178.
129 Benjamin, *Illuminations*, 100–101.
130 *Afternoon*, in fact, has become a canonical work. For instance, a fragment was included in Paula Geyh, Fred Leebron, and Andrew Levy, *Postmodern American Fiction: A Norton Anthology* (New York: W.W. Norton, 1998).

131 One of the persons that carried out the cracking presented it in the MindVox BBS saying that it was the last "Golden Fleece" of the hacker community. See Templar, "'Templar's Introduction to the First Online Copy of Gibson's 'Agrippa' Poem (December 10, 1992) (Item #D44) (transcription)," *The Agrippa Files*, October 23, 2005, http://agrippa.english.ucsb.edu/templars-introduction-to-the-first-online-copy-of-gibsons-agrippa-poem-1°992item-d44-transcription. This ulti-mately supports my claim that the work as a MacGuffin is a relevant aspect of the background of the *Agrippa* project.

132 Though Striphas suggests *Agrippa* is a forerunner of the DRM, others argue that the work was an early example of the increasingly common practice of cracking of books with DRM to release their digital circulation. Cfr. Urpo Lankinen, "Times Change for William Gibson." *Wolf Head of Self-Repair*. March 20, 2012, http://www.beastwithin.org/users/wwwwolf/blog/2012/03/times-change-for-william-gibson.html.

133 See, specifically between 21'25"–22'19", http://www.youtube.com/watch?v=drPpUlTypt4&feature=gv&hl=en.

134 Kevin Begos, Jr., "Press Release for 'The Transmission' (1 December 1992) (Item #D11) (transcription)" (New York, December 1, 1992), http://agrippa.english.ucsb.edu/transmission-press-release-item-d11-transcription.

135 *Mechanisms*, 226.

136 *The Late Age of Print*, 40–41.

137 This was never suggested by the creators of the project but it is more clearly explained in the context of the digital circulation of other products of the time such as video games. Striphas' interpretation of *Agrippa* as a forerunner of DRM had already been suggested in the MindVox BBS a few months after the on-line surfacing of the poem "Agrippa." In a post dated "Sat, 18 Jul 92 17:12:30 EDT," user ahawks@mindvox.phantom.com notes: "The interesting thing about Agrippa: A Book of the Dead is the protection against redistribution. 2 rumors are going around that either: 1, it deletes itself after being read (remember, this work is on a disk) or, 2, it is encrypted after reading. Last I heard, Loyd Blankenship posted to alt.cyberpunk that he will try and get a copy and distribute it to the net (which was *supposedly* intended for Agrippa)." The BBS post can be found in *Gopher Proxy* at http://gopherproxy.meulie.net/gopher.meulie.net/0/textfiles/bbs/MINDVOX/UNSEEN/vox04.log.

138 William S. Burroughs, *Electronic Revolution*. (Cambridge: Blackmoor Head Press, 1971).

139 Hayles, "Electronic Literature: What Is It?"

140 The entry for "computer worm" in *Wikipedia* indicates: "Unlike a computer virus, it does not need to attach itself to an existing program. Worms almost always cause at least some harm to the network, even if only by consuming bandwidth, whereas viruses almost always corrupt or modify files on a targeted computer." http://en.wikipedia.org/wiki/Computer_worm.

141 A picture of the item can be seen at http://upload.wikimedia.org/wikipedia/commons/b/b6/Morris_Worm.jpg.

142 Joshua Quittner, "When Art Resembles National Security," *Newsday*, June 16, 1992, sec. Read Any Good Webs Lately?, http://cyber.eserver.org/newsday.txt.

143 A transcript of the letter from Barlow to Begos is available at http://agrippa.english.ucsb.edu/letter-from-john-perry-barlow-to-kevin-begos-11-june-1992-itemd45-transcription. For more on Barlow's involvement see Kirschenbaum, *Mechanisms*, 229n39.

144 DuPont, "Cracking the Agrippa Code: Cryptography for the Digital Humanities."

145 Manovich, "From Borges to HTML," 14.

146 Steven E. Jones, "Agrippa, the Eversion of Cyberspace, and Games," Blog, *Steven E. Jones*, (April 23, 2012), http://stevenejones.org/2012/04/23/agrippa-the-eversion-of-cyberspace-and-games/.

147 Steven E. Jones, "Signs of the Eversion II: The New Aesthetic," *Steven E. Jones*, April 3, 2012, http://stevenejones.org/2012/04/03/201/. For a discussion on the New Aesthetic see also the long piece by Gibson's longtime collaborator Bruce Sterling, "An Essay on the New Aesthetic," *Wired.com*, April 2, 2012, http://www.wired.com/beyond_the_beyond/2012/04/an-essay-on-the-new-aesthetic.

148 Steven E. Jones, "Signs of the Eversion: QR Codes," *Steven E. Jones*, March 30, 2012, http://stevenejones.org/2012/03/30/signs-of-the-eversion-qr-codes/. Both ARGs and QR codes are an example of the phenomenon of normalization of the physical world and the enhancement of anticipation described in the first chapter.

149 *Mechanisms*, 38.

150 Slavoj Žižek traces this dichotomy outside the limited boundaries of science fiction, from the Nibelungs in Wagner's *Das Rheingold* [*The Rhine Gold*] to Emir Kusturica's 1995 film *Underground*, which he considers as a form of Dionysian rather than Apollonian aestheticization akin to a postmodern form of fascism. *The Universal Exception* (London: Continuum, 2006), 164.

151 Ibid., 270. For a discussion on transparency and opacity of cyberspace, also by Žižek, see the "Cyberspace, or, The Unbearable Closure of Being" in *The Plague of Fantasies* (London; New York: Verso, 1997), 161–213. This essay complements some aspects discussed by Kirschenbaum, especially regarding medial ideology.

152 Žižek, *The Universal Exception*, 273.

153 Lev Manovich, "What Is Digital Cinema?," http://manovich.net/content/04-projects/008-what-is-digital-cinema/07_article_1995.pdf, 1995.

154 Gibson, "The Art of Fiction No. 211."

155 For a history of the development of the computer-generated images and efforts to achieve a non-indexical realism through simulation rather than recordings, see Machado, *Máquina e imaginário*, 59–142. In his essays, he discusses the importance of randomness and the use of algorithm generated fractals in the quest of digital realistic images.

156 Kirschenbaum, Reside, and Liu, "No Round Trip: Two New Primary Sources for Agrippa."

157 Ibid.

158 It is worth noting that the "rough edges" may not be assimilated to the use of glitches in technological poetics. There are two different logics at play: the

first aims at dismantling aestheticization; the second, on the contrary, aesthe- tizes the emergence of the material contingency.

159 Kirschenbaum, *Mechanisms*, 218.

160 Regarding this last connotation, Kirschenbaum draws attention to the figure of Cornelius Agrippa, a scholar of the Kabbalah, i.e. another "decipherment method," only in this case of sacred texts. Cfr. Ibid., 230. See also Lindberg, "Prosthetic Mnemonics and Prophylactic Politics: William Gibson among the Subjectivity Mechanisms," 64–66.

161 One of the finest examples of the existence of records in time is the work of photographer Seba Kurtis mentioned in the previous chapter. Of particular note are his series *Shoe Box*, about the preservation of family memoirs, and *Drowned*, where the fate of the photographic copies imitates that of the undo- cumented migrants whose journey across the sea he represents; Kurtis threw all the undeveloped negatives of the series to the sea and only then he printed the result, some images survived, affected by salt and wear, just as the illega- lized migrants. And some pictures, maybe of great artistic value, did not make it. For the resulting images see http://www.sebakurtis.com/index.php?/immi grationfile/drowned/.

162 Hodge, "Bibliographic Description of Agrippa."

163 Friederich Kittler, "On the Implementation of Knowledge," in *Readme! Filte- red by Nettime: ASCII Culture and the Revenge of Knowledge*, ed. Josephine Bosma (Brooklyn, NY: Autonomedia, 1999), 67. It is no coincidence that Ital- ian philosopher Giorgio Agamben identifies this period as the time when mod- ern science is born and when also "experience," understood in the Benjaminean sense of a transmission of knowledge rooted in the context of daily life, loses value with the remission of experience and knowledge to a unique abstract subject, the Cartesian *cogito* causing a "death of experience." Cfr. *Infancy and History: Essays on the Destruction of Experience* (London; New York: Verso, 1993), 17–25. Kittler also locates the birth of technical knowledge in the same period: "Once Leibniz submitted the organizing of authors and titles to the simple ABCs, entire state and national libraries (such as those here in Berlin) were founded upon this addressability. At the same time, this alliance between text and image, book printing and perspec- tive, gave rise to technical knowledge per se." "On the Implementation of Knowledge," 68. As I have mentioned before, the "Prospectus" that was distri- buted before the *publication* of *Agrippa* explicitly mentioned the printing press and the *Luther Bible*.

164 Kirschenbaum, Reside, and Liu, "No Round Trip: Two New Primary Sources for Agrippa."

165 Cfr. "Printer's Copy of Genetic Code for Agrippa Body Text (1992) (Item #D2) (About)" at http://agrippa.english.ucsb.edu/genetic-code-item-d2-about.

166 Kirschenbaum, Reside, and Liu, "No Round Trip: Two New Primary Sources for Agrippa."

167 Begos, Jr., "Interview with Kevin Begos, Jr."

168 Neil Macmillan, *An A-Z of Type Designers* (New Haven, CT: Yale University Press, 2006), 90.

169 Begos, Jr., "Interview with Kevin Begos, Jr."

[170] Chartier, *Escuchar a los muertos*, 25.

[171] Before continuing with this section I recommend looking at the *Shoe Box* series at http://www.sebakurtis.com/index.php?/in-deep-water/fronts/.

[172] I owe this observation to César Lorenzano.

[173] Benjamin, *One-Way Street and Other Writings*, 243.

[174] John Berger, *Ways of Seeing* (London: Penguin Books, 1972), 85.

[175] Kirschenbaum, *Mechanisms*, 222.

[176] Kirschenbaum, Reside, and Liu, "No Round Trip: Two New Primary Sources for Agrippa."

[177] For archival documents on some of the exhibitions see http://agrippa.english. ucsb.edu/category/documents-subcategories/exhibitions.

[178] Jesús Andrés, "Agrippa (un Libro de Los Muertos)," Blog, *Ceci N'est Pas Un Cahier*, (May 15, 2008), http://cecinestpasuncahier.blogspot.com.ar/2008/05/ agrippa-un-libro-de-los-muertos.html; "IVAM exhibe los 'Retratos Genéticos' del estadounidense Dennis Ashbaugh," *Terra Noticias*, September 2007, http://noticias.terra.es/2007/genteycultura/0924/actualidad/ivam-exhibe-los-re tratos-geneticos-del-estadounidense-dennis-ashbaugh-00.aspx.

[179] The difference between hacking and cracking is subtle. As Garcia indicated specifically in relation to the encryption of *Agrippa*, "[t]he term 'cracker' de-notes specifically those individuals who engage in freeing information from ownership constraints. I prefer to use this rather than the oft-misused term hacker, which historically only refers to those individuals who enjoy seeking knowledge about the internals of computer systems. Being a 'hacker' and being a 'cracker' are truly orthogonal." Anthony Garcia, "What Gibson Is Say-ing With 'Agrippa': Some Guesses," *Future Culture*, December 16, 1992, http://www.noozoo.com/hometome/ blast.html. Throughout this work, I have referred to the way in which "Agrippa" began circulating digitally as a crack-ing, precisely because of the intention to "free" information. I have referred to the "hacker subculture," rather than "cracker," for being the most widespread term to refer to the communities linked to illegal or paralegal activities in the context of digital culture.

[180] Striphas, *The Late Age of Print*, 41–42.

[181] The transmission of video over the computer networks was not a practice in use in 1992, but that same cracking today most likely would not include the human typing intervention since it would surface directly as video in pages like *YouTube*.

[182] Kirschenbaum, *Mechanisms*, 237; Kirschenbaum, Reside, and Liu, "No Round Trip: Two New Primary Sources for Agrippa."

[183] For Garcia, the book object *Agrippa* is nothing more than a "hardware lock." In the next section I will address the concept of "dongle" and return briefly to Garcia.

[184] Garcia, "What Gibson Is Saying With 'Agrippa': Some Guesses."

[185] Kirvin, "Gone in 10 Hours."

[186] DuPont, "Cracking the Agrippa Code: Cryptography for the Digital Humani-ties."

[187] See the selection of lexias of *Afternoon* available at http://www.wwnorton.com /college/english/pmaf/hypertext/aft/index.html, a web complement of the book

by Geyh, Leebron, and Levy, *Postmodern American Fiction: A Norton Anthology*. The website of Eastgate Systems, the publishers of *Afternoon* is a clear example of the constant and controlled remediation process to which the digital circulation of the work has been subjected. As I write this, Eastgate offers the work on CD-ROM for Macintosh and Windows: "This title runs on Macintosh Mac OS X 10.3-10.6 (Panther through Snow Leopard) and on 32-bit Windows XP through Windows 7. It is not yet compatible with Mac OS X 10.7 (Lion) and 64-bit Windows 7. New editions for these systems, and for iPad, are in preparation. Contact Eastgate for details": http://www.eastgate.com/cata log/Afternoon.html.

[188] Chartier, *Escuchar a los muertos*, 7.

[189] It must be noted that the other elements of the book object *Agrippa* (the resinous box, the mortuary veil) also refer to the idea of a burial relic and a time capsule to be opened in the future.

[190] Kirschenbaum, *Mechanisms*, 97.

[191] *Labyrinths: Selected Stories & Other Writings*, 3–18.

[192] Ferrer, *Mal de Ojo*, 135.

[193] Kirschenbaum, *Mechanisms*, 219.

[194] See http://www.quut.com/berlin/scream/5.txt. Note that the University of Texas domain mail generates strong doubts as to who actually wrote the message.

[195] (Scott O. Moore) Scotto, "The Leri-L Issue. Scream Baby 5," e-zine, *Scream Baby*, January 3, 1993, http://www.quut.com/berlin/scream/5.txt.

[196] US@phantom.com, "AGR1PPA 2.01 - NEW & IMPROVED (Fixes Bugs from Version 2.00)," *Mindvox*, (December 1992), https://w2.eff.org/Misc/Publications /William_Gibson/agr1ppa.parody.

[197] Kirschenbaum, *Mechanisms*, 220n18.

[198] *A New Literacies Sampler*, 201–202.

[199] The video is currently available in archival documents of *The Agrippa Files*.

[200] Kirschenbaum, *Mechanisms*, 263.

EPILOGUE: Hybrid Genealogies in Digital Culture

[1] A wellknown example of instructions for a literary work is the already mentioned *Hopscotch* by Cortázar, one of the most frequently cited texts, along with Modernist avant-garde and the work of Borges, as forerunners of digital literature in particular, but also digital culture in general.

[2] As suggested in the preface, anyone who bought or copied a pirate game also had to lay hands on the "paragame" of photocopies and simulations of key displaying devices to be able to play them, or otherwise gain access to cracked software that allowed bypassing copy protections.

[3] For examples and comments on copy protection in computer games, see the post by Juan Gestal, "Las protecciones anticopia más curiosas" ["The Most Curious Anti-copy Protections,"] September 22, 2008, http://www.pixfans.com/ las-protecciones-anticopia-de-videojuegos-mas-curiosas/. For a discussion on anti-copy devices in the case of software in general, see Pingdom, "Wacky

Copy Protection Methods from the Good Old Days," *Royal Pingdom*, 2009, http://royal.pingdom.com/2009/08/26/wacky-copy-protection-methods-from-the-good-old-days/.

4 citrus!vector0!jon@csusac.ecs.csus.edu, "'Cracking' Agrippa," *Future Culture*, December 16, 1992, http://www.noozoo.com/hometome/blast.html.

5 The software supporting the lenslok was also easy to circumvent. For a discussion on the topic see Hewison, "Lenslok," *The Bird Sanctuary*, http://www.birdsanctuary.co.uk/sanct/s_lenslok.php.

6 For the packaging of this particular game see MoffRebus et al., "Indiana Jones and the Last Crusade: The Graphic Adventure - Indiana Jones Wiki - Raiders of the Lost Ark, Temple of Doom, Last Crusade, Kingdom of the Crystal Skull, Young Indy, and More!," *Wikia*, July 2, 2011, http://indianajones.wikia.com/wiki/Indiana_Jones_and_the_Last_Crusade:_The_Graphic_Adventure.

7 Associating dongles to *Agrippa* is not far-fetched because it illustrates the horizon of expectations in which the work was received. As Garcia's quoted posting stated, the book object created what he defined as a "dongle effect" inasmuch "every 'official' copy of the information is tied to a physical piece of 'hardware.'" Garcia, "What Gibson Is Saying With 'Agrippa': Some Guesses." The "hardware" here would be the book object.

8 Pingdom, "Wacky Copy Protection Methods from the Good Old Days."

WORKS CITED

With the exception of hyperlinks to some examples of images and videos without any clear authorship, the "References" list all the scholarly works, articles, papers, chapters, news articles, e-mails, and posts quoted or discussed in this book following the 16th edition of the Chicago Manual of Style with some minor alterations in the criteria to clarify if needed, especially regarding non-canonical sources. The extensive list of literary and artistic works mentioned, as well as other cultural products such as games and software is, however, not included. All online references were checked during the copyediting of this book in March 2015. Hopefully, they will persist.

For those curious enough, I provide here the translations for epigraphs in languages other than English. Since translations are one of the earliest examples of information lossy replication, in the body of the work I opted to remain true to the rather whimsical sources of my intellectual background and the peculiar synapses it favors. Any information lost in translation is my fault alone.

> For the trombone shall sound,
> And the dead shall rise incorruptible,
> And we shall be changed.
> -1 Corinthians 15:52, *Luther Bible*

> ...There I went for my *grincar*,
> I left leaving everything *pending*...
> -Indio Solari, "To beef or not to beef"

> ...My life goes on forbidden
> So say authorities
> -Manu Chao, "Clandestine"

...The universe (that others call the Library) is composed by an indefinite, maybe infinite, number of hexagonal halls, with wide ventilation shafts in the middle...

-Jorge Luis Borges, "The Library of Babel"

...What an insufferable story!
I do not want to read it twice
-Philippe Bootz, *little brush to dust fiction*

...With few but learned books together,
I live in conversations with the deceased.
-Francisco de Quevedo, "From Juan Abad's Tower"

...Your pride is like a city cop
It does not see me the way I am.
-Edilson Moreno, "Street Vendor"

REFERENCES

Aarseth, Espen. "The Culture and Business of Cross-Media Productions." *Popular Communication* 4, no. 3 (2006): 203–211.

———. *Cybertext: Perspectives on Ergodic Literature*. Baltimore, MD: Johns Hopkins University Press, 1997.

Adams, Tim. "Space to Think." *The Guardian*, August 12, 2007, sec. Books. http://www.theguardian.com/books/2007/aug/12/sciencefictionfantasyandhorror.fe atures.

Agamben, Giorgio. *Infancy and History: Essays on the Destruction of Experience*. London; New York: Verso, 1993.

Andrés, Jesús. "Agrippa (un Libro de Los Muertos)." Blog. *Ceci N'est Pas Un Cahier*, May 15, 2008. http://cecinestpasuncahier.blogspot.com.ar/2008/05/agrippa -un-libro-de-los-muertos.html.

Ashbaugh, Dennis, and William Gibson. "Dennis Ashbaugh and William Gibson." *Art Journal*, 1993, 79.

Auerbach, Erich. *Mimesis: The Representation of Reality in Western Literature*. Princeton: Princeton University Press, 1953.

Batchen, Geoffrey. *Forget Me Not: Photography and Remembrance*. New York: Princeton Architectural Press, 2004.

Begos, Jr., Kevin. "An Interview with Kevin Begos, Jr." Interview by Courtney Traub. *The Oxonian Review*, April 23, 2012. http://www.oxonianreview.org/ wp/an-interview-with-kevin-begos-jr/.

———. "Interview with Kevin Begos, Jr." Interview by Paxton Hehmeyer, February 19, 2006. *The Agrippa Files*. http://agrippa.english.ucsb.edu/hehmeyer-paxton-interview-with-kevin-begos-jr.

———. "On Agrippa (A Book of the Dead)," October 26, 2002. *The Agrippa Files*. http://oldsite.english.ucsb.edu/faculty/ayliu/unlocked/begos/letter.html.

———. "Press Release for 'The Transmission' (1 December 1992)(Item #D11) (transcription)." New York, December 1, 1992. http://agrippa.english.ucsb.edu/ transmission-press-release-item-d11-transcription.

Benjamin, Walter. *Illuminations*. New York: Schocken Books, 2007.

Benjamin, Walter. *One-Way Street and Other Writings*. Shorter. London: Verso, 1985.

Berger, John. *Ways of Seeing*. London: Penguin Books, 1972.

Bolter, Jay David, and Richard Grusin. *Remediation: Understanding New Media*. Cambridge, MD: MIT Press, 2000.

Bootz, Philippe. "La poesía digital programada: una poesía del dispositivo." In *Poéticas tecnológicas, transdisciplina y sociedad: Actas del Seminario Internacional Ludión-Paragraphe*, edited by Claudia Kozak, 31–40. Buenos Aires: Ludión, 2011. http://ludion.com.ar/archivos/articulo/2012_Ludion_Actas-1.pdf.

Borges, Jorge Luis. *Labyrinths: Selected Stories & Other Writings*. New York: New Directions, 2007.

Bosman, Julie. "Romance Books Are Hot in the E-Reading Market." *New York Times*. December 8, 2010, sec. Books. http://www.nytimes.com/2010/12/09/books/09romance.html?_r=0.

Buck-Morss, Susan. "Aesthetics and Anaesthetics: Walter Benjamin's Artwork Essay Reconsidered." *October*, no. 62 (1992): 3–41.

Bukatman, Scott. "Gibson's Typewriter." In *Flame Wars: The Discourse of Cyberculture*, edited by Mark Dery, 71–89. Durham, NC: Duke University Press, 1994.

Bürger, Peter. *Theory of the Avant-garde*. Minneapolis: University of Minnesota Press, 1984.

Burroughs, William S. *Electronic Revolution*. Cambridge: Blackmoor Head Press, 1971.

Cajueiro, Marcelo. "'Elite' Stirs Controversy, Box Office." *Variety*, October 19, 2007. http://variety.com/2007/biz/news/elite-stirs-controversy-box-office-1117974360/.

Calvi, Juan C. *¿Reproducción de la cultura o cultura de la reproducción?: Análisis económico, político y social de la distribución y el consumo de productos audiovisuales en Internet*. Madrid: Universidad Rey Juan Carlos I, 2008.

Capanna, Pablo. *Maquinaciones. El otro lado de la tecnología*. Buenos Aires: Paidos, 2011.

Carrière, Jean-Claude, Umberto Eco, and Jean-Philippe de Tonnac. *This Is Not the End of the Book: A Conversation*. Evanston, IL: Northwestern University Press, 2012.

Cassin, Barbara. *Google-moi: La deuxième mission de l'Amérique*. Paris: Albin Michel, 2006.

Chartier, Roger. *Escuchar a los muertos con los ojos: Lección inaugural en el Collège de France*. Buenos Aires: Katz, 2008.

Chartier, Roger. "Hay una tendencia a transformar los textos en bases de datos." Interview by Horacio González, Diego Tatián, María Pía López, and Sebastián Scolnik. *La Biblioteca*. 6 (Spring: 2007): 10–28.

citrus!vector0!jon@csusac.ecs.csus.edu. "'Cracking' Agrippa." *Future Culture*, December 16, 1992. http://www.noozoo.com/hometome/blast.html.

Clynes, Manfred E. and Nathan S. Kline. "Cyborgs and Space." *Astronautics* 13 (September 1960): 26–27; 74–76.

Dalenberg, Russel. "Adventure Family Tree." *Mipmip*, March 20, 2004. http://www.mipmip.org/adv/advfamily.shtml.

Dodds, Douglas. *The Book and Beyond. Electronic Publishing and the Art of the Book*, Ausstellungskatalog Victoria and Albert Museum, London, 1995.

Doueihi, Milad. *Digital Cultures*. Cambridge, MA: Harvard University Press, 2011.

Drucker, Johanna. *The Century of Artists' Books*. New York: Granary Books, 2004.

———. "Humanistic Theory and Digital Scholarship." In *Debates in the Digital Humanities*, 85–95. Minneapolis: University of Minnesota Press, 2012.

DuPont, Quinn. "Cracking the Agrippa Code: Cryptography for the Digital Humanities." *Scholarly and Research Communication* 4, no. 3 (2013).

Enriquez, Mariana. "Charly García: Cuando me empiece a quedar solo." *Rolling Stone Argentina*, June 11, 2008. http://www.rollingstone.com.ar/1020573.

Ferrer, Christian. *Mal de ojo: El drama de la mirada*. Buenos Aires: Colihue, 2005.

Flores, Leonardo. "Reading Agrippa: A 4-Part Series." *I ♥ E-Poetry. Short-Form Scholarship on Born-Digital Poetry and Poetics*, July 14–23, 2012. http://ilove epoetry.com/?page_id =7913.

Flusser, Vilém. *Towards a Philosophy of Photography*. London: Reaktion, 2005.

Franssen, Maarten. *Artefact Kinds: Ontology and the Human-Made World*. Cham: Springer, 2014.

Fyfe, Paul. "Electronic Errata: Digital Publishing, Open Review, and the Futures of Correction." In *Debates in the Digital Humanities*, edited by Matthew K. Gold, 259–280. Minneapolis: University of Minnesota Press, 2012.

Gallo, Rubén. *Mexican Modernity: The Avant-Garde and the Technological Revolution*. Cambridge, MA; London: MIT, 2005.

Garcia, Anthony. "What Gibson Is Saying With 'Agrippa': Some Guesses." *Future Culture*, December 16, 1992. http://www.noozoo.com/hometome/blast.html.

Gestal, Juan. "Las protecciones anticopia más curiosas," September 22, 2008. http://www.pixfans.com/las-protecciones-anticopia-de-videojuegos-mas-curiosas/.

Geyh, Paula, Fred Leebron, and Andrew Levy. *Postmodern American Fiction: A Norton Anthology*. New York: W. W. Norton, 1998.

Gibson, William. "The Art of Fiction No. 211." Interview by David Wallace-Wells. *Paris Review*, 197, Summer 2011. http://www.theparisreview.org/interviews/6089/the-art-of-fiction-no-211-william-gibson.

———. *Burning Chrome*. New York: HarperCollins Publishers, 2003.

———. *Count Zero*. New York: Ace Books, 1987.

———. *Distrust That Particular Flavor*. New York: Berkley, 2012.

———. "Interview with William Gibson." Interview by Mike Rogers. *Electronic Frontier Foundation*. https://w2.eff.org/Misc/Publications/William_Gibson/rogers_gibson.interview.

———. "Introduction to Agrippa: A Book of the Dead." *Official Website*. http://www.williamgibsonbooks.com/source/source.asp.

———. *Neuromancer*. New York: Ace Books, 1984.

———. "William Gibson: The Father of Cyberpunk." Interview by Alex Dueben. *California Literary Review*, October 2007. http://calitreview.com/263/william-gibson-the-father-of-cyberpunk/.

Gold, Matthew K., ed. *Debates in the Digital Humanities*. Minneapolis: University of Minnesota Press, 2012.

Hart, Michael. "The History and Philosophy of Project Gutenberg." *Project Gutenberg*, August 1992. https://www.gutenberg.org/wiki/Gutenberg:The_History_and_Philosophy_of_Project_Gutenberg_by_Michael_Hart.

Hayles, N. Katherine. "Electronic Literature: What Is It?" *The Electronic Literature Organization*, January 2, 2007. http://eliterature.org/pad/elp.html.

———. *Writing Machines*. Cambridge, MA: MIT Press, 2002.

Heinz, Federico. "De libros electrónicos, agua seca y otras quimeras." In *Argentina Copyleft*, edited by Beatriz Busaniche, 95–98. Villa Allende: Fundación Vía Libre, 2010.

Henthorne, Tom. *William Gibson: A Literary Companion*. Jefferson, NC: McFarland, 2011.

Hewison, Richard. "Lenslok." *The Bird Sancturay*. http://www.birdsanctuary.co.uk/sanct/ s_lenslok.php.

Hodge, James J. "Bibliographic Description of Agrippa (Commissioned for *The Agrippa Files*)." *The Agrippa Files*, November 6, 2005. http://agrippa.english.ucsb.edu/hodge-james-bibliographic-description-of-agrippa-commissioned-for-the-agrippa-files.

Hui, Yuk. "What Is a Digital Object?" *Metaphilosophy* 43, no. 4 (2012): 380–395.

In re Electronic Books Antitrust Litigation, 859 671 (Dist. Court, SD New York 2012).

"IVAM exhibe los 'Retratos Genéticos' del estadounidense Dennis Ashbaugh." *Terra Noticias*, September 2007. http://noticias.terra.es/2007/genteycultura/0924/actualidad/ivam-exhibe-los-retratos-geneticos-del-estadounidense-dennis-ashbaugh-00.aspx.

Jackendoff, Ray. *Consciousness and the Computational Mind.* Cambridge, MA; London: MIT Press, 1994.

Jameson, Fredric. "Fear and Loathing in Globalization." *New Left Review* 23 (October 2003): 105–114.

———. *Postmodernism, Or, the Cultural Logic of Late Capitalism.* Durham: Duke University Press, 1991.

Jerz, Dennis G. "Somewhere Nearby Is Colossal Cave: Examining Will Crowther's Original Adventure in Code and in Kentucky." *DHQ: Digital Humanities Quarterly* 1, no. 2 (2007). http://www.digitalhumanities.org/dhq/vol/001/2/000009/000009.html.

Jonas, Gerald. "The Disappearing $2,000 Book." *NYTimes.com*, August 29, 1993. http://www.nytimes.com/1993/08/29/books/the-disappearing-2000-book.html.

Jones, Steven E. "Agrippa, the Eversion of Cyberspace, and Games." *Steven E. Jones*, April 23, 2012. http://stevenejones.org/2012/04/23/agrippa-the-eversion-of-cyberspace-and-games/.

———. "Signs of the Eversion: QR Codes." *Steven E. Jones*, March 30, 2012. http://stevenejones.org/2012/03/30/signs-of-the-eversion-qr-codes/.

———. "Signs of the Eversion II: The New Aesthetic." *Steven E. Jones*, April 3, 2012. http://stevenejones.org/2012/04/03/201/.

Kaufman, Alejandro. "Imaginarios, lecturas, prácticas." *La Biblioteca* 6 (Spring 2007): 76–83.

Kirschenbaum, Matthew G. *Mechanisms: New Media and the Forensic Imagination.* Cambridge, MA: MIT Press, 2008.

Kirschenbaum, Matthew G., Doug Reside, and Alan Liu. "No Round Trip: Two New Primary Sources for Agrippa." *The Agrippa Files*, December 5, 2008. http://agrippa.english.ucsb.edu/kirschenbaum-matthew-g-with-doug-reside-and-alan-liu-no-round-trip-two-new-primary-sources-for-agrippa.

Kirvin, Jeff. "Gone in 10 Hours." *Writing On Your Palm.* http://web.archive.org/web/20011222005912/http://www.writingonyourpalm.net/column010827.htm.

Kittler, Friederich. "On the Implementation of Knowledge." In *Readme! Filtered by Nettime: ASCII Culture and the Revenge of Knowledge*, edited by Josephine Bosma. Brooklyn, NY: Autonomedia, 1999.

Knobel, Michele, and Colin Lankshear. *A New Literacies Sampler*. New York: Peter Lang, 2007.

Kozak, Claudia, ed. *Tecnopoéticas Argentinas: Archivo Blando de Arte y Tecnología*. Buenos Aires: Caja Negra, 2012.

Kraus, Elisabeth. "Gibson and Sterling's Alternative History: The Difference Engine as Radical Rewriting of Disraeli's Sybil." *Node9*, December 1997. http://web.archive.org/web/20020214220820/http://node9.phil3.uni-freiburg.de/1997/Kraus.html.

Langford, Martha. *Suspended Conversations: The Afterlife of Memory in Photographic Albums*. Montreal: McGill-Queen's Press-MQUP, 2001.

Lankinen, Urpo. "Times Change for William Gibson." *Wolf Head of Self-Repair*. March 20, 2012, http://www.beastwithin.org/blogs/wolfheadofselfrepair/2012/03/times-change-william-gibson.

Lata, Mike. "Return of the Tape: Sony 185TB Cassette Tape Packs a Wallop but for What Purpose?" *Tech Times*, May 6, 2014. http://www.techtimes.com/articles/6556/20140506/cassette-tape-tape-sony-185tb.htm.

Latour, Bruno. *We Have Never Been Modern*. Cambridge, MA: Harvard University Press, 1993.

Lindberg, Kathryne V. "Prosthetic Mnemonics and Prophylactic Politics: William Gibson among the Subjectivity Mechanisms." *Boundary 2* 23, no. 2 (Summer 1996): 47–83.

Liu, Alan. *The Laws of Cool: Knowledge Work and the Culture of Information*. Chicago, IL: University of Chicago Press, 2004.

Machado, Arlindo. *Arte e Mídia*. Rio de Janeiro: Jorge Zahar Editor, 2007.

———. *Máquina e Imaginário: O Desafio das Poéticas Tecnológicas*. São Paulo: Edusp, 1993.

Macmillan, Neil. *An A-Z of Type Designers*. New Haven, CT: Yale University Press, 2006.

Manovich, Lev. *The Language of New Media*. Cambridge, MA: MIT Press, 2002.

———. *Software Takes Command: Extending the Language of New Media*. New York: Bloomsbury, 2013.

———. "Understanding Hybrid Media." In *Animated Painting*, edited by Suzanne Buchan, and Betti-Sue Hertz. San Diego, CA: San Diego Museum of Art, 2007.

———. "What Is Digital Cinema?" http://manovich.net/content/04-projects/008-what-is-digital-cinema/07_article_1995.pdf, 1995.

Marx, Karl, and Frederick Engels. *The Communist Manifesto: A Modern Edition*. London: Verso, 2012.

MoffRebus, Jawajames, PaddleDee, Salla, Vetinari, PhilAnd, Adamwankenobi, Yodakenobi, Prymonek, and Charibot. "Indiana Jones and the Last Crusade: The

Graphic Adventure - Indiana Jones Wiki - Raiders of the Lost Ark, Temple of Doom, Last Crusade, Kingdom of the Crystal Skull, Young Indy, and More!" *Wikia*, July 2, 2011. http://indianajones.wikia.com/wiki/Indiana_Jones_and_the_Last_Crusade:_The_Graphic_Adventure.

Montfort, Nick. "Continuous Paper: The Early Materiality and Workings of Electronic Literature." *Nickm.com*, January 2005. http://nickm.com/writing/essays/continuous_paper_mla.html.

Montfort, Nick, and Noah Wardrip-Fruin. *The New Media Reader*. Cambridge, MA: MIT Press, 2003.

Owens, Trevor. "The Is of the Digital Object and the Is of the Artifact." *The Signal: Digital Preservation*, October 25, 2012. http://blogs.loc.gov/ digitalpreservation/2012/10/the-is-of-the-digital-object-and-the-is-of-the-artifact/.

Parente, Diego. *Del órgano al artefacto: Acerca de la dimensión biocultural de la técnica*. La Plata: Edulp, Editorial de la Universidad de La Plata, 2010.

Person, Lawrence. "Notes toward a Postcyberpunk Manifesto." *Nova Express*, 1998.

Piglia, Ricardo. "Las bibliotecas no sólo acumulan libros, modifican el modo de leer." Interview by Horacio González and Sebastián Scolnik. 6 (Spring 2007): 30–47.

Pinch, T. J., and W. E. Bijker. "The Social Construction of Facts and Artefacts: Or How the Sociology of Science and the Sociology of Technology Might Benefit Each Other." *Social Studies of Science Social Studies of Science* 14, no. 3 (1984): 399–441.

Pingdom. "Wacky Copy Protection Methods from the Good Old Days." *Royal Pingdom*, 2009. http://royal.pingdom.com/2009/08/26/wacky-copy-protection-methods-from-the-good-old-days/.

Poe, Edgar Allan. *The Works of Edgar Allan Poe*. Vol. 2. New York: Widdleton, 1871.

Quittner, Joshua. "When Art Resembles National Security." *Newsday*, June 16, 1992, sec. Read Any Good Webs Lately? http://cyber.eserver.org/newsday.txt.

Schwenger, Peter. "Agrippa or The Apocalyptic Book." *South Atlantic Quarterly* 92, no. 4 (1993): 617–626.

Scotto (Scott O. Moore). "The Leri-L Issue. Scream Baby 5." E-zine. *Scream Baby*, January 3, 1993. http://www.quut.com/berlin/scream/5.txt.

Simondon, Gilbert. *Du mode d'existence des objets techniques*. Aubier: Editions Montaigne, 1958.

Soler, Chimo. "eBooks: La guerra digital global por el dominio del libro." *Real Instituto Elcano*, September 6, 2010. http://www.realinstitutoelcano.org/wps/portal/rielcano/contenido?WCM_GLOBAL_CONTEXT=/elcano/elcano_es/zonas_es/lengua+y+cultura/ari92-2010.

Sterling, Bruce. "An Essay on the New Aesthetic." *Wired.com*, April 2, 2012. http://www.wired.com/beyond_the_beyond/2012/04/an-essay-on-the-new-aesthetic.

Steyerl, Hito. *The Wretched of the Screen*. Berlin: Sternberg Press, 2012.

Stiegler, Bernard. *Symbolic Misery*. Vol. 1. Cambridge: Polity Press, 2014.

———. *Technics and Time, 1: The Fault of Epimetheus*. Stanford, CA: Stanford University Press, 1994.

Stone, Brad. "Amazon Erases Orwell Books from Kindle Devices." *New York Times*, July 17, 2009. http://www.nytimes.com/2009/07/18/technology/compa nies/18amazon.html?_r=0.

Striphas, Theodore G. *The Late Age of Print: Everyday Book Culture from Consumerism to Control*. New York: Columbia University Press, 2009.

Svensson, Peter. "Harry Potter Breaks E-Book Lockdown." *Yahoo News*, March 27, 2012. http://news.yahoo.com/harry-potter-breaks-e-book-lockdown-205343680. html.

Tabbi, Joseph. "Locating the Literary in New Media." *Electronic Book Review*. http://www.electronicbookreview.com/thread/critical ecologies/interpretive.

Taussig, Michael T. *Mimesis and Alterity: A Particular History of the Senses*. New York: Routledge, 1993.

Taycher, Leonid. "Inside Google Books: Books of the World, Stand Up and Be Counted! All 129,864,880 of You." *Google Books Search*, August 5, 2010. http://booksearch.blogspot.com.ar/2010/08/books-of-world-stand-up-and-be-counte d.html.

Templar. "'Templar's Introduction to the First Online Copy of Gibson's 'Agrippa' Poem (December 10, 1992) (Item #D44) (transcription)." *The Agrippa Files*, October 23, 2005. http://agrippa.english.ucsb.edu/templars-introduction-to-the-first-online-copy-of-gibsons-agrippa-poem-1992item-d44-transcription.

Testoni, Laura. "E-Book italiani: Quale bibliodiversità? Lo stato dell'arte 2011." *Bollettino AIB: Rivista italiana di biblioteconomia e scienze dell'iinformazione* 51, no. 4 (2011): 347–367.

Thomas, Angela. "Blurring and Breaking through the Boundaries of Narrative, Literacy, and Identity in Adolescent Fan Fiction." In *A New Literacies Sampler*, edited by Michele Knobel and Colin Lankshear, 137–166. New York: Peter Lang, 2007.

Trettien, Whitney. "A Deep History of Electronic Textuality: The Case of English Reprints Jhon Milton Areopagitica." *DHQ: Digital Humanities Quarterly:* 7, no. 1 (2013). http://digitalhumanities.org/dhq/vol/7/1/000150/000150.html.

———. "Zombie Editions: An Archaeology of POD Areopagiticas." *DIaPSaLMaTa*. http://blog.whitneyannetrettien.com/2010/12/zombie-editions-archaeology-of-pod. html, 2010.

US@phantom.com. "AGR1PPA 2.01 - NEW & IMPROVED (Fixes Bugs from Version 2.00)." *Mindvox*, December 1992. https://w2.eff.org/Misc/Publications/Wil liam_Gibson/agr1ppa.parody.

Vara, Vauhini. "Project Gutenberg Fears No Google." *The Wall Street Journal Online*, December 10, 2005. http://www.wsj.com/articles/SB113415403113218620.

Vera Barros, Tomás, ed. *Escrituras objeto: Antología de literatura experimental.* Buenos Aires: Interzona, 2013.

Von Ahn, Luis, Benjamin Maurer, Colin McMillen, David Abraham, and Manuel Blum. "reCAPTCHA: Human-Based Character Recognition via Web Security Measures." *Science* 321, (2008): 1465–1468.

White, Steve R., Jeffrey O. Kephart, and David M. Chess. "Computer Viruses: A Global Perspective." In *Proceedings of the Fifth International Virus Bulletin Conference,* Boston, 185–191, 1995.

Witmore, Michael. "Text: A Massively Addressable Object." In *Debates in the Digital Humanities*, 324–327. Minneapolis: University of Minnesota Press, 2012. http://dhdebates.gc.cuny.edu/debates/text/28.

Wood, R. Derek. "A State Pension for Daguerre." *Annals of Science*, 54, no. 5 (1997): 489–506.

Wray, Richard. "Bloomsbury Buys Arden Shakespeare." *The Guardian*, January 6, 2009. http://www.theguardian.com/business/2009/jan/06/bloomsbury-buys-arde n-shakespeare.

Žižek, Slavoj. *The Plague of Fantasies*. London; New York: Verso, 1997.

———. *The Universal Exception*. London: Continuum, 2006.

INDEX

Colin Lankshear & Michele Knobel
General Editors

New literacies emerge and evolve apace as people from all
walks of life engage with new technologies, shifting values
and institutional change, and increasingly assume 'postmodern' orientations toward their everyday worlds. Despite many
efforts to take account of such changes, educational institutions largely remain out of touch with the range of new
ways of making and sharing meanings that increasingly mediate and shape the lives of the young people they teach and
the futures they face. This series aims to explore some key
dimensions of the changes occurring within social practices
of literacy and the educational challenges they present,
with a view to informing educational practice in helpful
ways. It asks what are new literacies, how do they impact on
life in schools, homes, communities, workplaces, sites of
leisure, and other key settings of human cultural engage-
ment, and what significance do new literacies have for how
people learn and how they understand and construct knowledge. It aims to challenge established and 'official' ways
of framing literacy, and to ask what it means for literacies
to be powerful, effective, and enabling under current and
foreseeable conditions. Collectively, the works in this series will help to reorient literacy debates and literacy
education agendas.

For further information about the series and submitting
manuscripts, please contact:

Michele Knobel & Colin Lankshear
Montclair State University
Dept. of Education and Human Services
3173 University Hall
Montclair, NJ 07043
michele@coatepec.net

To order other books in this series, please contact our
Customer Service Department at:
(800) 770-LANG (within the U.S.)
(212) 647-7706 (outside the U.S.)
(212) 647-7707 FAX

Or browse online by series at:
www.peterlang.com